HIGH
SPIRITS

HIGH SPIRITS

Peter Funk

Doubleday & Company, Inc.
Garden City, New York
1983

Library of Congress Cataloging in Publication Data

Funk, Peter
  High spirits.

  1. Farm life—New Jersey. 2. Funk family. I. Title.
S521.5.N5F86 1983   630'.92'2 [B]

ISBN: 0-385-18935-4
Library of Congress Catalog Card Number 83-45118
Copyright © 1983 by Peter Funk
Printed in the United States of America
First Edition
All Rights Reserved

Edward Zanza said, "After heaven's gates were shut them in, then Abraham, in a vision, spoke of and the names of their Dachau concentration camp was written on the concentration camp so that the had hope in...

Harold Zasius, Machlis Edition Pacific Guard Code, from ... apply, ... guilty and ... for credit...

... that the ... forward submission

Acknowledgment

Thanks to you, Jean Wiggs, for so cheerfully typing and retyping and retyping ad infinitum the growing manuscript.

HIGH SPIRITS

1

John yanked open the kitchen door. "Dad!" he yelled. "The wind's making the field catch on fire. We need you. Hurry!"

I'd been trying to repair a balky dishwashing machine that came with our old house. Dropping the tools, I sprinted the hundred feet or so up the driveway.

Near an outbuilding which we planned to use for some farm equipment, we'd found a perforated steel barrel for burning trash. At the moment, crammed with flaming paper, the barrel roared ominously, shooting showers of sparks into the air. Caught by gusts of wind, the sparks and partially burned scraps fluttered past us.

Fresh from suburbia, Mary, I, and our seven children had moved to our farm the previous week. We'd moved to find a particular way of life and poured everything we had into it—emotionally and financially.

When I followed John through the door that Saturday afternoon, I realized the hazardous combination of fire and wind. I'd put Peter and John, at fourteen and thirteen our oldest children, to work burning the piles of paper used for our move from one house to another. Sparks flew out of the barrel we used for burning like a Fourth of July pinwheel, igniting the adjacent tufts of dry grass left over from winter.

They tried to extinguish the small ring of smoldering, creeping fire by stamping on it. When John's foot quenched a flame, his body stiffened with excitement, his hands waving as if he were a bird about to take off. "Got you!" he said with vigorous enthusiasm to the burned-out spot.

I joined them. Sparks snapped at my ankles. Puffs of ashes dusted new work shoes. The fire moved faster than we could. We needed help.

"Peter, please get your mother. Tell her to bring brooms . . . As many brooms as she can find. And tell her to get moving! It's an emergency." In one of the myriad pamphlets the government sent me on farming, I'd read you could put out small fires successfully by sweeping the flames back into the burned area. "And tell the other kids to get up here too," I called after him.

John and I continued pounding the ground with our feet around the rim of the fire. Our dog, Laddie, a mixture of Border collie and just plain collie, barked enthusiastically.

"What do you think, Dad?" John's blue-green eyes sometimes glitter with intensity.

"Don't know . . . Probably depends on the wind."

The strong, midafternoon winds of March rushed large silhouettes of cloud shadows across the land. When they flew beyond the sun, for a few brilliant minutes the air around us burst into a gloriously radiant light. Then just as quickly a chilling dusk draped around us as the clouds again blocked the sun, blotting out the light. For me the wild shadows represented a symbol of imminent misfortune.

I kept my back to the adjoining field. I didn't even want to think of what might happen. We had 110 acres. But that five-acre field behind me contained our principal hope of hanging on to the farm—a barn and three small cottages we rented.

We wanted to farm but we weren't playing games about making a living from farming or being farmers. We counted on the place carrying itself so we could live there. With high spirits, and high hopes, we'd bought Good Ground Farm on a "shoestring" with a first and second mortgage. Without the modest rental income from the cottages, we couldn't keep it. Now these structures were endangered by the fire.

Furthermore, my office in the barn contained my files, research notes, incomplete manuscripts, a book in the works, dictionaries, and reference books. For a vocabulary specialist and writer many of these items were irreplaceable.

Mary hurried up the hill, holding two brooms in one hand and pulling Eleanor along with the other one.

"I can go myself!" three-year-old Eleanor insisted loudly, trying to disentangle her hand.

Celine, Estelle who carried her black cat Licorice, and Mark ran after Mary. "Paul's been throwing up and his temperature's 104 . . ." Mary began.

When she saw the low, flickering flames edging toward the field and buildings, her blue eyes filled with alarm. "Oh my Lord!" She threw me one of the brooms and took the other. "Eleanor . . . Stay back."

We flailed our brooms desperately. The children stamped. Laddie barked incessantly. Yellow-eyed Licorice watched us dispassionately, now on the low limb of a tree.

"I'm getting some boards," Peter said in his unruffled voice, going to a stack of old wood that lay piled next to the nearby outbuilding. "Maybe they'll smother it . . . And then we'll all be *bored* with the fire," he added with a grin. He enjoyed playing with words and punning.

"You guys are pretty stupid to set the field on fire," our redheaded seven-year-old Mark observed. At that age, tact was not his strong point.

"If you're so smart, figure out a better way to put it out," John said.

"Rub your foot back and forth like this. It smears the fire and it goes out even better."

"Watch out for your sneaker that it doesn't get on fire," Mary panted, smacking the broom on the burning grass.

Celine, at ten our oldest girl, usually piled her blond hair on top of her head. "I just washed my hair. It's getting all smelly and dirty."

"Maybe it'll catch on fire and burn up," John teased. "And guess what? You'll be bald . . . The only bald girl in your class."

"Forget *that!*" she cried, stepping away in horror.

"Keep stamping," I said. "We're just holding our own . . . This crazy wind!" Normally we would have exulted in the wild beauty of the day. Now it menaced our future.

"Licorice is having so much fun watching us, aren't you?" Estelle said, looking at her cat appreciatively, her mind happily focusing on her pet. A year younger than Celine and as blond, she had the curious paradox of sturdiness in a delicate bony structure. "Look at him, Mother."

"Forget Licorice and keep working," Mary said, catching her breath from the exertion.

"Mother, better give me your broom," John offered. "You're getting tired. We have to work fast."

"I'm trying," she said.

"I don't want my mother die'n try'n." He took the broom. "Your turn to stamp."

Each time we seemed to make a modicum of headway in one area, a blast of wind ignited another spot. We rushed to it. More flailing and stamping.

"What an appalling sight," I said.

"What's that mean?" John asked.

" 'Horrifying' . . . 'Frightening' . . . 'Dismaying' is probably a good meaning for *appalled* at the moment . . . Wonder what its Latin root might be?" Instinctively my hand reached for the bulky, battered paperback dictionary I usually stuffed in a pocket Mary enlarged for that purpose. But I caught myself in time, continuing to swat the fire. Mary glanced at me, *appalled* at my temptation.

The tiny tendrils of flame inched to within a few feet of the tall field grass. Previously I'd relished its warm, russet beauty as its slender leaves moved gracefully in the wind, never suspecting its lethal potential.

The rim of fire grew larger. "Call the fire department," I said to Mary. "We're really in trouble now. We can't handle it."

She grabbed Eleanor in her arms and ran down the slope to

the house. "One of you children ring the bell," she shouted back. "Maybe Amory and the others will come and help."

Amory Neilson, an architect, rented an office in the barn. Naturally it contained all his files, plans, and models.

Why didn't I think of asking for help sooner? I never should have let the boys burn trash on a day with so much wind. I was furious at myself.

Celine tugged on the old farm bell's rope, ringing it with surprising vigor for a ten-year-old-girl. You could hear its clanging for at least a mile.

The rim of the fire stretched into the field. The grass went up with a terrifying *whoosh*. Roaring and crackling, the smoke and flames seemed to streak toward the barn.

Stunned, I envisioned a catastrophe, the type of event that makes up local folklore for years to come. The barn and cottages would burn to the ground. The banks would take everything else. I saw our family migrating to Australia to start a new life. Our dream of a new way of life was burning up.

In the office barn window an astonished face appeared and abruptly withdrew. Help was coming, but too late.

In desperation I snatched at another plan.

On the side of the field near us, a shallow, picturesque fieldstone well stood beneath a large maple tree. Actually this was more of a cistern than a well.

Grabbing a coil of rope and two pails from the outbuilding, I called for Peter and John to follow me. We skirted along the edge of the fire and reached the cistern, looking over the side into its dank depths. In the dim light we saw a pile of heavy timbers lying at the bottom, surrounded by water.

"John, I'm pretty sure you can stand on that pile of wood while you fill the pails with water. We'll let you down by the rope. If the pile is firm, untie yourself and then tie the rope on the handle of the pail." Though heavy boned, John was somewhat lighter than his older brother, who tended to be husky. *Well-fed*, his siblings teased. I decided John would be easier to lower into the well.

However, John preferred organizing things. "I've got an

idea. Since Peter's the strongest, he should go down. I'll go get
the other kids . . ."

Peter interrupted. "Since you say I'm the strongest, I
should be pulling up the pails because with all that water in
them they'll be heavy," he added with irrefutable logic.

As John peered over the edge into the gloomy hole, his
enthusiasm waned. Characteristically, he quickly assessed the
possibilities and reached an immediate conclusion. "It's not going to do much good, Dad."

The conflagration poured heat over us. My words rushed.
"You might be right, but it's worth a try. It's the only place we
can get water."

"Well . . . Okay, I guess." Doubt lingered in his voice.

Peter's eyes searched the bottom. As usual, rather than
automatically assenting to a proposal, he considered other options. "John's right. It'll be too slow. If we had a submersible
pump . . ."

"We don't," I said, tying the rope around John as fast as
possible.

"We need more pails and other people . . ."

"No time . . ."

Peter still hadn't given up thinking. "Better watch out for
rats."

"Rats!" John said, scrambling back off the edge. "I'm not
going down there. No way!"

"There *aren't* any rats down there," I insisted. "I've never
seen a rat there."

"You've never even *looked* down there until today," John
countered just as emphatically. "You don't *know* if any rats are
down there."

"I know a *lot* about rats. They keep away from holes like
this. How would they climb out? How would they get down?
Listen," I pleaded desperately, "we need water. There's a disas-
ter going on . . . You're brave. You'll go down in the history of
Good Ground Farm . . . And there are no rats down there
. . . *No* rats. But there *is* water."

As his blond head disappeared courageously beneath the

rim, we heard a shriek from Mary as she ran up the hill toward us. "What are you doing?"

Too late. John stood on the bottom.

We threw a pail down after him. He tied the rope on it, scooped water in, and we hauled it up to dump the water into the other pail. Alternately, Peter and I would take the pail, run to the fire, and soak the grass in front of the blaze. We'd race back to the well for a refill, an exhausting routine.

Mary helped haul up the bucket. As long as her son worked in that Stygian darkness, she wasn't going to leave.

If it hadn't been for a strong gust of wind, we might have contained the fire. In a few seconds that gust shot the flames beyond us. We were beaten.

"Where is that fire department?" I shouted as we watched the broad line of flame creep toward our buildings. "Call them again."

Mary ran back to the house.

I glimpsed people near the barn. Someone wetted the walls with a garden hose. Others scurried around, but I couldn't see what they were doing. Where *was* the fire department? Minutes were hours.

"I'm going down to the house to see why the firemen aren't here," I said to Peter. "Just be sure to keep the kids away from the fire. I'll be back in a couple of minutes."

Knowing he'd take the responsibility of watching over his brothers and sisters, I ran to the house.

As I banged open the kitchen door, Mary stepped in from the dinette where she'd been telephoning. "I called the Lambertville fire department by mistake. They said I should have contacted West Amwell Township. That's ours. I didn't know. But they've taken care of everything and help is on the way. They'll probably be here in a few seconds."

Our two multicolored parakeets lived in a large, white, semicircular cage hanging over the dryer and washer. They made more noise than our entire family combined. "Quiet!" I stormed at them.

Mary keeps her equanimity in the midst of calamity. She may be worried and intent. But there's no choking up or panic.

"Help's on the way," she repeated. "I don't dare leave Paul and I'll keep Eleanor with me. If you want me to do something, send one of the children to tell me."

As she hurried from the kitchen, her forehead slammed against the sharp corner of an open cabinet door. Blood spurted across her face. She staggered to a chair, holding her head, bending over. Blood dripped through her fingers to the floor.

I grabbed a damp dishrag and wiped away the blood. The ragged gash immediately gushed blood again.

Upstairs our youngest son's groans and retching were painfully audible. Beyond the kitchen I heard shouts of people as our new world burned out of existence. Though we'd fallen irrationally in love with the place, the genesis of our move was rooted in a passionate longing to live more of a family life. In suburbia we worried about the questionable influences and pressures trying to mold our children's lives. We felt we would have a better chance to sort out the deeper values of life as a family in a country setting.

Mary had realistic apprehensions about this move. It seemed much too large and complex for us to handle, especially since I could give it only a portion of my time. But the area fell within commuting distance to New York, the acreage offered us scope, and the beauty of Good Ground's setting made it irresistible.

We were losing it before we had time to try.

And here was poor Mary, dazed and bleeding. I worried she might have a concussion.

I found a clean dish towel, which she held against the cut. "We've got to get you to a doctor." We'd been so busy this week, it never occurred to us to locate a family physician. "I'll call the rescue squad. At least they'll get you to the hospital."

"No, no . . . I don't want to go. I'll be all right. Just give me a few seconds." She moved her free hand vaguely as if shooing me away. "Just go . . . The children."

"They're okay for a few minutes. Peter's taking care of them." I said a quick, firm prayer for Mary and then ran up the driveway, which extended alongside the field. By now the fire was halfway to the barn. Dense, dark smoke streamed from the earth. The grass crackled in the burning heat, sounding like someone snapping giant sticks.

The barn and two of the cottages formed a grouping about fifty yards from our driveway. The other cottage stood at the corner of our drive and a short lane going to the barn.

Amory Neilson and his six-year-old son, Max, lived in the cottage adjacent to his barn office.

As I approached, incredulously I saw the architect's old Studebaker turn off the driveway, bumping and lurching across the field straight at the fire. His secretary and two young men who worked for him jogged alongside.

I cut across the field, catching up with the car. "Get your car off this field. It'll burn up!"

He waved at me cheerfully. "I'm bringing water."

Heroic man! I'll never forget his gesture. We opened the doors, grabbing at the four pails. They were mostly empty. Water sloshed around the bottom of the car.

"I'll get more." He was the epitome of insouciance.

He gunned the car violently, whirling it around so it faced back toward the driveway. A spray of mud squirted over us from the spinning wheels. The engine thundered, the wheels spun, showers of mud gushed like a miniature oil well. But the car didn't move. Mired, the wheels sunk deeper and deeper into the ground, soft with the dampness of spring.

We pushed. The fire was hot on our backs. The car was hopelessly stuck.

Someone shouted from the edge of the driveway. "Get out of there. The car may explode."

We ran.

A slow, full-throated wail sounded from Mule Hill Road. Two magnificent fire engines turned majestically into our driveway, their intercoms crackling with voices and static. For me the cacophony became a beautiful sound of hope.

A line of ten or so cars followed the trucks, parking behind them. People swarmed toward us.

Dexterously and without fuss, the volunteer firefighters uncoiled hoses that resembled monstrously long boa constrictors.

I went to the man who seemed to act as Chief. "Glad you're here," I said gratefully.

"Got a pond we can draw water from?" he asked. Taller than I am and about as lean, shirtsleeves rolled up over arms knotted with muscles and ridged with veins, he kept hauling the hose with the other men as he talked to me.

The fact of not having water available hadn't occurred to me. Despair kicked open the door again. "We don't have a pond . . ."

"Don't matter none," he said unperturbed. "Trucks carry water. Guess we got enough."

Under the pressure of gushing water, the hoses writhed and stiffened as if awakening.

Two men grunted as they picked up the nozzled end of one of the hoses, bracing themselves for the recoil from the water exploding through the opening.

Suddenly there it was! Water sprayed over the charring field like a small cloudburst.

The barn and houses might be saved.

But for the Studebaker, help came too late. The fire swept over and under it. We held our hands ready to shield our faces if it blew up.

"I'm sorry, Amory . . . I really appreciate your trying to help. You have to be one of the nicest guys going," I murmured. I'd make it up to him in some way. A new car, I guessed.

Attention riveted on the vehicle. The automobile's hazy, ghostly form nearly lost in the shimmering heat seemed to bend and twist in a metallic agony.

For a few seconds the fire swirled about it. Then the flames ran past. The old car, virtually unsinged, unaccountably survived its ordeal by fire.

"I can't believe it," Amory whispered. "I just *can't* believe it!"

I patted his back, relieved both for him and me. Sometimes we do luck out. "Let's say it's been a filipendulous moment," I said, letting out a long sigh.

He returned to reality. "A moment filled with what?"

"A moment hanging by a thread."

"I've had it." He shook his head, walking slowly to his cottage.

Along with the fireman, fifteen or twenty men, women, and children left their jobs and homes to see if they could be of help. They stamped on smoldering areas and were ready to move personal belongings from the barn and cottages.

We found this reaction to be typical of many of our country neighbors. They always appeared during an emergency. The word *neighbor* took on an added connotation for us. Later, out of curiosity, I looked up the origin. It comes from Old English *neighbor—neah* ("nigh" or "near") and *gebur* ("dweller"). We were grateful to our "near dwellers."

They were friendly in a dignified, reserved way. Few words were exchanged with us. My effusive thanks were accepted silently, although I caught a mild amused expression on some of their faces. After all, we were "city folk" and wouldn't be expected to know you never burned anything during high winds. I felt, somehow, we seemed typically naive suburbanites who tend to think they don't need advice from "country folk."

The men and older boys began winding the hoses back onto the trucks, while the other neighbors prepared to leave.

Worried about Mary, I hurried across the field to go down to the house when I saw her walking toward me, a large piece of gauze on her forehead.

"You shouldn't be up here," I said, gently chastising her. "You should be lying down."

"I'm all right. I really am. It's not a bad cut. You know how scalp wounds bleed. They look a lot worse than they are. I'll just have a goose egg up there for a while," she said, touching the bandage. "What's happening?"

I tried to discern if she was hiding her pain but decided she was telling the truth. "They finished. The fire's out. No damage, thank God . . . How's Paul?"

"He's stopped vomiting. I think he's better. Boy, is he a mad little five-year-old— He's missing all the action."

"After today I have a feeling he'll have plenty of opportunity for action."

A small, plump woman stopped in front of us, holding the

hand of a skinny young boy who seemed about Eleanor's age, three. Ashes smudged one of her cheeks. Her brown eyes expressed concern as she looked at Mary. "You've hurt yourself. Are you all right?"

Mary explained.

"That's terrible. You're lucky you didn't put out your eye," the woman said, speaking with a soft and curiously flat intonation common to this area. People call it a Lambertville accent. "Too bad about the fire. You have a beautiful place."

"Thanks for helping us," I said. "I'll tell you one thing. I'll never let *that* happen again."

She looked down at her youngster, her voice turning shy. "Oh, Roy and I didn't do much. We were here just in case . . . Anyway, field fires happen a lot around here this time of year. You're not the only one." Her friendly ingenuousness infused the moment with a needed reassurance for us.

"You were so nice to come over," Mary said, putting out her hand. "I'm Mary Funk and this is my husband, Peter."

The woman's alert, soft eyes reflected a cheerful warmth. "I figured as much." She took Mary's hand. "I'm Tess . . . Tess Snedeker."

A sturdy, large-chested woman walked over the field toward us, her hair a yellowish white, cheeks pink, lively blue eyes behind real granny glasses. "Looks like you tried to put out the fire yourself," she said to Mary, her voice clear and energetic.

"I didn't watch where I was going. It looks much worse than it is," Mary replied.

"This is Mrs. McGillian," Tess explained. "One of my best friends."

"We've known each other for a long while," the woman answered.

"Well, all I can say is, thanks for coming to help," I reiterated. "We really appreciated it."

"If you ever need a sitter, call Mrs. McGillian. She's real good. She's had six of her own," Tess said.

Mary brightened. "How great! I didn't know whom to call. You'll be hearing from me."

Eventually the fire trucks rumbled back to their stations

and our neighbors left to resume whatever activities they'd interrupted. I overheard one of them as she walked to her car. "I wondered what the folks were like. This was sure a good way to get to see them."

An hour previously bedlam engulfed us. Now we were blanketed by quiet. Even the wind became less blustery. The occasional wisps of blue smoke rising and vanishing from the charred field, the heavy, sour smell of wet ashes, Amory's car sunk in the mud, evoked the sense of having lived through a scorched-earth campaign.

We stood by the blackened field talking with Rex and Melissa Etherington, who rented our cottage nearest the driveway.

Rex took the curved pipe out of his mouth, pointing the stem toward the abandoned car. "Amazing about Amory's old Studebaker . . . That's the kind of crazy thing that's always happening to him. A great scene . . . Just a great scene." A chuckle rippled through the six-foot-two man.

"Maybe the spilled water in the car helped keep it cool," I offered. Exhaustion made it difficult for me to think. Right now even talking was hard. All I wanted to do was collapse on our couch.

Melissa, not as tall though certainly as lean as her husband, continued laughing. "Who knows why it didn't explode . . . It was awfully funny . . . But only *after* we realized the fire department had everything under control." She looked at Mary as if seeing the bandage on her forehead for the first time. "What *happened* to you? Are you okay? Shouldn't you be sitting down or something?"

Again Mary explained what had happened. "And actually it doesn't hurt a bit right now."

"Endorphins . . ." Rex replied, taking the pipe out of his mouth.

"What?" Mary asked, puzzled.

"Endorphins . . . 'Substance put out by the brain to suppress pain.' Like morphine. Happens in shock."

Mary laughed. "Well, whatever. Anyway it doesn't hurt."

"Listen, come on in for a drink. You two look as if you need it," Melissa said. If I looked anything like Mary, I did need it. We accepted, following them into the cottage—just to sit down would be a relief.

I telephoned Peter, telling him where we were. "We'll be about a half hour or so. Keep the kids in the house. If you're hungry, have John make up some sandwiches.

"John . . . Make up sandwiches?" Peter asked slowly. "Remember when he made them up for school our lunches? A slice of cheese between two pieces of bread . . . No butter, no mustard, no lettuce."

I couldn't help laughing. "I suspect a bit of skullduggery there. It was an easy way to get rid of the sandwich-making chore. Don't forget, garnishes never matter much to John."

"The garnishes are what make a meal a treat instead of just fuel . . . No *fueling,*" Peter also laughed as he reached out for a pun.

"You win. Why don't you put together one of your creative concoctions for all of us for supper. Your mother and father are out of gas—no fueling." I made a feeble attempt to carry on the game though I wasn't up for word play. "Put John in charge of the children."

I looked around the cottage, once again appreciating it. We hadn't been in it since we'd mortgaged our lives to the farm. This was an ideal place for a couple—a small, well-set-up kitchen, twelve- by sixteen-foot living room with a fieldstone fireplace at one end, and two bedrooms, one large enough for a double bed. A stone terrace, the length of the house, faced the fields, distant woods, and hills.

Photographs of Rex lined one part of the living room wall. "I remember now . . . You're an actor," Mary said.

He nodded.

"I should probably know . . . Are you in a TV series or a film?"

"I'm a sort of staple with The Tent Theater . . . That's the local summer theater here. Sometimes I act in TV soaps and once in a while do some commercials." He began lighting his pipe.

"That's so interesting," Mary replied, studying the pictures.

"You're certainly photogenic. Are you playing in anything on TV now?"

"Rex is thinking of changing," Melissa answered from the kitchen, her voice tightening. "Acting's a pretty hard field. Unbelievable unemployment."

"Like writing," Mary murmured.

I took my dictionary from my pocket, squinting at the pages as I turned them. "I don't have my glasses. Did I give them to you?" I asked Mary.

She shook her head.

"A magnifying glass help?" Rex asked, picking up one from his desk and handing it to me.

"Thanks . . ." I found what I wanted. *"Appall* comes from Latin *palir*—'to grow pale,' " I read to Mary. "The prefix is an intensive."

Mary smiled, turning to Rex. "Imagine! In the midst of that conflagration, Peter almost pulled out his dictionary to look up the root of *appall.* He must have looked at me!"

"She was a perfect illustration of the word," I laughed.

"Your word addiction was almost the death of us."

"Ah, but we would have died with *meaning.*"

"You always carry a dictionary around with you?" Rex asked carefully.

Mary started to explain. "Logomaniacs . . ."

She didn't have time to finish, for Melissa appeared with a tray and four glasses. "I realize I never asked. I just mixed up what I wanted and assumed . . . If you want anything else . . ." With her attractive smile and looks she might have been a model or actress—perhaps more successful than Rex.

"You have a wide choice of drinks in this bar . . . this brew straight up . . . or on the rocks," Rex said, quietly pleased with his words.

"I'll take mine on the rocks and I won't guarantee what might happen," Mary said.

I took the glass in both hands and gulped the drink. This one was the coolest and dryest I'd tasted in a long while. On principle I stay clear of them. Mary sipped hers and placed it on the table.

Melissa put her glass on a side table. "Mary, someone, and I can't remember right now who . . . Anyway. Someone said you'd been asking where you could find a little donkey and this person said she knew where there might be one. I think she said it was *white*. I'll try to think who it was." She rushed her words, moving her hands in rhythm.

"Calm down, Melissa. Lay back," Rex said carefully, taking the pipe from his mouth.

I looked at Mary. A donkey! For us? She hadn't said anything to me.

Mary laughed. "I was going to surprise Peter and the children. He loves animals."

"I'm *sorry*," Melissa said. "I didn't know this was meant to be a surprise. My friend didn't tell me that. She only said you might be looking . . ."

Pipe between his teeth, hand moving up and down as if in a slow-motion wave, his voice soothing, Rex smiled. "Calm down. You don't have to rush."

"Melissa!" I said. "No apologies needed. Let me put it this way. There are surprises and then there are *surprises*. And there's one thing I know. A donkey is one surprise I won't miss."

Mary reached over and patted my hand reassuringly. "Darling, you're just upset about today . . . You remember a little while ago you saw a donkey and said how cute it was and it'd be perfect for any farm on Mule Hill Road? . . . And I thought maybe we could get one to surprise Eleanor and Paul on Easter Day."

The chilled drink glass cooled the palms of my hand and I felt myself being eased into relaxation.

"The last thing we want is a stubborn donkey to contend with. Amory's car gave us enough problems . . . Could you see us trying to prod a donkey out of the field?"

Remembering the car's survival, we laughed again as we relived the incident.

"Maybe someday . . ." Mary said.

"Maybe someday," my words echoed hers.

"When that day comes, you'll love the animal," Mary

laughed. "I know you . . . Keep looking, Melissa. Easter's not that far away."

The telephone rang. Melissa answered and handed it to me.

"You left John down the well . . ." Peter began with a touch of glee in his voice.

"Oh, Lord . . . I'll be home right away."

Alarmed at my voice, Mary stood up ready to go—hair a nest of unbrushed wisps and curls, blood-smeared bandage across her forehead, circles of fatigue beneath eyes bright with sudden apprehension, ash-smudged clothes. Her response was living proof of a mother's fortitude.

Peter continued. "Don't worry. We got him out. He was down there an hour and no one heard him yelling. Eleanor was the one who missed him. "He's *really* mad. And he *did* see a rat." I nodded weakly, replacing the telephone. "Everything's okay," I muttered.

Mary collapsed in the chair rather than sitting.

One more quickly gulped drink and the world slowly and inexorably closed in on me. I focused my fading concentration on Mary. "We've got to go home," I announced with deliberate care. Mental and emotional exhaustion from worrying about Mary, the children, the farm, and everything, left me with no tolerance for alcohol.

"Stay for dinner," Melissa urged graciously. "We'll have potluck. We have plenty."

I shook my head slowly and murmured a thanks, *but* . . . My vision became a narrow focus and the periphery a haze of indefinite shapes.

Mary read the situation clearly. "That's so nice of you, Melissa, but I have to get supper for the children." She linked her arm firmly with mine and we walked the hundred yards home.

Avoiding the children as much as possible, I had just enough strength left to crawl up the stairs to our bedroom. The mattress to our double bed still lay on the floor. I'd been too busy that week to put up the bed frame.

While the grandmother's clock in the living room chimed six o'clock, I rolled onto the bed.

Outside the closed door, a child whispered, "What's wrong with Dad? He's acting so funnily."

Mary's soft voice whispered, "Shh'h. He's *very* tired. It's been a terrible day for him."

The telephone rang. I heard Mary's amused reply. "Oh . . . His dictionary. We'll pick it up tomorrow. Don't worry, Melissa. He's not going to be using it tonight."

As I drifted into the nirvana of oblivion, a question clung to the thin vanishing edge of thought.

Was this the way it was going to be? If so, I wasn't sure we could handle it.

I fell asleep to the cheerful muted sounds of children's laughter mingled with the contented barking of Laddie.

2

During the year, we catapulted ourselves into activity, repairing the cottages and barn, reclaiming fields, adding chickens and two horses to our menageries. Also, we planted ten thousand fir trees, expecting to harvest them in six or seven years as Christmas trees.

"This life on the farm comes about as close to a long-distance cross-country race as anything else I know of," I said to Mary after supper one night as we cleaned up the kitchen . . . It's more of a workout than I thought it would be."

"Well, you always said your forte was endurance, so I guess you're in the right spot . . . Anyway, this happens to be one race you're not running alone. You've lots of help." She indicated the teeming, noisy, cheerful, robust activity in the kitchen. All seven children helped and all seven inherited our predisposition to an enjoyment of talking.

"Let's go outside for a few minutes," Mary said to me when we were finished. "It's such a clear, beautiful evening. Remember in Stamford when sometimes we couldn't even see the stars because of the trees or the smog?"

Knowing her as well as I did, I sensed there was something else she wanted to talk about.

In the stillness we heard our two horses, Talla and Babe, cropping the grass, a soft, swishing sound. Cows lowed in the distance, a kind of soothing, bovine lullaby.

The word *low* interested me and I wondered why it was spelled like the *low* which meant "not high." English is a hornet's nest of homonyms. My dictionary gave the origin of *low,* the sound of cattle, as coming from Old Norse *hloa,* meaning "to roar." Somewhere along the route to modern English, the *h* was dropped and a shift in pronunciation changed the *a* to *w.*

Mary linked her arm in mine. "I'm sure you think it's a little crazy of me . . ."

I wondered what she was going to say.

"I haven't mentioned it for a year, but I just know how much fun the children would have with a donkey, and Easter Day would be the perfect time for a surprise like that. Can't you see their faces when it arrives? I know Eleanor would be wild about one. Every time I see a donkey when I'm driving in the car, I want to bring it home."

"Glad they don't fit into shopping bags," I said. "Anyway, let's be patient. When it's the right time, the right beast will show up . . . One of our biggest problems is that we're both impetuous. Sometimes we push too hard for things and then they don't turn out the way we expect."

"We have Good Ground," Mary replied. "We were looking for a better way of life and I think we found it."

"You're right. I agree. It is. At least so far. I love it . . . But I can sure say this. The work's a whale of a lot more than I thought. It's us against nature and she has an uncanny way of finding out our weak points."

Mary smiled. "And she never sleeps either."

"Yes, most of the work has to be done *now* and not later when you feel like it . . . Especially with animals."

We walked up the driveway slowly, holding hands.

"The funny thing is, we didn't really know *what* we were looking for," Mary continued. "We couldn't articulate what we felt was missing. We knew that important values are somehow being eroded and family life threatened . . . These are such fragmented times . . . But we *did* know we wanted to live a family life with a firm center of values."

We stopped, listening to the sounds filtering through the darkness—a dog barking in the distance, a horse snorting, the quiet call of an owl.

We looked behind us at the lights in our house, throwing yellow shadows on the lawn. Mary still continued her thought. "Before we moved here, I can't tell you the number of times I felt as if we'd been dumped into a centrifugal machine that whirled us away from one another . . . Either the older kids would be scattered throughout the neighborhood, or we had a thousand of their friends racing through our home."

We neared Melissa and Rex's cottage.

I nodded. "I came across a good statement the other day. I can't remember who said it, but she talked about the *failed relationships* of today . . . between members of a family . . . between people. I don't want failed relationships in our family."

She squeezed my hand. "We won't . . . Don't worry. I like *our* 'good life.' "

Mary referred to the good life touted by the entertainment and advertising community, which almost always turns out to be shallow and tawdry. Their slick promises are merely words wrapped around hollow assurances, like the empty, gaily colored Christmas packages under trees in shopping malls.

We wanted a sense of family unity. We longed for a happy and wholesome family based on love, awareness, and individual responsibility. Vaguely, we longed for an old-fashioned American way of life—the kind we thought must have been lived on farms in the past—independent, hardworking, fulfilling.

We wanted to be rooted in nature's timeless cycles.

God saw all that he had made, and it was very good. We intended to try to recapture that exuberant sense of creation.

However, there was one aspect of my life that troubled me —my career.

Mary looked at me. "What was that sigh for?"

"Guess . . ."

She knew. As the author of the monthly feature in *Reader's Digest,* "It Pays to Enrich Your Word Power," my reputation as a lexical semanticist (vocabulary specialist) was growing. Also, I'd written some other books, including fiction. One of them, *My Six Loves*—about six orphaned children—was doing reasonably well.

Yet, attempting to earn a living from writing is a precarious business. So, with such a large family, I felt the only fair thing to do for everyone was for me to have a reasonably secure job. There are times when your personal desires are of secondary importance.

Mary understood. On the other hand, if I decided to take the chance with the typewriter, she would back me completely. She felt that if I were happy in my work, the family would be better off.

Incongruously, I became sales manager of two mutual funds, and though this was far from being my métier, did fairly well. All during this time, however, I held on to a delusive hope that a *deus ex machina* would pluck me out of my dilemma and set me down before my books and typewriter full time. I didn't dare make the move myself.

In retrospect, and something I could not have anticipated at the time, I should have taken the plunge. Hanging on to the Wall Street job was partly responsible for creating as dreaded a situation as I could possibly imagine.

When we reached the Etherington's cottage, we saw that the lights were on in Amory's office in the barn.

"These architects work long hours, don't they," I said to Mary.

"No longer than you . . . You're not getting up at four again tomorrow morning, are you?"

"I really have to . . . It's Saturday and we're doing the fencing. But tomorrow will be easier than commuting."

My writing and studying had to take place in those early hours, on trains to and from New York, in university courses during the weekend and other moments snatched out of the day and night.

In my studies I struggled with the arcane, unfamiliar symbols and sounds of Sanskrit. The abstruse and often poorly written monographs dealing with the new field of psycholinguistics excited me. I tried to refurbish my Latin. I pondered Noam Chomsky's theories of transformational grammar and his idea of the way a child's mind handles the abstractions of language. Some books on semantics had me yawning and nodding as I picked my way through long, convoluted, virtually impenetrable sentences. Others snapped me awake with challenging perceptions.

"I wish you'd get back to painting," I said, thinking of how much I enjoyed writing.

"Painting! How? When?" She sounded amused. "Listen, for now my artistry's going into creating a good family life. I'll pick up my painting later on. I'll have the time. Don't worry . . . I'd much rather have this dream come true."

"I know . . . That's why I'm willing to commute . . . I remember lying awake at night dreaming of an old-fashioned farm. You know, the wild thing is I actually visualized us high on a hill which sloped toward a nearby river . . . And here we are . . . Well, we'd better get back to the house. I want to be sure the boys are set for the fencing. It's important to get that field done."

After breakfast the next morning, we unloaded a 150-pound, five-foot-high roll of wire-mesh fence, setting it upright on the ground, struggling with its ungainly, heavy mass.

We're working together as a family, I thought enthusiastically. I'd always liked the Jewish concept of working as a family unit.

"Hey guys, you're doing a great job . . . Couldn't do it without you," I called to them. They had the satisfaction of knowing they were needed in a practical sense.

Fourteen-year-old John unwound the fence slowly along my sight line, a three-hundred-foot string attached firmly at either end. When he got it lined up correctly, his lithe body tensed with pleasure, his face intent with concentration.

Peter, more "laid-back" in personality, drove the green John Deere tractor which pulled our lopsided wagon along the new fence. He daydreamed occasionally, leaned on the wheel slouching a bit, his large blue eyes reflecting contentment. His arms, chest, and shoulders were larger than those of his younger brother because of lifting weights.

In putting up a wire-mesh fence, the trick is to make sure that the entire five-foot width of wire is equally taut. Since it's easier to stretch the top rather than the bottom, the tendency is for the top to be pulled farther ahead. When this happens, you end up with a slant to the mesh. The wire doesn't hook onto the stakes evenly and the fence tends to buckle in places, losing its effectiveness.

These are the things you learn, and you delight in your ability finally to be able to do a job like this efficiently and well. So many of us forget such joys, the satisfaction of accomplishing a simple physical task with competence.

Standing on the wagon and using a heavy sledgehammer, I pounded in a metal stake every ten feet and to which we fastened the fence. Mary held the stakes in position with understandable reluctance.

Unexpectedly, one of them vibrated violently, banging painfully against Mary's hands. My hammer bounced and slid off the end of the steel post.

"Ow!" she cried, letting go, shaking her stinging hands. "That hurt!"

"Sorry. Must have hit shale."

"I don't know what happened, but there's got to be a better way. You're going to have a wife with mashed potatoes for fingers."

I looked at her hands. "No wonder that hurt. I didn't know you weren't wearing gloves . . . Peter, I left a pair of my work gloves on the toolbox in the garage . . . How about running down to get them for your mother?"

"I've got an idea," John called out, winking at Peter. "Why doesn't Dad hold and Mother can pound?"

"I have a much better idea . . . *You* hold the stake and let Mother do *your* job," I replied.

"Dad . . . ! Come on! She couldn't push this stuff around . . . Let Peter hold for you." He gave an extra grunt as he moved the roll of wire, grimacing for effect.

Peter burst out laughing. "John, you could roll out all the wire at one time and then come back and hold for Dad."

"Maybe John's right," Mary said. "I bet I could use the sledgehammer."

"It wouldn't be good for you. It's too heavy."

"I can try."

"Peter, run on down and bring the gloves, please." I stepped off the wagon, handing her the tool. "If you get into the habit of swinging that hammer, you're going to end up the strongest girl in Lambertville."

She took hold of the handle. But it slipped out of her hands, thumping on the ground, barely missing my foot.

"We'll find a better way," I said, climbing back on the wagon. When Peter returned with her gloves, I tempered my enthusiasm and tapped the stake carefully until it was deep enough to stand without being held and Mary could release it. After she let go, I could pound as hard as I wanted.

When we felt the stake blocked by shale, we moved it a few feet in either direction until it could be driven into the ground more easily. Sometimes we had to pound our way through the thin rock. I liked swinging that twelve-pound hammer. I could almost feel my arms growing stronger.

At one point we ran out of stakes. Peter and John drove the tractor and wagon back to the barn to pick up what we needed.

As we waited, Mary and I walked to a tangled, rocky hedgerow separating two of our fields. We sat on a fallen cedar, gray and hardened by weather and time. We welcomed the respite.

Our farmland fell in quick, esthetic swoops through fields and woods to the river, three quarters of a mile away. You could glimpse the river through the trees in pieces of glistening silver. Beyond, we saw a barn resembling an Eric Sloan painting with muted shades of reds and mauve-colored stone.

Against the horizon, seven or eight miles away, your finger could trace the outline of softly undulating hills. In between were stretches of pines and spruces, splashing the countryside with variegated shades of green. Below us stood our long white barn. Other fields surrounded it.

Animals grazed or lay on the ground, enjoying the unexpectedly warm March weather. The bright voices of children were like echoes of sunlight.

Above, the great wheel of sky and clouds turned slowly like a giant carousel. Its shadows briefly crossed over the land and us. We felt the sudden chill.

I wondered if those shadows presaged something darker in our future. Almost too often to be merely coincidental, good fortune seems to be counterbalanced by its opposite. Perhaps we're not meant to live in extremes. I recalled a friend who won a cherished Pulitzer Prize at the time his wife was dying. In the midst of depressing difficulties Mary and I would frequently discover a small oasis of happiness.

At the moment we were surrounded by joy.

Mary took the opportunity to renew her current campaign as she reached into her pocket, taking out a page she'd torn from a magazine. "I've been reading about these donkeys. They're tiny and would make such an adorable pet for Paul and Eleanor . . . Wouldn't they love one?" She handed me the page. The advertisement extolled the charm of having a Sardinian donkey. "Nothing can compare with one of these little gray donkeys no bigger than a large dog. They will capture your heart."

After a year on the farm, my heart hardened easily against such seductive phrases. "I don't know," I shrugged, not wanting to be negative. "But don't you think that maybe we have enough pets." I counted on my fingers. "Two horses, a duck, chickens who hide their eggs, cats, dogs, gerbils, a hamster, tropical fish, Thompson the Java Temple bird . . ."

"Anyway, I've written for information. We can think about it."

A few days later while Mary took a bath, the telephone rang —a long-distance call from Wyoming. The ranch had received her letter and the caller wanted to tell her personally about these unusual animals. As the bathwater dripped on the rug and she chilled, she began to understand how the man could afford to telephone during expensive daylight hours. The animals were selling for about two thousand dollars.

Vast disappointment. "That's about $1,975 more than we were thinking of spending."

The conversation ended quickly.

But a beautiful vision is hard to shake off, and Mary still had an image of a donkey arriving on Easter Sunday.

One night after we'd put the youngest children to bed, she took my hand, leading me quickly into our bedroom, closing the door behind us. She bounced herself cross-legged on our four-poster double bed. Its fringed canopy nearly touched the low ceiling.

"Guess what . . . ! I've got the most exciting news. I *found* the white donkey Melissa told us about the day of the fire."

When relating an experience, many people just give the salient facts. Others, like Mary, create a narrative. They're the born storytellers. They take you with them on their adventure. Blue eyes merry with excitement, she told me about the event.

"I took Celine, Estelle, and Mark with me. When we found the place, I was really worried and didn't think we should go in . . . Honestly, it looked just like a tornado had whipped through. You've never seen such junk lying around. *Every-where.* Rusted engines, dilapidated farm equipment, old cars, the frame of a pickup truck, pieces of metal, rotting boards. You think we have trouble with *our* fencing. You should see his. Posts were leaning every which way with wire all over the place.

"We didn't dare get out at first. You should have seen the enormous German shepherd chained to this wobbly post. He kept barking at us, and I was positive the post would pull right out of the ground.

"Then a man came out of the house and all I could think of was that he looked like one of the odds and ends he sells. His clothes were the same color as all that rust and grease. You know how some people look so stiff . . . as if their heads and necks were welded together? That's the way he is. I was positive he'd have to turn his whole body if he wanted to look around. He has a huge head and it's set on a neck as thick as a wrestler's. And his stomach . . . it hangs over his belt in the most marvelous way.

"I could tell he was trying to figure out why we were there. I told him I'd heard he had a white donkey. He nodded and I could see him trying to size us up. Then I told him the children would like to see her and he guessed it might be all right.

"We had to walk down a kind of hill because his barn is on a slope and one side is buried in the higher ground. When we went around to the other side, the barn has a big overhang. Everything looked so dreary and dark. You could hardly see inside. The windows were all smoky with dust and cobwebs.

"And he has goats in there too. You know how *they* smell! Then I saw her. This darling animal. She looked as if she were dozing. Her eyes were closed. She rested on one hind foot with the other one forward. Of course, the children went right up to the side of her stall and they put out their hands to her.

"She's really very intelligent. You could almost see her wondering who they were and why they were here. Her ears came forward. She looked *adorable*. I wish you could see her eyes. They're so soft and dark. Just like velvet. But you know what? They have a sadness to them. They really do. A kind of patient, sad wisdom.

"Then I guess curiosity got the best of her and she took a step toward us. But not *too* close. And she put out her muzzle, sniffing the children's hands. I was amazed at the breadth of her forehead.

"Anyway, our eight-year-old redhead almost ruined everything. You know Mark! He can't stand seeing an animal being mistreated . . . Well, he looked at all the rotting straw and manure. He said to the man, 'Sure is dirty and smelly in here. Bet you wouldn't like it if you had to stay in her stall. Don't you ever clean them out?'

"And did that man look surprised. I didn't know what he'd say, but I think he liked Mark's honesty. He mumbled something about not having the time. Poor Celine. She almost died. I know she thought he might tell us to leave.

"Then Estelle asked him how long he'd kept her in the stall. Do you know what he said? I couldn't believe it. Two years! Two

whole years. He said the reason he didn't let her out is she'd run
away. I don't blame her. I'd run away too.

"Darling, I mean it. I've never seen an animal with a pret-
tier face. She reminds me of a fairy tale. You know . . . When a
witch's curse imprisons a beautiful girl inside an animal! When
she's freed, she'll change into an exquisite princess." Mary
leaned forward, laughing at the fantasy. Then she frowned. "I
think I made a mistake."

"You opened the stall door and let her out?"

"I asked him if she was for sale and so he knew I wanted
her."

"And he said he'd trade her for one of our children?"

"He wants three hundred dollars for her. He's asking *three
hundred dollars!* Imagine!"

"Don't."

"Then Mark asked if she was like a horse people could ride.
He said you could ride her. And even more than that, she was
trained to pull a cart."

I could see the snare of desire had entrapped Mary. Her
imagination flared, creating an idyllic image of the children
driving the burro around the farm.

Mary sighed, her strong, artistic hands smoothing the bedspread. "I told him you were *very* firm about not wanting any
more animals."

I nodded, yawning. We were past our bedtime, and 4 A.M.,
my usual rising time, looked too close at hand. "At least for
now."

We were both tired. Quickly we checked the house and
children.

Even in bed, Mary's mind didn't want to leave the day's
adventure. "Her name is Jenny."

"H'mm . . ." My mind rummaged around for information.
"An appropriate name since a *jenny* is a female donkey."

After a bit. "He bought her at an auction." A pause. "Darling . . . ?"

Most of my thoughts had been put on the shelf for the
night. "H'mm."

"Would you just go see her and maybe talk to him?"

We were holding hands. I had no desire nor inclination to refuse.

She squeezed my hand, having read my mind as she so often did.

3

From the moment we met, the junkman and I were antagonists. He had the bulk of an ancient brown rock. I knew he'd be hard to move. A tough old bully, he needed to go to the Wizard of Oz for a heart.

When I saw Jenny, that little white burro in that black hole of a stall, I knew I'd lost the battle. But no matter what, I refused to pay three hundred dollars. That was a ridiculous price.

I asked him for a lead line so I could bring her out into the light. He mumbled about this being a bad idea because she was so d—— smart and could jerk the rope out of your hands. If she did, you couldn't catch her for days. She'd go all over the country. And he let me know that I'd have to be the one to catch her.

I insisted. He put a rope around her neck, handing it to me. She was delighted to be out of the stall. Immediately, she tried to bolt, nearly yanking me off my feet.

"Told you so," the man gloated. I think he hoped she'd break loose. It would serve me right.

It took all my strength to hold her. She was amazingly strong. Whenever I moved close to her, she sidled away. With the children, however, her ears came forward and she remained quiet, putting up her darkly colored muzzle, searching their hands, sniffing them, her breath blowing on them gently.

I studied her. Burros and donkeys have larger heads in relation to their bodies than horses. Perhaps this is one reason why they're so much more intelligent than horses. She stood on gracefully slender legs. Though spotted and dirty from her stall, her winter coat had come in full and white. When I patted her rump, it felt as hard as a board—all muscle and sinew. The tip of her ear missed a crescent-shaped piece, probably from a horse bite. A dishlike dimple decorated her nose.

I found Jenny's feet packed with manure and in very poor condition and her hooves long and chipped. She needed them trimmed. I wondered if she had thrush—a softening and inflammation of the center sole of a horse's or donkey's foot.

"Maybe God sent us to rescue her," Estelle observed.

I cleared my throat, turning to the man. "My problem is we have the farm, and the last thing I need on it is a useless burro."

With mocking disbelief he glanced at my clean khaki pants, my sport shirt and loafers. He saw nothing of the farmer in me. I came clad in the wrong armor.

"I'm going to be on the level with you. I really don't want her," I continued, momentarily discombobulated. "But my family does. I'll take her off your hands for one hundred dollars."

He didn't say the words, but his expression suggested the phrase *You've got to be kidding*. With unruffled confidence he looked at the eager, expectant expressions on the faces of my family. Almost amiable, the man shook his head. "Told your missus the price was three hundred dollars and I was doin' her and the kids a favor."

I had no confidence in my bargaining position. In fact I had no confidence. He seemed so much more sure than I. In this situation he dealt with facts. I negotiated for a family's sentiments without a firm base.

"Okay . . . Let's say one hundred and fifty dollars. You've had feeding expenses and you'll probably want some extra remuneration."

He glared at me angrily, a sudden and unexpected change

in his demeanor. I couldn't understand why. What had triggered the almost violent hostility? Had I inadvertently said something offensive? A particular word? Maybe *remuneration?* But how could he be insulted by *remuneration?* Nothing pejorative about that word. Perhaps he didn't know what it meant. Sometimes we take offense when we think someone is "high-browing" us. Maybe I'd misused it in some way. I didn't think so, but on the other hand, why not make sure?

Wrapping Jenny's lead line around one hand, I reached into my pocket for the dictionary. "Anyone seen my glasses?" I asked, patting the other pockets.

The children groaned. "Oh no! Not now!"

"Darling, don't you think . . . ?" Mary began. She turned to the man. "My husband's a writer and he works with vocabulary."

Another facial expression. *So that's what's wrong with the guy!*

I handed Mary the crumpled paperback. "Well, you probably want to get back the cost of feeding her," I began again.

"She don't eat much. Only a handful of oats," he replied in a testy voice.

I came up to one hundred and seventy-five dollars. He wouldn't budge. Frustrated and exasperated after additional increments of ten dollars each, I made my final offer. "Two hundred and twenty-five dollars . . . Take it or leave it."

He put his hefty hands on his hips. "Mister, I guess you and me don't understand each other. I told you she's worth three hundred to me. If you don't pay it, sometime somebody will. *You* take it or leave it." He snapped back his words at me with equal annoyance.

What an unfeeling, stubborn turkey! I threw him the lead line.

Jenny stood quietly, as if resigned to her fate. She tucked her body slightly back into itself, her ears in a neutral position, her head low.

"Oh, no . . ." Estelle cried, a ten-year-old with a shattered heart.

In anger, the man yanked at the rope. The animal resisted

as well as she could, planting stubborn, slender legs, sliding in the mud. He cursed her, jerking on the rope, which tightened around her neck, choking her.

Walking toward the car, I looked at the faces of my family. I had no recourse. I returned to Jenny. I swear there were tears in her eyes. That was to much.

I resumed bargaining. The negotiations were one-sided. After a series of futile efforts, I capitulated.

Jenny was ours and we belonged to her. The junk dealer didn't even have the grace to give up a few dollars to save my face in front of my family. Celine, Estelle, and Mark rushed to Jenny, jubilantly hugging and patting her.

I wrote out a check for three hundred dollars, reducing our bank balance to about ten dollars. He agreed to deliver the burro on Easter Day.

To my surprise, I didn't think of myself as having been defeated. After all, we'd rescued a most unusual animal.

Mary marked off the days on a calendar until we'd arrived at the one circled in red—Easter.

"If *that man* doesn't bring Jenny soon, I'm going to cry," Mary said, looking at her watch for the tenth time in as many minutes. "It's almost one o'clock and he *promised.*"

"Maybe I paid him a little extra *not* to bring her."

"I know you. She's going to end up your favorite pet . . . Do you think he forgot today is Easter? I called him Wednesday and he said 'no problem.' He'd bring her at one o'clock."

"The time I begin to worry is when people tell me 'no problem.' "

We stood on the kitchen side of the house where we could see up the driveway. Mary had suggested an Easter egg hunt which she hoped she could time in such a way that the arrival of Jenny would be a dramatic climax.

We were both tired. Sunday mornings were never particularly peaceful times in our home. Ideally, perhaps, they should be. But they weren't. Reluctant to get up, the older children slept as long as possible. We'd try to have a leisurely breakfast. It rarely worked out that way. The crescendo of pace increased rapidly, for we went to a 9:15 church service. Getting nine of us fed, dressed, and out in time inevitably ended in frenzied activity. By the time we got to church I really felt I needed it!

We had daily schedules as to who would feed what animals, set the table, wash dishes, and the like. But sometimes the list was either ignored or misplaced. Nor were clothes always where Mary hoped they'd be.

"Mark, can't you find a pair of socks that match? You've got a red one on one foot and a blue on the other and the blue one has a big hole in the heel."

"All I have," the eight-year-old replied untroubled, rubbing Laddie's back. The dog gave rumbling sighs of contentment. "It's good for his arthritis," Mark explained.

"I washed a lot of socks this week."

"Don't know," he shrugged."

"Maybe Laddie took them," Paul joked, punching his larger brother, who jumped up and grabbed him. Laughing and shouting, they scuffled around the kitchen.

"Stop it! Stop this right now . . . Somebody's going to be hurt," Mary cried out, pulling them apart. "We're late already . . . Paul!" she sighed. "You *can't* go to church wearing a sneaker on one foot and a shoe on the other."

"I can't find the other shoe."

"Wear both your sneakers. You've got the right one on your left foot anyway."

"Can't find the other one," the six-year-old explained patiently. "Somebody put them somewhere."

"Well . . . I know who that somebody is. You have to be more careful of your clothes. You leave them all over the house . . . Every place except your room."

"Paul, do you know you're the messiest-dressed boy in school?" Estelle asked amused, commenting rather than criticizing, walking into the room in a slip. Our ten-year-old had a knack of looking neat and trim whatever she wore. "Mom, this hem has a rip and I can't get it right."

Mary examined it. "No one will notice. It's under your dress. We'll fix it later."

"But I don't like it that way."

"Estelle . . . We have to leave. We're late. Your father wants to go. You can't see it."

"Let's get in the car," I called.

"But I want it to look right." She grew teary.

Mary sighed. "Estelle, I'm telling you, you're the only one who will know. There are times when it's not important to be a perfectionist. It's a good quality, but you have to judge when . . . Now finish dressing. Please!"

Frequently, parts of shirts hung outside pants, and ties were askew. Some of the nine heads were brushed and combed and others weren't. Mary's and the girls' always; mine, Peter's, and John's most of the time; Mark's and Paul's occasionally.

Mary got us through this weekly crisis with an unruffled humor, bringing a modicum of order out of incipient chaos.

This particular Easter Sunday began at an even earlier and faster pace. First, before breakfast, the younger children hunted for an Easter basket filled with small presents and candy, then church, and now the egg hunt.

"I'm really upset," Mary said, watching the younger children scurry around trees and under bushes looking for the brightly painted eggs.

"You still have about ten minutes to go before *Jenny hour.*"

"What're you whispering about?" Paul asked. He held a large, floppy, one-eyed bear, low on stuffing but high in character. He and his friend were inseparable.

"Something tells me we might be in for a surprise." Mary's voice implied a mystery.

"What kind of a surprise?"

"Something pretty special."

"How do you know?"

"Just one of those feelings . . ." In an aside, she added, "I'm beginning to feel that *I'll* be the one surprised if there is a surprise."

"Is the Easter Bunny bringing *me* something special?" Eleanor asked, munching jelly beans.

"Maybe . . . We'll just have to wait and see."

Paul bit off a piece of chocolate rabbit, warm and smearing

from being handled by sticky fingers. "There's *no* Easter Bunny. That's baby stuff."

"There is so an Easter Bunny . . . There is so. Isn't there an Easter Bunny, Mommy? Isn't there?"

"Well . . . Some people think so," Mary hedged.

"They'd call her a baby in school if she said she believed in the Easter Bunny. She's four years old!" Paul stated firmly.

"Paul, why don't you see if you can find more eggs? I think there might be a few more out there," Mary suggested, trying to change the topic.

"How come *you* know there are more eggs out there if the bunny put them out?" Paul asked, his logical mind catching the discrepancy.

"Because mothers happen to know a lot of things other people don't know," she replied with mother logic.

Perched on a branch high in a spruce tree, redheaded Mark shouted, "Hi Paul. I'm looking for Easter eggs up here."

Celine ran to her mother, whispering. "Don't worry, Mom. I'll climb the wall in the center circle and watch for the truck. I'll let you know when he's coming." Her sensitive, inner radar so easily detected nuances of feelings in facial expressions and voices. So often she'd ask, "Why are you looking at me that way?" We wondered about her ability to be self-protective. Was she too sensitive, too trusting?

"Hey Mom . . . I see something," Celine called.

"It's a truck," Mark said.

We heard an engine slowing down as if turning a corner. Gears grated.

"It's coming down the driveway, Eleanor. I wonder who's coming to see us," Celine said with an anticipating smile.

An ancient truck appeared over the rise. As it drew closer, Paul's attention riveted on two large white furry ears projecting beyond the top of a cab.

"The Easter Bunny!" he whispered, incredulous—an Easter Bunny so large it had to be carried around in a truck. He watched in stunned awe as the apparition approached.

"I told you so, Paul! I told you so," Eleanor shrieked. "I told you there was a real Easter Bunny."

As the truck stopped, Paul backed away prudently. When
he saw Jenny, he shook his head as if waking up. "It's only a little
white horse. I *knew* there wasn't any Easter Rabbit. It's a white
pony . . . Whew!" he sighed in relief.

Eleanor ran and hid behind me. I picked her up. She
pushed her face against my chest, clinging tightly to my arms.

I turned around. "Look, Eleanor . . . It's a white burro for
you and Paul."

She wouldn't look, keeping her head buried in my sweater.

"Her name is Jenny. She wants to say hello to you."

In between her sniffles, I heard her whisper, "There is so an
Easter Bunny."

John put his head close to his sister's. "Eleanor . . . Now
we have a little donkey. And you can take care of her."

She turned her head slightly, peeking sideways. The other
children surrounded the truck, excited about the new addition.

"It's got rabbit ears," Eleanor murmured defiantly.

Cheerfully, the junkman swung down off the torn sagging
seat in his cab. "Well folks, here she is."

In her joy and relief Mary nearly hugged him. "You're right
on time. Thanks *so* much. She's precious."

Jenny kept her ears forward, looking about her with curiosity. She'd tucked her short tufted tail between her legs, a characteristic of hers we noticed whenever she became uncertain,
angry, or fearful.

Eleanor won her bout with disappointment and embarrassment. She wriggled free of my arms, edging close to the truck.

Like a sail bulging with too much wind, the man's clean,
white, and tieless shirt, which he buttoned to the collar, barely
stretched over his mountainous chest. His jacket, something
approximately a tweed, must have been older than the truck.
Apparently his gray, frayed work pants had received a recent
press.

Jenny stood quietly. He'd scrubbed away the yellowish
manure stains. She almost glistened in the sunlight.

"She's beautiful," Estelle said softly, gingerly patting her
soft nose.

"You gotta remember to hang on to her," the man warned,

glancing at our fields. "Hope you got good fencing, mister. She's smart. Once she's out, she's the devil to get back in."

"She'll be okay. We put in some new fencing last month, and the latches on the gates are strong," I said.

"She's a real good little critter. Won't never hurt no one. Wouldn't have sold her to you if she was dangerous. Not with kids around." His proud smile reached into all the crevices of his face. "Anyway, she's yours now. Just remember she's what you call a real escape artist." Shyly he put out his hand, which wrapped itself around mine firmly.

Quickly, he pulled it away.

"Thanks a lot," I said. "We really appreciate that you arrived on time. And she looks great. We're happy you sold her to us."

Flustered, but obviously pleased, he swung himself back into the truck and drove off.

For a few seconds we were silent as we looked at Jenny. "Guess we'd better introduce her to the rest of the family," I said.

I held the lead line firmly, while Jenny walked after me daintily, switching her tail. She flicked one ear forward and the other back. I wasn't sure what that meant. She looked around her with curiosity.

"Will the other animals hurt her?" Mary asked.

"Don't know." I too had some apprehensions. Like many animals, horses establish hierarchies and frequently attack intruders.

Our two horses, Talla and Babe, stretched their necks over the fence, bending it down, apparently trying to examine this small stranger.

I closed the gate behind us, releasing Jenny. The horses stalked slowly toward the burro, ears flattened, heads down. We could hardly believe these were our two lazy, slow, peaceful animals.

As they approached, Jenny stood her ground, ears forward, soft, dark eyes watchful.

Within a few feet of her, the horses stretched out their necks, teeth bared and ready to bite.

Unexpectedly Jenny hunched up her back, suddenly lashing out with her feet in a sideways motion, just missing the horses—missing them as if deliberately. Startled, they skittered away, galloping across the field, tails flowing behind them, heads held high and to one side so they could see if they were being followed.

We all burst out laughing.

Now that she'd straightened out that situation, switching her skinny tail back and forth, she settled down into doing what we discovered she enjoyed most—nibbling on green grass. She never stopped for the next fifteen years.

For a while, the children played with Jenny, taking turns sitting on her, while someone led her by the halter.

After supper, hoisting Eleanor on my back and with Estelle holding my hand, the three of us went up the field. We had an inviolable rule that all animals must be checked at the very least each morning and evening. Left too long on their own, they can create all kinds of panic parties. Since the weather forecast predicted a relatively warm evening, we decided the animals could remain outside.

"Do you think Jenny's happy?" Estelle asked as we went back down to the house.

"Probably happy as a clam."

"A clam?" Eleanor asked, puzzled. "She's not a clam."

"That's just a saying your grandmother uses all the time."

"Clams can't be happy. They're just clams."

"They smile . . . Ever look at one to see how the line between their shells curves up?"

"Daddy, you're teasing."

That night with Mary comfortably nestled next to me in bed and wedged in with her many small pillows, she held my hand.

"Now, aren't you glad we have Jenny? And wasn't that junkman a darling?"

I sighed. "What bothers me is how wrong first impressions can be."

"At least you have the capacity to change your mind."

"I have to admit I didn't like being beaten down by him. He

didn't give an inch. He really wanted that three hundred dollars. Guess he could use it though."

"So could we."

"Sure could . . . But then it turned out to be a kind of happy trade-off, hasn't it?""

She squeezed my hand.

The next day, the day after Easter, we understood the junkman's warning to us about her being an escape artist.

I'd been up since 4 A.M.

I read the Bible, prayed and meditated, cooked a hamburger and brewed a strong pot of Hu Kwa tea (I know now a lethal diet), and settled down to study and write.

I didn't relish getting up so early, but I found it the only period of the day when children, animals, and telephones were reasonably quiescent. I could concentrate on my work. Often at six I'd do some necessary work around the farm for forty-five minutes or take a run.

In the meanwhile, those children who were slated for farm chores that week were up by six. They worked in pairs. The job included mucking out stalls, putting out grain and bales of hay, filling water troughs, feeding the fowl, finding eggs, and making sure the animals were safe.

At seven Mary fed all nine of us—*her* livestock—an old-fashioned breakfast of fruit, hot cereal, eggs, toast or muffins, milk, and whatever else she thought we'd need to keep us going.

By 7:15 I rushed out of the house for a ten-mile, twelve-minute dash (exactly . . . unless with bad luck I found myself behind a school bus) to a railroad station in a neighboring town with about a minute to spare.

Mary faced her own formidable morning obstacle race to get the children off to school on time.

This Monday after Easter, I'd been working on completing a "Word Power" quiz for a future issue in *Reader's Digest*. Usually I work four months ahead.

At about six, the telephone rang.

"Peter, this is Melissa," her hurried voice told me. "One of your horses just put his head through the open window over our bed and almost licked my face . . . He and the other one and Jenny are heading for Mule Hill Road."

I heard Rex in the background. "Calm down, Melissa . . . Calm down." I envisioned him lighting his pipe.

Dropping my work, I hurried to the kitchen to tell Mary. Celine and Mark shuffled sleepily down the stairs. This week they were scheduled to feed and care for the barn animals. I explained the situation.

"How could they get out?" Celine yawned. "The gates were all closed yesterday afternoon. I checked them."

As we ran to the barn, Mark laughed and said, "Dad, you're still in your pajamas and bathrobe . . . You look so funny."

We weren't the only ones up. The light from Amory Neilson's office window shone brightly in the still partly darkened early morning. He too kept long hours. Opening the door, he nodded. "Ah . . . Up for your morning run, I see."

"Up for the morning chase. The horses are out."

"You know, I saw the gate open a few moments ago . . . Thought you or the kids might be out riding."

"I'm sure it's that burro we just bought. But I don't see how. The spring on the gate is strong. Keeps the horses in."

"Hope you resolve this *enigmatic hugger-mugger* . . . Words out of this month's 'Word Power' quiz," he said, waving cheerfully. "Stop in for a cup of coffee when you've rounded them up."

"There they are," Mark yelled, pointing to the field bordering Mule Hill Road. They grazed near the edge of it. We hurried across the field. Underneath the knee-high grass stiff stubble poked at my feet through my slippers. Cold water soaked through them. During the spring many parts of our fields were soggy.

I glanced at my wristwatch—an hour before I had to leave. It would be a tight fit, but I didn't anticipate a problem in returning the animals to the barn. "Let's work it out this way. One of you get Babe and the other Talla. I'll take care of Jenny."

Nibbling the grass, Jenny watched us. Almost casually she

moved between us and the horses. As we approached them, she moved and the horses shifted away from us with her.

Advancing slowly, I spoke to her quietly. Every few steps I took toward her, she took the same number away from me. And so did the horses. We were coming closer to the road.

I glanced at my watch. I could still make the train. Breakfast would be out of the question.

We edged. She edged, always pushing the horses with her.

"Get on the other side of the horses and you can probably get them. I'll stay where I am."

Jenny must have read our minds. As soon as the children changed direction, she lifted her head high, suddenly trotting toward our unfenced upper field. The horses immediately followed.

Jenny and the horses kept a steady distance from us. We couldn't get closer to them. At this rate, the children would miss their school bus. I doubted whether I could even make the last train, which left at 8:30. That meant I'd have to drive to the city, getting in about noon, missing all of my morning appointments.

An acquaintance raised sheep. During lambing season he and his wife found it necessary to stay up a good part of the night helping the ewes give birth. Too often he arrived in the New York office late and tired. At one point the firm he worked for gave him a choice: the sheep or his job.

I didn't want to be in the same position. The question flickered through my mind again whether we'd been precipitous in taking on Good Ground. If I'd had a job in a nearby town, the constraints of time would not have been so stringent.

One thing I was sure of now, however. Life would never be the same *with* Jenny. I shouted at her in frustrated anger. "Will you stop moving around!"

"Dad, you'll scare her if you yell. Then we'll never get her," Mark said.

"I wish we could be so lucky."

The animals followed the border of the road toward the upper limits of our last field.

"Here come Peter, John, and Estelle," Celine said. "Maybe

we can all get on the other side of her and then she'll head back to the barn. I think we're pushing her in the wrong direction."

"Uh! Oh! . . . There's the school bus," Mark called out.

Halfway down the hill from us, the bus stopped at our gate, picking up Bart Fowler's two children. The Fowlers rented the cottage next to Amory's. The bus lumbered past, crowded with children. Seeing us, they laughed and shouted.

"I'm *so* embarrassed," Celine said, looking at me in my yellow bathrobe with its red Chinese designs, a pocket bulging with my paperback dictionary.

Startled by the noise, Jenny suddenly veered and galloped across the road onto our neighbors' property, which was owned by two retired bachelors, brothers who reminded us of gnomes. They lavished care on their several acres of property, cultivating a peach and apple orchard from dwarf trees.

"We've got to get them out of there," I said urgently.

Already the horses and Jenny were nibbling the budding fruit. A window banged open. "Hey! Get your ass and horses out of our orchard," a voice bellowed, sounding like the fierce troll in Anderson's fairy tales.

"Okay . . . Okay . . . We're trying," I called back. "Don't worry, Joe. We'll get them out. Jenny!" I commanded. "Enough is enough. Stay right there."

At times Jenny's facial expression could epitomize angelic innocence. She looked at me, her velvet eyes gentle and pure. I took a hopeful step toward her. Quickly and daintily she moved a few steps away, always out of my reach. She continued nibbling the small buds.

"If you don't get your ass and horses out, we're going to call the police," the voice trumpeted from the window.

"And I'm going to let them take you back where you came from," I said to Jenny angrily.

"Dad . . . Dad . . ." Peter ran up to me. "You're going about it all wrong. You've got to appeal to her *greed.*" He carried a cup of grain. Approaching Jenny slowly, he poured some of the grain in his hand, holding it out to her, talking to her quietly.

Jenny lifted her head, ears forward, nose sniffing the enticing aroma of the molasses-enriched grain. For a critical second she hesitated. Then, moving a few steps closer to him, she stretched out her neck, licking the grain off his palm. With his other hand, he reached out and easily took hold of the halter.

Smiling happily at me, Peter led Jenny out of the orchard, relishing the success of his ploy. The horses followed dutifully.

The next week, the gnome brothers constructed a monstrously large fence, topped with barbed wire, around their property.

4

The telephone call came on a weekend.

"Peter Funk . . . This is Jerry Collins. I'm a partner in . . ." and he named a prestigious brokerage firm in New York. "A friend of mine in the theater liked your novel *My Six Loves* in *Redbook* magazine and gave me a copy. It has possibilities . . . Would you like to make a musical comedy out of it?"

On a drizzling Saturday morning someone asking me if I wanted to turn *My Six Loves* into a musical? What a question! Would I mind if my goose laid a golden egg each day? Did Ponce de León want to find the fountain of youth? Would the Mets, nearly always at the bottom of the barrel, like to win the National League Pennant?

You bet I wanted to do a musical. But I didn't tell him in those words. I said the idea sounds interesting and let's talk about it.

"Could you join us Sunday afternoon in my apartment in New York? I want to bring together a few people to meet you who would be involved . . . Some of us backed a show you've probably seen." He told me the name. A fabulous success. It still ran to capacity audiences.

Mary, the children, and I flew on euphoric wings. We had it

made. In my imagination we were already at the theater on opening night. Limousines lined the curb. The glamorous and the not so glamorous walked into the theater between rows of excited, curious onlookers. Television lights illuminated the moment. An interviewer asked me questions. I gave sage and witty replies. Mary looked more beautiful than ever. The children, a bit self-conscious, enjoyed every second of it.

I telephoned Sheila, my literary agent. She reacted in a matter-of-fact way. Why did she have to be so low-key and businesslike at such a time? Don't get your hopes up, she advised. The theater's a jungle for the unwary and innocent.

The genesis of my novel *My Six Loves* involved the actress Mary Martin. We knew her slightly through an interview. During a backstage conversation once, she mentioned she would have loved to have been the mother of a big family like ours. Serendipitously, the following day I read a brief news story about a family of six orphans trying to stay together as a family. The incident moved me intensely. Then I began to fantasize what might happen if someone like Mary Martin felt so touched by their desperate situation that she agreed to take them on for the summer to give them a few months respite. The actress in my story knew nothing about children. Would she grow to love them? I wanted to write about love—its joy, its anguish, and paradoxically, its hard edge of reality.

I settled down to do the fastest writing of my life. I completed a fairly lengthy book in a month and then rewrote it several times.

The fiction editors of *Redbook* magazine enjoyed the story's offbeat characteristics and suspense and used it as the book selection for the month.

The following Sunday: A fashionable apartment on top of the world. A blur of people standing, talking, holding drinks. Sheila waved to us from the other side of the room. Mary and I felt we'd walked onto a stage set.

Jerry Collins, dressed in a blue blazer, tan trousers, tan espadrilles, and an open blue shirt. Smaller than I am, he had the thin, alert face of a successful ferret.

Lola Rae, past middle age, wide bottomed and buxom,

wore a casual brown caftan. Her hair, a darkish henna, was a
mess of loose curls. Square faced with confident eyes, she came
across as the preeminent member of the group. In one hand she
brandished a long, gold cigarette holder, out of which a cigarette smoldered. In the other she held a fat Welsh corgi. I
learned she would be the producer.

Lola put down the dog. "General, don't you dare pee on
Jerry's beautiful potted plants." When she spoke to me, in her
mind she was on the stage and I in the audience. She talked
rapidly in a husky voice. "Peter, I want you to meet Don Saint
John . . . We pronounce it *Sinjin* . . . He was a child prodigy
in France and played in concerts all over Europe." She paused,
inhaling her cigarette deeply, tapping the ornate holder, flicking the ashes in the air.

"You probably already know. Don's the assistant conductor
of the State Ballet Theater . . . He composes music, teaches,
and even choreographs some of the ballets. And sometimes he's
a soloist on the piano with the most famous orchestras in the
world . . . And I don't know what else he does." She paused,
smiling benevolently at this paragon. "He's charming too."

Don batted long brown eyelashes at me, ducking his coif-
fured, curly head, a pleasant smile on his round, boyish face.
"Hi, Peter . . ."

"Hi, Don . . ." I couldn't think what else to say to a possible collaborator. We shook hands. The party stopped talking
and watched. Someone took a picture of this historic moment.

Satisfied, Lola continued, her voice slower, emphasizing
the words. "We feel we might have a terrific success here if you
and Don think you can *work* together."

I've worked with a lot of different people in my life and saw
no reason why Don and I couldn't have an amicable partner-
ship. He seemed to be pleasant.

"Let Don teach you," she said as others listened. "Don
knows how to put lyrics and music together. He may look like a
child. But let him be the parent and you the child. Let him be
your teacher . . . Don, why don't you play some of your music
for us. Sing a few songs."

Dressed in a white shirt, white pants, and white loafers, he sat down at a white piano. Don played with style and vivacity. I felt people watching me for my reaction. I applauded at the end, congratulating him.

We met the guests—theater people, potential investors, and the like. Mary and I have never had much to do with theatrical types and the whole thing seemed somewhat stagy to me. But after all, this was theater and to be expected.

A touch on my elbow. "Mind if I make a comment?" The sharp, nervous voice belonged to one of the palest faces I've seen. Her eyes were black and oval, her nose thin, her jet black hair cut in bangs. A black turtleneck sweater and skirt wrapped around a thin body and dark stockings around thinner legs.

"Not at all," I said, wondering.

"She's *unreal.*"

"Who?"

"Mary."

"My wife?"

"Your heroine."

"How . . . ? What do you mean?" I asked.

"Nobody's *that* nice."

"Mary is."

"Mary?"

"My wife . . . She's over there," I said pointing. "By the way, what's your name?"

"Jena . . . I'm Don's wife."

"Glad to meet the other half of the musical family . . . What instrument do you play?"

"I'm a painter."

"Portraits?"

"Abstracts."

"Is painting a hobby or do you sell?"

She nodded. "I sell. Some people seem to think they're nice."

"If your paintings are abstracts, they're *unreal* even if they are *nice,*" I teased. She didn't pick it up. "Well, guess we'll all be seeing quite a lot of each other."

"I guess."

Lola Rae took charge again. Standing in the large living

room with its window forming one entire side, she looked at me. "What we'd like to propose to you, Peter, is that we all work together on spec."

I didn't understand. I glanced at Sheila, who stood next to me.

"Speculation," she said. "No contracts."

"Correct . . ." Lola nodded. "Let's see how the project goes and then we can firm up things later on."

I shrugged. "Sounds all right to me."

Sheila shook her head, her voice crisp. "Sorry . . . As Peter's agent, I can't go along with that. You should take an option on his work. If you're interested in using *My Six Loves* as a basis, that's the least you should do."

Lola waved her golden cigarette holder around. "But my dear, we don't work that way."

"Sorry, but that's the way I'm advising Peter to work."

My stomach began to cramp. Svelte Sheila, with her gleaming hair pulled back into a meticulous bun, was going to wreck everything. Whose career was it?

"I feel it's all right, Sheila."

She shook her head. "Miss Rae, if you want to do it on speculation, that's up to you. But I want you to know I'm working on other deals. For example, if a movie comes along, you have no claim on Peter, his work, or anything else involved in this . . . Are you prepared for that? Do you understand what I'm saying?"

"Absolutely, my dear . . . No ties at all. If Peter wants to take another deal, it's all up to him. He won't have any obligations to us at all," Lola acknowledged breezily, waving her cigarette holder. "Anybody's free to leave at any time."

"I just want to make positive we all understand," Sheila responded. "We know that a musical at this stage is very iffy. If something that looks more solid comes along, I'm going to advise Peter to take it and he owes you nothing."

"But of course! That's what I've been telling you . . . Don agrees. We all agree." She looked over at the window where her dog pressed against a curtain. *"General!* You should be ashamed. Naughty! Naughty!"

"G———!" Jerry said angrily. "I asked you to leave that leaky faucet home. If he ever comes over here again, I'm really going to fix him!"

When we were in the elevator, Sheila emphasized her position again. "It's not a good deal. They may be successful, but I don't like the way they work as far as you're concerned. If they want your story, they should put down money for an option to hold it."

"But if they're successful with this *modus operandi*, why fight it? I can't complain."

"I hope you can say that in six months," she fired back.

Plunging into a cauldron boiling with ideas and techniques new to me, I studied the musicals of Rodgers and Hammerstein and those of Lerner and Lowe, analyzing how they integrated the lyrics with the story and the personalities of the characters.

Don and I worked primarily on weekends. He'd arrive on a Friday night and a blizzard of creativity inundated our home. This put pressure on Mary and the children, for they took over many of my normal chores. We explained the importance of a family working together like this, each helping the other when a particular need arose. In the long run everyone would benefit.

However, in the short run it certainly didn't benefit Mary, who now had ten people to feed every weekend plus those times when Jena, Don's wife, and others from the group joined us. Occasionally we'd persuade Don to play, and for a few moments we'd relish the rare privilege of having a personal concert of magnificent music ranging from classical to pop.

Our usual method of working would be for me to outline a scene for him, giving him its mood and action and the spot where there should be a song. We'd discuss a scene definitively. Then he'd compose the score, either during the week or while we worked together, and I'd match the lyric to its beat. A few times we reversed the process.

I found that working in New York at a high-pressure job and at the same time trying to put together a musical became an exhausting routine. I not only had Don to contend with, but there were also Lola and her partners and advisers. Quite naturally, everyone had suggestions.

Don and I felt sanguine about the music and lyrics, but the story line worried me. I didn't like the way we were adapting it from the book. To add to the strain, I wasn't used to working with an artistic temperament. Mary spoiled me. She's gifted with talent in art. She's spontaneous and romantic. Yet she's so reasonable and intelligent. Paraphrasing Henry Higgins in *My Fair Lady*, "Why couldn't Don have Mary's reasonableness?"

Don was nervous and emotionally unpredictable, needing an array of pills to keep him together. He didn't like working at our home. The irrepressible energy radiating from our spirited family and the hubbub situations we sometimes fell into unnerved him.

The fastidious care he gave his skin and hair fascinated our children. "If your father would use this cream every day on his face, he wouldn't have all those wrinkles."

Celine put her arms around me. "I like my Dad's wrinkles."

"You're my favorite *eleven*-year-old daughter and you get a ten-percent increase in your allowance immediately," I said laughing.

"Why is Celine your favorite?" Eleanor asked, hurt to near tears.

I picked her up. "Celine's my favorite *eleven*-year-old daughter and *you're* my favorite *four*-year-old daughter." It took a few seconds for that to sink in.

Estelle walked past Don's chair in the dinette. She stopped, looking down at his head. "Don, did you know you have a piece of dandruff?"

"What!" he said, his voice rising in disbelief. "Where? Where?" He leaped up from his chair, asking for a hand mirror, examining his hair minutely, muttering, "That's insane. It's not possible. Never. I must have caught it here." He rushed out of the room to wash his hair.

One day as we worked at the piano, he placed his fingers on the edge and looked at me. "Someday you and I are going to have a fight . . . a terrible fight."

"A fight?" I couldn't understand him. "Why should we have a fight."

"Collaborators *always* have a fight at some point."

"Well, this is one time it won't happen," I replied cheerfully. "I don't like to fight."

"You'll see."

"No, *you'll* see."

A few days later he wrote a hauntingly beautiful melody. I wanted to do a lyric that would catch its spirit. We'd worked together Friday afternoon and evening. After he'd gone to bed, I continued to fuss with the lyric, pouring cups of coffee in me. When Don played the music on the piano, I taped it. Now I played it back *ad infinitum*, absorbing its rhythm, matching my words to the beat.

I worked all night. Not really satisfied with what I now thought of as a poem, in the early morning I took a walk. I came out of the woods in one of our lower fields.

The sun blazed over and on and through the dew-drenched wildflowers. I'd never been in the midst of such delicate, exquisite, ephemeral beauty. For an irradiated second I was part of God's heart.

At that moment the entire lyric fell into a whole. I rushed home to complete it.

By the time I finished, I was strung out from too much creative excitement, too much coffee, and no sleep. I couldn't turn myself off. Like an electric current pouring through wires too small to carry the load, energy pulsed through my network of attenuated nerves.

I wandered into the kitchen where Mary had begun to make breakfast. The expression on her face told me that she was about to say, *enough is enough.*

Grabbing a piece of bread and another cup of coffee, I hurried to the playroom before she could say anything about the circles under my eyes. I could hardly wait until Don woke up. I'd placed the sheet of paper with my lyric on the music stand above the keyboard.

Finally he walked down the steel spiraled staircase, sauntering into the playroom still shedding sleep.

He rubbed his eyes. "Hi . . ."

"I finished the lyric. It took me all night."

"Really . . ." He sniffed. "I smell something cooking. You know, I never was much of a breakfast eater, but I love her breakfasts." He moved his neatly combed head in a circle, loosening his neck. "You look sleepy too. Forgot to comb your hair? Just get up?"

"I've been up all night working," I said carefully and tapped the piece of paper on the music stand. "I just finished about an hour ago."

"Really . . ." He yawned, stretching.

My nerves trembled. "I must have rewritten it fifty times."

"Really . . . Last night was the first time I haven't used sleeping pills in a long while. By the way, you know that book you gave me . . . your father's poems. They're fantastically clever. I loved them."

"I think this lyric is the best I've done." I tapped the sheet of paper again. "It matches your beat exactly."

"Really . . . Let's have breakfast and then we can go to work . . . Somehow I'd rather sit around today. Put my feet up . . . read."

"Why don't you play the piece *now*. We can say the words and you'll see how it works in with your music." Riding the crest of creation, I yearned for his approbation. To match a rhythm is one thing. But to have content in the lyric as well is something else. Of course, it's what you strive for.

He shrugged. Sitting down at the piano, his trained fingers skillfully picked out the notes. Leaning forward, he partly sang and spoke the words. He played it through again, dropping his hands to his lap.

"You're half a note off on your meter here," he said, casually pointing to a word.

No acknowledgment of what I'd tried to do artistically. No mention of the intensive work. Not a single word about all that. Only that my meter was off by half a note. An invisible winch began tightening everything inside of me.

"No . . . You're wrong. I'm not off," I said with forced

control. "I paid particular attention to that section. Play it again."

He did. "You're off right at that spot."

"I am *not* off."

"You are."

"I am *not.*"

"Peter . . . You are. *I* should know."

"It's the way you're playing it."

He'd swung around on the piano stool, facing me with what I interpreted as an arrogant expression. *"My* playing!" he said with amused scorn. *"Me! I'm* the musician. I'm the expert, not you."

The inflammatory words ignited a raging fire within me. In its light I saw his fingers. "Don . . . ," I said with quiet, ferocious intensity. "Do you know what I'm going to do to those fingers that earn your living and that express your life . . . ? Do you see your fingers . . . ? I'm going to take each one and I'm going to *break* them one by one . . . *Like this."* I stressed the last words slowly, making twisting motions with my hands, and made a snapping noise with my tongue. I reached toward him.

He stared at me, paralyzed. Then, with a shriek, he lurched off the piano bench, streaking out of the playroom. "Mary . . . Mary . . . Peter's gone crazy . . . He's going to mutilate me . . . He's lost his mind . . . He's going to kill me . . . Help!"

Surprised and elated he would take me seriously, I chased after him, my bellows reverberating through the house. "Even your precious little pinkies," I shouted.

No alarm could have pulled the children out of bed faster. They poured down the stairways.

Don ducked behind a bewildered Mary, who held a pan of muffins she'd just removed from the oven.

"Save me," Don screamed. "Save me from him. He's gone crazy. He's going to mutilate me."

The coffee perked, the bacon broiled, the parakeets chattered, Oliver, the gerbil, twirled on his treadmill, the mesmerized children crowded behind me.

"What's going on?" Mary cried out. "What in the world's happening?"

"Every single finger, Don," I said menacing. *"Every one."* I took a step forward.

With his hands on Mary's hips, he shoved her directly in front of me. "He's gone crazy . . . He's insane . . . He's a wild man . . . Call the police."

Mary stamped her foot angrily. "Stop it! Stop it! Both of you. What's going on? Will someone *please* tell me."

"Nothing much," I said, now calm and enjoying myself. "I'm just going to break his fingers. That's all. He can still conduct, but he won't be playing the piano for a while."

"Wow!" Estelle gasped.

Mary relaxed. "You two! You're just like Mark and Paul when they start roughhousing . . . You've both been working *too* hard . . . Now get washed up. Breakfast is almost ready."

I walked outside. I needed to breathe fresh air. Don remained with Mary.

The children followed me to the terrace.

Peter yawned and stretched his muscular arms, holding a small barbell. Morning was the slow point of the day for him. "Well, that's one way to get us out of bed."

"I bet if Mother hadn't stopped you, you would have done that to Don. Wouldn't you?" Paul asked, as if sorry the excitement ended so undramatically. He tripped on the hand-me-down pajamas that were too big and covered his feet.

"Maybe not *all.*" I winked. "Just one or two."

"God wouldn't have let you do that," Estelle said.

"I wouldn't have let myself do it."

"Why are you always talking about God, Estelle? If Dad wanted to break Don's fingers, God couldn't do anything about it. That's so stupid to say that," Mark said, ready for an argument.

I tousled Mark's red hair and put my arm around Estelle. "Estelle knows what I mean and I know what she means," I said cryptically, not sure of what I meant, though it sounded like something. It seemed to defuse an incipient dispute. I'd had enough contentions for the day.

Celine's meditative blue eyes saw through me, and they grew bright with an inner amusement. "Daddy, you were ridiculous." She began laughing and we all joined in.

Relaxed by now, I decided to apologize to Don. He was a splendid musician and may have been correct about the meter of my lyric. And we had a fondness for him and his crotchets.

One Saturday, Lola and her photographer, Una Betts, came for luncheon. Jena stayed in New York for an art exhibition. Una took pictures of Don and me. Don wore white ducks and a white shirt. He leaped and ran barefoot over the grass, Una's camera clicking away. Mark and Paul couldn't resist tackling him, causing a small, green stain on his trousers. Don fussed over it awhile and then went into the house to change, annoyed.

Lola, dressed in a black and gold blouse with purple pants, her tousled hair needing a touch-up, commanded our terrace. She expounded on her experiences in the theater, talked of a famous director she hoped might be interested, and admired Don's capers. She'd fastened General's leash to the chair.

The terrace extended the length of our house, overlooking the river valley and the countryside beyond. Large and beautifully formed boxwoods grew along the edge of our terrace.

Lola turned and sniffed at them, wrinkling her nose. "They smell like dog piss," she said, referring to the bushes.

Mary winced.

The tan Welsh corgi, lifting his leg toward them, fell off the edge, dangling by his neck from the leash. Lola twisted around to extricate him, and her chair slipped over the side. Like a sack of potatoes tumbling off a ledge, she fell back into the bushes. We helped her up. She was unhurt.

Breathing heavily from her exertions, she scolded General. "Next time don't pee on Peter's boxwoods. They're dangerous." Quickly she regained her aplomb and chatted about her plans for the musical.

Those bushes grow slowly, and for years the gap in one of them brought back memories.

Sheila called one evening. "Peter . . . Some great news. Paramount Pictures is interested in *My Six Loves*. They want to buy it."

What sweet words! Our project worried me and I'd been losing confidence in it. The musical needed my full time and I considered leaving the job in New York. "Think we should go ahead?" I asked her.

"Yes . . . I told them they'd pulled me back from vacation and unless they offer . . . ," and she specified an amount. ". . . I wasn't going to bother talking to them and you wouldn't be interested."

When I heard the sum, I didn't take more than a nanosecond to make up my mind. "Let's go."

The following day she telephoned again, saying they agreed to the price. Mary and I were jubilant. This happened on a Thursday. "Tell them to hold off until Monday. I'm going to let Don, Lola, and the others know. I feel I owe it to them . . . And by the way, if the deal goes through I want to give Don about five percent. He's worked hard."

"You don't owe them *anything,*" an exasperated Sheila told me. "Paramount's ready. Don't fool around."

"It's only until Monday. I'll talk to the group and then report back to you."

Lola spent her mornings working in bed. The maid showed me into her large bedroom, a mélange of untidy elegance. She wore a rich purple bedjacket and waved her long gold cigarette holder at me. Ashes floated over the paper-littered bedspread.

"Peter dear . . . What can I do for you?" She put her cheek forward to be kissed.

I explained the proposal from Paramount.

Lola smiled. "It was thoughtful of you to tell me. If the offer's a firm one, take it. We won't stand in your way. That was our arrangement, wasn't it? Good luck, dear."

I called Sheila from a phone booth in Penn-Central station. "She couldn't have been more gracious . . . They may be a little eccentric, but I guess that's show biz."

"Who says *you're* not eccentric . . . ? Anyway, I have some bad news." She explained that the executives at Paramount were angry at my delay and had dropped the offer to one half.

"Well, tell them to go to Hades, then," I said irritated. "I was just trying to be fair with the others."

"You mean it?"

"I sure do . . . The original price or nothing. I'll go back to the musical. I've been thinking of giving it my full time."

When I reached home, Sheila called to say the film company had come back with the *full* offer. She'd meet with them the following day to work out the contract.

When we finally realized what this meant, Mary and I were stunned. We simply could not believe our good fortune. No way could we stay home for dinner. We called Mrs. McGillian to sit for us and celebrated at the best restaurant in town. For the first time in our married life we didn't bother computing the prices on the right-hand side of the menu.

When we'd finished eating and talking and lay in bed with our arms around one another, visions of sugar-coated money plums tumbled around our heads.

In my office Monday morning, sitting at my desk in New York, I appreciated the fabulous view of the river and of the boats from all over the world that traveled up and down its waters. How often had I watched a small sailboat, longing to be on it. Maybe now we could be the ones sailing.

My secretary handed me an envelope delivered by special handling. The return address spelled out the name of a law firm I didn't recognize. Probably some mutual fund sales agreement.

After opening it, I had to read the letter several times before I could grasp the contents.

Lola, Don, and the others were suing me for breach of contract!

These people with whom we'd been friends, whom we'd entertained and worked with, whom we knew intimately, were suing over a contract that never existed.

Sheila had the good grace not to say the obvious. She explained their action was pure blackmail. Paramount would not go ahead with the film as long as a lawsuit threatened. The group knew that.

We hired a lawyer specializing in such cases and came to an out-of-court settlement. The group's lawyer, someone well known for his expertise in theatrical matters, recognized this as a trumped-up accusation. He looked sheepish and apologetic.

To my astonishment, Don called me several weeks later and in his boyish, offhand way wondered when we might work on something else.

Mary and I invested the money at the time the stock market decided to drop.

Day by day it dropped and dropped. Several times I spoke to members of our firm about selling my shares. "Don't be a sissy," I was told. "This is just a technical correction . . . It's going to turn up."

The market didn't take their advice and continued to drop.

"Stay with it," I was told. "The market's fundamentally sound."

The market "sounded" the depths and my bank called our loan, which had been secured by the stocks. And that was the end of our windfall. However, we had tangible evidence of our experience—a superb tennis court!

Many months later we received an invitation for a private viewing of the film.

At the Paramount building in New York, the nine of us were elaborately ushered into a small theater with plush, red comfortable seats.

My moment of moments began.

The title MY SIX LOVES flashed on the screen before us. Peter Nero's bright, rippling music was perfection. You knew you were in for a merry adventure.

My name appeared in Broadway-size letters. Mary squeezed my hand. Paul said, "Wow . . . That's Daddy's name." Later, however, when the film was released, you had to look fast to see who'd written the book—a few seconds of tiny print.

The first ten minutes caught the essence of the story and I sat enthralled. But then, as if we'd been driving along a road I knew well, the film began to take unfamiliar twists and turns. I couldn't recognize the landscape. Occasionally something familiar would surface. But the scriptwriters had eviscerated the story. They'd cut the guts out of it.

I tried to write about love—not just physical love but the kind of love that's filled with compassion and concern; love freely given for the sake of another; love that wipes away tears and comforts and protects; love that accepts responsibility. But they'd made an *Our Gang* type of comedy.

Admittedly, it had a number of good, humorous scenes. Not all bad. But not all mine. I ended the preview with a burning stomach. Later I asked the film editor why they'd made all the changes.

"Don't know . . . I think it was a mistake. But that's Hollywood for you."

In truth, I had few complaints. I'd been paid well for a story I enjoyed writing.

A paperback publishing company asked me to do a book for them based on the film version. I refused but suggested instead they print my original manuscript. They did, and when I first held the book in my hand it became mine again.

One day on the early morning train to New York I realized the tall, lank man next to me would occasionally burst out laughing at a book he was reading. To my surprise I saw it was mine, and I entertained myself watching the shift of his emotions.

"Did you tell him who you were?" Mark asked at supper.

"I shook my head.

"You *didn't?*" Peter said. "Why not?"

"Daddy . . . You should have," Celine added. "He would have been so surprised. Next time it happens, you tell the person."

It's hard to believe, but the following morning the same man sat next to me, still reading *My Six Loves* and still laughing at parts. Following the encouragement of my family, I introduced myself. When he looked at me, I could read his thoughts in his eyes: *What kind of nut is riding this train?* I explained about yesterday and what my children said, apologizing for interrupting him.

He was polite and restrained, and I extremely embarrassed. When the train reached New York we shook hands.

He joined someone he knew on the platform, moving rapidly away from me. As they walked up the exit ramp, he looked back over his shoulder and pointed in my direction. Then, turning to his friend, he tapped his head, shaking it.

5

_____

When we so eagerly take on pets for our own joy, the thought rarely occurs that sorrow often walks hand in hand with love. We learned this too often on our farm.

As Mary and I looked around our household menagerie, we felt like curators of a miniature zoo.

One early winter morning, eight of us crowded around the table in the small dinette, finishing Mary's farm-sized breakfast. We had no fussy eaters. If you didn't like it, there was nothing else. What one didn't eat, another would finish.

Celine was outside feeding her rabbit, Popcorn. We'd set the animal's cage in a grove of trees and bushes at the back of the house. She felt uneasy about the place and mentioned it several times.

In a few minutes I'd be racing off to New York and the children would be getting ready for school. Quickly, Mary and I reviewed various plans and errands for the day, writing notes to ourselves. The youngsters talked and joked, some more awake than others. Peter muttered to himself as he wrote hurriedly in a workbook.

Eleanor's two gerbils inhabited the waterless fish tank on the side table. Oliver considered his occupation to be twirling tirelessly in his wire treadmill, while Lady worked incessantly at building her nest.

Mark peered into the tank intently. "Aren't they cute . . . I think she's going to have babies. She looks kind of fat."

John leaned on him, looking over his shoulder. "I think you're right. You know what, Mark. Since you want to be a doctor, Lady can be your first patient. You can be her obstetrician."

"I hope I'm here when it happens," the eight-year-old said with a quiet wistfulness. He pressed his forehead against the tank, reddish curls spreading over the glass. Mary and I observed that though Mark could be annoyingly argumentative and stubborn, he was an unusually caring and gentle youngster.

In an adjacent cage, old Sir Tom, Paul's hamster, as calm and steady as an ancient hermit, munched his breakfast seeds. On the same table, next to the telephone, multicolored fish swished around in their tank, darting around the air bubbles, the flora on the bottom waving slowly in the miniature currents. The two cats, with tails curled neatly around them like fur pieces to warm their haunches, ate out of dishes in a corner. Mark had fed Laddie earlier.

"By the way," Mary said, "who remembers what happened in 1066? We studied it last night."

To give the children a sense of history, each night at supper we went over an important date.

"I'm tired of learning things when we're home. That's what school's for," Paul complained. "When I'm at the Jenners' house, they don't have any of this learning stuff."

"Paul, you're just a sport's jock," Estelle said. "Something to do with England?" she answered her mother. The child's hair turned up in a graceful wave above her shoulders.

"Battle of Hastings when France invaded England," Peter said, not looking up from his work.

"And changed the English language from Old English to having more French words . . . Became Middle English," John added, glancing at me, his body tensing with the pleasure of knowing.

I nodded. "Right . . . It's when English truly became more of an international language."

"Peter, you haven't taken out the trash," Mary reminded.

"Let John do it. I've got to finish my homework."

"Why should I do your jobs when you *always* leave your homework to the last minute?"

"John, we're not all as well organized as you," Peter said with mild, brotherly sarcasm.

John was organized. He went immediately to work when he arrived home from school. One of his teachers told us he'd never known a boy who could concentrate so intently.

"Yeah . . . Well, you spend all your time reading instead of doing your homework."

"Peter, the trash is your job this week," I said.

"I don't know why John . . ." he grumbled, getting out of his chair.

Mark came up to his mother. "I'm all ready for school. I can help you."

"Oh . . . Thank you. Your poor old mother can stand some help this morning."

"You aren't so poor," he said with sly humor, obviously ignoring *old*.

Mary laughed. "Thanks a lot." She looked at Paul. "Why don't you see if you can find your brother a pair of clean pants. The ones he has on have holes in them. And that sweater! Paul, how can you be so messy?"

"It's easy," the six-year-old grinned, carrying his plates to the sink.

The radio competed with Eleanor's noisy, loquacious parakeets. During periods of questionable weather we left it on because a farm is directly influenced by the vagaries of weather, especially when livestock is involved. Today had the feel of a storm. When I tapped the barometer in the library, the needle jerked downward. Usually barometers rise in the morning and drop in the afternoons.

". . . and heavy snow is expected to begin falling this morning," the announcer intoned.

I turned the radio louder, asking the children to be quiet

even if the birds would not. ". . . probably continuing through the night. High winds are predicted by early afternoon."

"Sounds like a big one . . . Did you leave the animals in the barn after you fed them?" I asked Estelle and John. This week they had the barn chores.

John nodded. "The way the wind's whipping around up there, they didn't want to go anywhere. We decided to leave them in. The water froze in the buckets."

"Did you give them fresh water?"

"*Dad!*" John said reproachfully. "Sure we did. By the way, the warming wire around the water pipe was unplugged. We plugged it in again."

Where we'd lived previously, a storm was simply a storm. Perhaps school would close for the day. Watching the weather news on TV, the children would have only a remote, second-hand feeling about it. Today, however, they were fully a part of the experience. Their decisions affected the safety and comfort of animals.

When Celine opened and closed the kitchen door to the outside, we felt the fresh, cool air puff past our faces. She pulled off the red and white knitted hat from her head and the long blond hair tucked underneath tumbled to her shoulders. Her eyes seemed bluer against her cheeks pink with the morning cold. Her hair, eyes, coloring, and slightly high cheekbones created a portrait Renoir would have appreciated.

"Do you think Popcorn will be all right?" she asked, taking off the worn work jacket. Her face reflected a worry.

"We can bring him in this afternoon after school," Mary suggested. "We'll fix up a nice place for him in the playroom."

"He looks kind of unhappy . . . Maybe I should do it now."

"He'll be all right till you come home. He has a good warm box with lots of straw . . . and his cage is practically as big as all out of doors." Mary looked at me and laughed. I amused the family with my carpentry exploits. Somehow everything I build doubles in size, and we had to dismantle the cage before we could get it out of the cellar.

"Couldn't I put him in a cardboard box until we come home?" Celine asked.

"He'd chew his way out of there in no time. You better think about getting ready for school. We're running late."

Reluctantly I left for New York where I was still sales manager for a couple of mutual funds.

Later that morning, from my office high above lower Manhattan, the heavy mist of tiny, swirling snowflakes looked as if the Milky Way whirled past my window.

I watched the thickening snow gradually obscure that part of the bay formed by the juncture of the East and Hudson rivers. Governor's Island became a vague shadow in the distance and then no more. Fierce winds rattled our windows. We were caught in the belly of a mighty storm.

Everyone in the office welcomed the announcement we could leave by three o'clock. I'd planned to go anyway. It wouldn't be long until our country roads became impassable. Actually my happiest moment of the day was when I left the office. I couldn't wait to get out of there. As a writer and linguist I felt awkward in Wall Street, as if I lived a double life. I was a closet writer.

I can, though, understand the excitement people have about business. Putting together a successful deal can be as satisfying in its own way as creating a painting or a piece of music or writing.

By the time the delayed train reached my station, thick night wrapped around me. It seemed as if I drove through a snow tunnel surrounded by blackness. High-crowned roads threatened my car with a slide into a ditch. I passed several abandoned cars hopelessly stuck. Growing drifts stretched across sections where the gusting winds blew across open fields.

My headlights beaming down our long driveway through the dust of eddying snowflakes indicated that in a couple of hours no car could get through. Snow streaking across the field to my right poured over the bank, spilling on the road in an airy waterfall.

A warm, yellowish light glowed from the windows of our home. I knew Mary would be anxious about me. There's an excitement to a storm, though you enjoy it most when you know you're safe.

I walked into a kitchen steaming with warmth and enticing fragrances and brimming over with life.

Estelle, Mark, Paul, and Eleanor gave me an enthusiastic cheer. "Daddy's home . . . Daddy's home . . . Guess what . . . ? Do you know what happened to Celine . . . ?"

Slender Mary put strong arms around me. They got their strength from lifting children and from the house and farm work. One time, in her delight at having me home, her squeeze cracked one of my ribs. "Thank heavens you're home. I've never seen a worse night."

"Guess what happened . . ." Mark said.

"Let me tell . . . I want to tell," Eleanor cried out.

"Popcorn's *gone,*" Paul's voice shot out from behind me.

"*I* wanted to tell Daddy," Eleanor complained. "That's not fair."

"Poor Celine," Mary explained. "I feel so terrible about it. I can't get her to come in out of the storm. She's looking for Popcorn."

"And she keeps crying," Eleanor said.

"What happened?" I asked.

"The biggest branch of the tree fell on the cage and knocked it over. The cage got all broken . . . ," Estelle began.

"And Popcorn got out and ran away," Mark finished.

"The winds have been terrible. Celine's been out there ever since we've been home," Mary said. "We've all looked . . . But how can you find a white bunny in the snow at night? And I feel so awful. As if it's my fault because I didn't really think about it. She wanted to bring him in this morning. I should have let her."

"There weren't even any tracks. The wind and new snow covered them," eight-year-old Mark said, his face flushed almost the color of his hair.

Taking a flashlight and putting on my galoshes, I walked around to the back of the house. Since the storm blew from the northeast, that section was temporarily protected from the full force of the wind.

I found Celine on her hands and knees, crawling through the bushes, lumps of snow falling off the branches on her. "I can't find him anywhere, Daddy. He's going to freeze to death."

"Maybe not. Don't forget he's used to being outside. He's not like a house rabbit and he does have a fur coat."

"But he's not used to being outside of his cage. And he could get lost. I'm scared he'll die." Tears and melting snow flowed down her cheeks. One of her gloves had fallen off, and her small hand looked blue in the beam of my flashlight. I put my glove on her hand. "It's my fault," she said. "I knew I should have taken him inside this morning."

"It's not your fault. It's *our* fault."

"I could have put him in my room with newspapers on the floor," she sobbed.

I took her frozen face in my hands. "Let's do this. You go back to the house and get warm. I'll keep on looking. And I'll put some feed in front of his house . . . Maybe make a little trail of it to bring him home."

She nodded, resigned. "All right . . ."

A half hour later, my feet cold, my fingers stiff, my business suit soaked from crawling through the bushes, I felt Popcorn had to be a most perverse rabbit. He couldn't have gone far. He had to hear us calling. Life was much safer in a cage. What was wrong with the stupid animal!

I kept going a while longer, even though I felt sure this was no time to look for him. But I had a vision of an eleven-year-old's face spilling over with joy as I walked in with the wriggling bundle of fur.

I gave up. Passing the cage, I noted with some satisfaction that at least it took a *big* branch to smash my creation.

The blazing fire in the hearth, keeping us snug against the surging winds, couldn't dispel our concern for Popcorn. Celine kept getting up, cupping her hands against the black window-panes, peering out into the raging night.

At one point, I put an arm around her shoulder, pulling her to me. "You know, I've been thinking about something. Maybe he's having an adventure he's always dreamed of. I've never liked seeing animals in a cage, anyway. They can't talk. But they have feelings . . . I watch Oliver running around his tank, trying to climb out or going around and around in his treadmill . . . Why wouldn't they like to be out, feeling the earth under them, nibbling grass, being a part of what they were meant to be . . . ? I don't know. Maybe it's worth the danger for Popcorn."

As Celine and I looked out into the night storm, worrying about Popcorn, I thought about the unexpected sadness pets bring into our lives. I wished I could reassure our child about the little rabbit.

There's nothing quite like waking up to a clear morning after a heavy snow storm. The world's been transformed by nature's magic gift. Above you the sky is an azure blue of such purity that you're afraid your eyes may mar it if you look too long. The snow glistens as if trillions of diamond slivers sprinkled the surface. The pristine whiteness surrounding you is so bright you squint your eyes. Then there is the antithesis—the dark trees whose branches stand out in the snowscape like the ribs on a Halloween skeleton.

Celine was first outside. Carefully she searched the area but found no sign of Popcorn. She left more lettuce and pellets in front of his wooden house.

Mary tried to comfort her. "Maybe he dug a hole in the snow to keep warm. Animals do that and so do Eskimos."

She shook her head, her long, finely sculptured fingers touching the corner of an eye. "He died . . . I dreamt he died."

"Listen, most of the time those kinds of dreams never come true. They're just worry dreams."

"I bet God will take care of him," Estelle said.

We knew there'd be no school, and no way could I get to New York. Even if we plowed and dug out our driveway, there was no guarantee the county plow would get to Mule Hill Road. Our road always seemed to be last on the list. We were jubilant. We'd been handed a free day.

"I've got an idea," John said at breakfast. "Let's go skiing at Trapper's Mountain."

All the children, except Celine, shouted in happy agreement.

We joked about our Trapper's Mountain ski area. The "mountain" was only a six hundred-foot-high hill. But it had a dangerously precipitous slope, the length and width of a football field. Because the slope bottomed out almost at the edge of the road, bales of straw created a protective barrier of sorts. There were times when gratefully I ended up draped over a bale instead of the hood of a passing car.

The county went all out on the project, putting in a snow machine, a rope tow, and, to our amusement, a chair lift. A *chair lift* for six hundred feet!

On weekends the slope became as crowded as a Los Angeles freeway during rush hour.

After breakfast clean-up, the children raced upstairs to get ready to go out. Celine stayed with us.

How revealing a child's eyes. How much more than tears. The inner sorrow is told without words, without sound. In a child's eyes is the essence of feeling.

Though she said nothing, Celine's blue-gray eyes reflected poignant distress. She moved listlessly during the bustle of cleaning up the kitchen after breakfast and while completing her various other chores.

Mary tried to divert her. "Celine! *Look* at this window . . . ! You're my little artist. Isn't it exquisite?"

She pointed to the kitchen windowpanes, completely layered with ripples of ice of varying thicknesses and textures and with rough ridges as if poured from a silver candle. Subtle, barely discernible shadows of light touched the surface. The early sun glowed through the center pane, the illumination becoming a golden halo spreading across the ice fabric, a vision of breathtaking beauty.

"Oh . . . ! It is," Celine murmured, entranced.

"Mom . . . Do you know where my gloves are?" Estelle called, ready to go out. She paused. "What're you looking at?"

"The windows . . ."

"Wow . . . That's beautiful . . . It's just as if God was coming into our house."

The other children trooped into the kitchen, dressed for outside, skis and ski poles rattling, banging against the furniture and walls.

"Hey Celine! Aren't you coming?" John asked. "We're going to be leaving in a second."

She shook her head. "I don't think I want to go."

"It's going to be *great!* This is the best skiing day we've had all year. You'll really have fun."

"I don't feel like going."

"Sure . . . ? We'll wait for you."

"John's right," Mary added. "It'll be so good for you to go out. And you love skiing."

She shook her head.

"I want to go," Eleanor cried. "I want to. Paul's going. Why can't I?"

"You don't know how to ski, Eleanor," Paul explained.

"I'm always left behind," she cried. "I hate being the littlest.

Peter bent down to her. "When I come back, I'm going to take you out on our hill and I'll show you. There's a small pair of skis in the garage we've all learned on."

When the door closed, they left silence behind them.

Mary and I glanced at one another, each knowing the other wondered how we might comfort Celine.

"Why are you looking like that?" the child asked. We found Celine especially sensitive to moods and facial expressions in others.

Mary took her hand. "We feel so bad for you . . . I'm just so darn sorry I didn't listen to you about bringing in Popcorn yesterday."

"It isn't your fault."

"It is . . . I guess I get so busy sometimes . . . ," Mary sighed wearily. My sister Joan, knowing Mary's daily schedule, jokingly called her *weary dearie.*

"Listen, I have an idea," I said. "Last night I was fooling around with a theme for the next 'Word Power' quiz . . .

Come on up with me to the barn office and you can help me. I'll show you the way I work."

I put my arm around Celine's shoulder, walking out of the kitchen with her. "Put on your boots. The snow will be deep."

Mary took Eleanor out to sled on our small hill.

The barn office was almost too ideal as a workship with its windows on three sides of the room. My concentration often wavered whenever I looked up, pulled away by the different panoramas.

The room had no rugs or curtains and was furnished sparsely with a couch, a couple of office-type chairs, three desks —two of which were hollow doors on iron legs. Bookshelves lined one wall. I liked the simplicity.

One of my desks, a dark oak one with a myriad of small drawers and cubbyholes, belonged to my grandfather, founder of Funk & Wagnalls. I placed a picture of him sitting at his desk on its corner, a desk as cluttered as mine now. His office seems a jumble of papers, books, manuscripts, rows of card files which were probably citations of different words to be used for an updating of the dictionary.

One time I studied the picture closely with a magnifying glass and he became a reality for me, more than merely a photograph of a grandfather I never knew.

I wondered what work engaged him when the photographer took the picture. What manuscript is that on his desk? A powerful man with large, strong hands, wearing a frock coat, he's poised holding a pen. His sturdy body is ready for action. The magnifying glass shows a big ink spot on his thumb. His hair and beard are white and he has a prominent nose.

He looks at me with an alert, questioning, penetrating glance. But those eyes look a little tired, meditative, and even sad. He'd been a minister before turning publisher and I've wondered what his sermons were like.

The picture gives me a sense of personal history and a feeling of continuity. My father, Wilfred, continued the tradition of lexicography, passing it along to me. There's a certain satisfaction in carrying on a family trade.

"Here, sit beside me," I said to Celine, pulling another

chair to one of the flat tables, littered in much the same fashion as my grandfather's desk. "We'll talk a little bit about the theme for the next quiz and then we'll select some of the words . . . By the way. Do you know what *theme* means?"

She shook her head, watching me attentively.

"Well, let's see." I searched for a metaphor that might be helpful. "You know how one song is different from another?"

She nodded.

"It has its own tune. Like 'Happy birthday to you; happy birthday to you,'" I sang. "And so on."

She nodded again, her sweet face observant.

"It has its own special notes you can sing . . . Anyway, a theme is similar. It's more or less a single idea. And for the 'Word Power' quiz, I look for one particular idea or theme. Then I pick words that fit into that theme. And I try to think of what will interest my readers, what words they might like to know about."

"How can you tell?"

"I've had a lot of experience," I replied, thinking about her question. "I study a lot. I read the letters people write me. I guess I've developed a feel for it."

She nodded again and laughed. "Your desks are kind of messy. You're lucky you're not us. Mother would make you clean up."

"You're right. They are messy. Maybe sometime you can help me pick up. The trouble is I start working on something and forget . . . Now the theme for this quiz is going to be based around words that are fun to say or have an interesting sound." I paused, trying to think how she could feel a part of this. "Are there any words you think are funny or have a funny sound to them . . . ? Or maybe words you like?"

She looked away, her eleven-year-old face frowning a little in thought. Then she smiled. *"Bluckmush!* Remember Paul used to say *bluckmush* a couple of years ago?"

I repeated the word, laughing, remembering it well. "He used it whenever he didn't like something."

"Mother told him that rhubarb tastes good and he said it was *bluckmush* and then he'd laugh because we would."

"That's a perfect example of what this business of words is all about," I said enthusiastically. "Perfect! You see, a word's nothing more than a symbol. The only reason the sound has meaning is because we've *given* it a meaning."

A wondering, baffled expression crossed Celine's face. I knew I'd lost her.

"Does *bluckmush* mean anything to anyone outside the family?" I asked.

She thought about that, shaking her head.

"But it does to Paul."

"When he doesn't like something."

"And Paul made up the word," I continued. "You know what *house* means?"

"Oh Daddy . . . That's so easy."

"Sure it is, because everybody who speaks English uses the same word. But if we called it a *diddlydink* . . ."

"Diddlydink . . . !" she laughed. "Diddlydink! What's that?"

"Well, if everyone used that name for a house, that's what it would be and we'd know what it meant. A word is only a symbol for something. That's all. *Bluckmush* was Paul's verbal symbol for 'I don't like it.' *House* is our symbol for 'a place in which we live.' If we were French, we'd say *maison.*" I glanced at her. "I have a feeling I'm confusing you."

She looked uncertain. "Kind of, I guess."

"Well . . . why don't we talk about the theme for this quiz? Since part of the fun of speaking comes from the sound of words, I've been thinking about words that might fit . . . Now where did I put my glasses, darn it?" I stood up, patting my pockets.

Celine laughed. "Daddy, you're always losing them." She reached under some papers and pulled them out. "Here they are."

"Thanks . . ." I glanced at the notes I'd made last evening.

"Some words might make you laugh when you say them. I've always found *flabbergast* funny . . . Other words may sound as smooth and round as a stone. Doesn't *avuncular* seem that way?" I pronounced it slowly. "Or a word can be as pointed

as a sharp stick, maybe like *gawk,* or there's *dillydally* that
always reminds me of a nursery rhyme . . ."

"What's that mean?"

"To dawdle or waste time in doing something . . . I try to
encourage people to use colorful words. You like to paint pictures. Supposing you only had a couple of colors to use. You
couldn't do what you wanted to."

"I could mix them and get some more."

I smiled at the sensibility of her reply. "You're right . . .
But you still wouldn't have as much fun as if you had a lot more
to use. And that's the way it is with words. The more words you
know, the more color you bring to your writing and speaking
. . . Maybe we'll start with *flabbergast.* Know what it means?"

She shook her head.

I tried to think of a way to help her know it, to have the
word become more a part of her. "Maybe we can act it out," I
mused, standing up. "Flabber . . . Now what would flabber be
like . . . Something limp?" She watched me with an affection-
ate, amused look which I interpreted as *Here goes Dad again
with his words.* "How would you do it?" I asked. She stood up
and let herself wilt to the floor, smiling a bit shyly as she did.

"That part of the word comes from *flabby* and when you're
flabby you're apt to be a little limp and soft, aren't you."

"I guess so."

"Let's go to the other part of the word . . . *gast.* I think it
comes from *aghast,* 'a feeling of being amazed or stunned.' At
any rate that's one of the meanings. Another one is 'horrified.'
But for our purposes now we're interested in the meaning of
amazed or surprised because it's involved with the meaning of
flabbergast . . . How would we act out *aghast?*" My thespian
talents are meager, but Celine is clever at mimicking or depict-
ing something accurately. She caught *aghast* exactly and we
burst out laughing.

"Do you remember," I said, "when Rex Etherington came
to the house dressed up as a ghost on Halloween. He was about
to ring the doorbell when Mark, who was going outside for some
logs, unexpectedly opened the door. Mark was so surprised he

sagged down to his knees . . . *That's* what it means to be *flab-bergasted.*"

"This is a fun way to learn words. I wish they'd teach us like that in school."

"I do too . . . You can do this with a lot of words. Now that we know exactly what the word means, we want people to play a game. And so we need to think up three other answers that *sound* right. They aren't right, but they may fool some readers. We have a list of twenty words, and each word has one correct answer and three that aren't . . . So, let's see what else *flabbergast* sounds like."

Celine thought for a moment. Standing up, she yawned, stretched, and finally sprawled on the couch, closing her eyes.

I clapped my hands at the performance. "You're a great mime. *Exhausted!* Perfect!"

She looked proud.

"We need two more," I said. We thought awhile. "When Mark collapsed in surprise, how do you think he felt?" She sat curled up on the couch, head in her arms, trying to imagine. "How would you feel?" I asked.

"If it happened to *me?*" She sat up, her eyes opening wide. "I'd be *so* embarrassed . . ."

I interrupted her. "Alternate answer number two and it's a good one . . . Hey, you're terrific. I'm going to have you help me every time . . . We need one more. Let's see. What could be another feeling you might have . . . ? You've been *surprised* and you're *exhausted* and you've been *so embarrassed* . . . Let's set a scene. Geoffrey's visiting you . . . That guy in your class who thinks you're super. You ask him to help you get a log. You open the door and find Rex standing there about to knock. You collapse on the floor right in front of Geoffrey . . ."

"In front of *him* . . . ! I'd die. I'd absolutely die. I'd be *so* mad at him for being there . . ."

I wedged my voice in between the exited spate of words. "Not *mad.* Maybe annoyed."

"I'd be *mad.*"

"Well, the problem with *mad* is that it also means 'crazy.' 'Enthusiastic' is another meaning. I'm *mad* about words . . .

So let's stick to *annoyed."* I looked at my notes. "Good . . .
Now we have to find out where the word comes from and after
that to work out a sentence to illustrate how it's used." I pointed
to the row of dictionaries on the shelf, the ones on my desk, and
all the other reference books. "I'll be going through at least
seven or eight of those to get an up-to-date consensus of the
meaning."

"There're so many words I don't know," Celine said, looking distressed. "What's consensus?"

"It's when a majority of people agree about something
. . . On some words I'll go through a dozen or more reference
books."

She looked at the array of books on the shelves. "All those
have to do with words?" she asked.

"In a word, yes."

She collapsed on the floor. "I'm flabbergasted."

I laughed at her. "I wonder how you'll feel when you get to
word number twenty."

"That's too many. I'm exhausted."

"The thought of it *discombobulates* you."

"What?"

"Dis-com-BOB-you-late," I said, pronouncing each syllable,
stressing the accented one.

"What does *that* mean?" She made a face, blinking her eyes
at me in the unhurried way Licorice, our cat, did. I'm not sure if
she taught him or if she'd been a copycat.

"It means you've 'been thrown into confusion.' " I looked at
my watch. "Maybe that's enough for today. I'm pretty sure the
county will have Mule Hill Road plowed out later this afternoon
. . . Want to help me plow with the tractor? You might have to
do some digging in the snow. But that will work up an appetite
for a *scrumptious* dinner."

"I know what that means. Mother uses it sometimes. She
says that something is *just* scrumptious. Doesn't it mean 'something's really good?' "

"Right . . . ! 'Very pleasing and delicious.' Used mostly
with food."

We kept the John Deere tractor in the barn. Fortunately,

I'd put the chains and snowplow on the previous week. Snow-plowing is similar to mowing a field or lawn. You have the visible satisfaction of having accomplished something.

Initially we had to punch our way through the drifts near the barn, the snow falling off the edge of the plow in white cascades. Eventually, however, a snow wall would build up that stopped us. At that point I jumped off the tractor and Celine and I dug away the high mass of snow.

Gradually we worked down the driveway, the snow piling up on the side of the road into relatively high banks. Celine sat alongside of me. When we reached Mule Hill Road we shoveled away the accumulated mounds. Turning the tractor around, we reversed the process, now clearing the snow off the other half of the road.

I loved that faithful old machine. It was a glorious, two-cylinder green monster. Occasionally its nervous system went awry when wires crossed. But that happens to all of us. And it made a lot of noise. But that was all right too, because it spoke with authority. That tractor meant business. No lollygagging for it. The red-hot muffler caused the snow-mist coming from the plow to hiss and disappear. The chains clanked heavily, biting solidly into the snow. It was a grand day to be plowing.

As we chugged by Amory Neilson's office in the barn, he opened the door. "Any words to describe today?" he challenged, waving to us.

I thought a moment. Sometimes the pages of my mental dictionary stick together and I can't think of the word I want. Today, however, I lucked out. "It's a day of irrefragable beauty," I called back.

"I'll check it out in the next 'Word Power' quiz," he chuckled and returned to his office.

We parked the tractor and shut the barn door.

"What if my prayers about Popcorn aren't answered?" Celine asked as we went through the feed room. The rich smell of molasses in the grain sweetened the air.

It seemed to be my hour of sighs. "That's the age-old cry of hurting hearts . . . It's a tough question. A very tough one . . . Well, for me I know by this time that my prayers are answered. *But* the truth is, not always the way I thought they'd be. And I have to admit I haven't been a hundred percent happy about the results. But then most of us spend our life in the dark with only a weak flashlight. We can't see very far ahead. Sometimes it's taken me years to understand how a personal prayer has been answered . . . It's a matter of trusting God. *Really* trusting God . . . I keep working at it."

We walked through the barn past the horses' stalls. They kicked their feet against the doors, trying to get our attention. Jenny brayed loudly, and Hubert, the gander, arching his neck and lifting his white body, honked.

"Later, guys," I said. "Be patient."

Holding hands, we walked across the field to the house. "Are you ever afraid of dying?" Celine asked me in her direct, gentle fashion.

I stopped, wondering just how honest I should be. I looked around at everything I loved—everything that created this beauty; that created Mary, my daughter standing beside me, the other children, my work—everything. Everything.

"I'd be sad to leave. Even when I'm unhappy I'd rather be right here . . . Sure I'd be a little scared . . . No, that's not right. I'd be scared to death . . ."

We looked surprised and then laughed at the unexpected play on words. "I'd probably be *very* scared to die right now. It'd be like taking an examination when I'm not prepared."

She searched my face as if expecting more.

I thought of the many faces of death. "The word *death* is an interesting one. I mean, for some people death is the end . . . the end of everything. For me and others it means the beginning of something exquisitely wonderful . . . Can you see what I mean now when I say a word is only a symbol? For example, for doctors death is a clinical term that describes the time when a body stops functioning. Like turning off the tractor. But it's not an end. There's no end of anything, really. Only different kinds of beginnings, and death triggers a new type of birth for all of us . . . For us *and* Popcorn."

Celine placed the palms of her hands together and against her lips. Strands of blond curls strayed from the knitted woolen cap. The color of her cheeks poured out the glorious health of youth.

"How do you know?"

"How do I know? . . . Well, anyone who knows the least bit about atoms and electrons and matter and antimatter and space knows anything's possible." I felt my way. "I know from what Jesus, Buddha, and other great religious thinkers say . . . I know from my own mystical experiences. In times of certain inner quiet I become filled with something I can't explain. When it happens, I *know*. I know as much as I want or need to know."

She nodded.

But I wasn't sure whether she agreed or felt answered or even understood. "Popcorn and prayer . . . It's turned out to be an interesting combination."

When we entered the kitchen, Eleanor called out to us. "Hurry up! Look what's happened! Hurry!"

We found Mary and Eleanor hovering over the glass gerbil tank.

"Lady's had *babies!*" Eleanor shouted with a four-year-old's wonderment and delight. "Real, little, teensy babies . . . And Mark wasn't even here to help."

The animals, about as big as my thumbnail, squirmed around their mother. Instead of passing out cigars, Oliver twirled vigorously in his wire treadmill.

Celine reached her hand into the tank, touching one of the tiny wiggling creatures, the trace of a smile lighting her face for the first time that day.

The following spring I found a rabbit's skeleton among the taxus bushes, just beneath our library window—about twenty-five feet from where the cage had been.

6

She told me about her day.

The children fought. They shouted. They sulked and talked back. They roughhoused. The boys pummeled one another. None of them obeyed her. They were all as obnoxious as only children can be at times.

A chair turned over. A lamp broke.

Mary pleaded. Mary ordered. Mary grabbed an arm, a leg, a shirt, and pulled. Mary's voice was fading.

Finally. *"All right . . ."* She stamped her foot on the kitchen floor and pounded the table with her fist. "That's enough . . . I've *had it.* You're on your own. I'm leaving," Mary said loudly in a rare state of exasperation.

She grabbed the car keys and rushed to the red VW bus, starting it quickly and uncharacteristically roaring down the driveway, gravel spurting against the side of the house from the spinning tires. The car raced between the fields, past the long white two-storied barn, past Jenny stuffing herself on grass, past Hubert the gander, who raised his head and honked, past the horses and chickens, past the Etheringtons' cottage. Melissa, reading a book on the terrace of the small fieldstone cottage, looked up, startled, at the speeding car. The car passed the field of growing Christmas trees. Then coming to the end of the driveway it stopped out of sight from the house.

Mary hadn't planned to go beyond the driveway. She didn't want to see anyone. Didn't feel like driving anyplace. She just wanted to be alone for a while to rest. She was so tired and at times lonely. And on days like this everything became too much.

Turning on the radio, she picked up a station playing music. The romantic tune "Ebb Tide" splashed over her, the gulls calling, the waves washing the beach.

Mary began to cry.

When she returned later, she found a neat kitchen and a quiet house.

In the early evening, as we talked about her day, its memory gradually vanished. Life with children can take a 180-degree turn. We were leaning out of our open windows watching what could have been a scene from Shakespeare's *A Midsummer Night's Dream.* Or a children's ballet choreographed and staged by nature.

A full moon, misty and ringed behind high, thin clouds, illuminated the dark velvet mantle of evening. Showers of fireflies sparked on and off as if drifting in and out between tall columns of darkness.

On the lawn the girls in their nightgowns and the boys in their pajamas played and chased one another barefoot over the soft, damp grass, leaping, dancing, their laughter spinning through the air like silvery shards of moonlight. One or another would pause breathless for a moment and then with a cry of delight dart among the others again. Watching through the pale gauze of light, we found it easy to believe in the fairies of mythology. They must have been children playing.

We lived this magical moment of poetry, living it beyond the bounds of time. But the spell was brief, for as all evanescent beauty must, it vanished, becoming a shadowed memory for the inward eye.

Since no words could recapture the enchantment, after the children were asleep we went to bed in peaceful silence.

The following morning, Mary awoke, thoughtful. "Yesterday's experience with the children started me thinking about something. They're children and sometimes they're impossible. That's normal. It's not that that's bothering me . . . You know I love our place, but we're missing something very important in our lives."

"Hmmm . . ." I heard her, though my attention centered more on business plans. My schedule called for a sales trip throughout the Midwest. A few weeks later I'd be in the Southwest and California. I dreaded these lonely times. It meant leaving Mary to cope with everything. Sometimes I'd literally run from sales call to sales call, missing a meal here and there, saving enough time to get back a day or so earlier. I identified with Oliver the gerbil, who twirled endlessly on his wire treadmill.

Frequently the routes of the planes I took flew over our area, causing me a particular anguish, for I could always pick out Good Ground. I considered asking for a parachute.

As I pulled on my shoes, I noticed one sock was brown and the other blue. Who cares! Probably either Peter or John had the others.

Mary continued. "Do you realize that the only time we're alone together is when we're in bed? That is, unless we have our little visitors, which is almost every night . . . I love our children and parents, but they're about the only people I see, except if I pick up the children at school I talk to some of the mothers . . . And I almost *never* see you. You're at business and when you come home you're either working on the farm, or writing and studying. And then you're on the vestry at church, which means meetings . . . I'm lonely . . ." Mary seemed close to tears.

I stood up and we put our arms around each other. "I know. Things have gotten out of balance. I feel it."

"We have a quality of life in one way. But we don't in another. Do you know what I mean?"

I did. I understood too well. Sometimes an uneasiness shadowed me that perhaps we'd made a mistake. Neither one of us actually voiced it. We didn't want to think that way. And yet . . .

She sighed. "I want time *with you*. We're never alone together. I can't even go to the bathroom alone. Someone suddenly needs something and scratches or knocks on the door. 'Mom, I can't find . . .' whatever. Or they shove pieces of paper under the door with notes or with drawings on them."

"At least *that* doesn't happen in my office in New York," I said.

Mary took a deep breath, looking out the window to the valley, where the shades and shadows were giving way to morning's light. "I feel . . . Well, it's hard to explain, but it's as if we're being left behind in some way . . . Sometimes I want to be more than a mother or daughter, or a housekeeper, or a neighbor. And I don't want to talk about fencing in another field, or how to keep that rascal Jenny from breaking out, or how we're going to afford a new roof on one of the cottages, or worrying about whether we can pay the mortgage . . . I want us to enjoy just being together . . . Just two people in love."

A wistful sadness touched her voice, spreading from her gentle blue eyes throughout her face.

We held hands. "I know," I said. "Sometimes I feel as if everything is getting away from me." I tried for a smile. "We can always lock the door and drink champagne in bed all day." Whenever we felt hemmed in we'd joke about that silly impossibility.

She did smile. "When I really think about it, I'm not sure I'm *that* fond of champagne . . . Anyway, I have an idea. I had to take a long way around to get to it." Mary glanced at the clock. "Oh dear. We're late. We'll have to get the children up." Her voice hurried. "Anyway, it's not a big idea, but it's at least something. Maybe it's a start." She went to the closet, looking for clothes, still talking. "Today is Friday. After supper tonight we'll all go out in the field and pick wild strawberries for dessert. And then tomorrow you and I . . . *Just* you and I *alone* will go on a picnic. And I mean *alone!*"

I caught an earlier train from New York that afternoon. With supper finished, we took off on our wild strawberry expedition. The best of the tiny berries grew on a field south of our

home. Mary handed out plastic containers. "Let's pick enough
to freeze, so we can have them this winter."

The wild strawberries proliferated in the fields I kept
mowed. We found a large patch by accident one day during a
walk. The berries are tiny, about a quarter of the size of a
commercial strawberry. Since we're chary about eating anything we're not sure of in the wilds, we tested the berries first.

There are a few simple rules of thumb to see if a plant or
berry is poisonous. Generally, be careful of anything white.
Next, see if it irritates the skin, has a milky juice or a strong odor.
If so, stay away. Bite off a small piece and hold it inside your
lower lip for five minutes. If there's no soapy or bitter burning
sensation you're fairly safe. But eat only a small amount and
then wait twelve hours or so. If you've had no bad effect, it's
probably eatable.

We were almost positive at once these were strawberries.
They tasted that way from the first nibble. Also, the plants are
easy to spot. They're very small with clusters of white flowers.
In the fields they spread by a network of runners.

"Hey, we forgot to leave Laddie home," Paul complained
when we reached the area. The old dog had the same passion
we had for the berries.

"Just don't tell him where the best ones are," John advised.

"But he keeps following me."

"Go to a place where there aren't many and then leave
him. He'll be so busy looking he won't think about where you've
gone."

Paul sighed. "Not for long."

"Mom, guess what! I found the *best* place ever," Eleanor
shouted happily. "There's a whole bunch and don't anyone
come over here."

The trick was to find clusters like that because then you
didn't have to keep crawling on your hands and knees across the
ground, prickly with the spreaders and stubble of cut grass.

Suddenly she cried out. "Laddie, go away. Daddy, he's
eating *all* of them. Make him go away." The dog had an uncanny instinct for the person who found the lushest area.

"Let's entice him to go to another place," I suggested.

"Entice? What's that mean?" Mark asked. "Nice or something."

When I pulled out my paperback dictionary I saw it was about to shed a few dog-eared leaves. I thumped around in my pocket. "Anyone seen my glasses."

"Daddy, why don't you tie them on. You're always losing them," Estelle laughed.

"Hope I haven't dropped them out here. Maybe I didn't bring them." I handed the dictionary to eight-year-old Mark. "Could you please read this for me." I pointed to the entry word in larger type.

He peered at the pages closely, speaking slowly. "To tempt or . . . or . . . What's this word?"

John looked over his shoulder and read with impatience. " 'To tempt or *allure* by arousing hope or desire.' "

"I can do it . . . Dad asked me," Mark complained. He looked at me. "That's confusing. What's *entice* mean?"

"More or less to tempt."

"Why doesn't it say so right away then?"

"Because *entice* means more than just tempt . . . If I entice Laddie I'm trying to persuade him that he'll find more strawberries in another place, which may or may not be true. But if we tempt him, we might be trying to get him to do something wrong or foolish. There's an ambiguity to *tempt* . . ."

Mark's attention slid away and he massaged the old dog's back; Laddie groaned appreciatively. "It doesn't sound fair, Laddie. You can eat some of my strawberries. Don't worry. We'll find a good patch."

John's eyes glistened with good humor. "That's *enticing* him."

"Mom! Are these strawberries fattening?" Celine asked.

How different from life in the suburbs or cities. Had we remained in our former house, probably tonight the children would be watching television. Or the older ones would be at someone else's home. Here we were together as a family exploring and enjoying the mysterious abundance of nature. This is what we'd hoped for. It counterbalanced the inconveniences of commuting and other difficulties.

We picked until it was too dark to see the minute, juicy berries and then returned to the kitchen.

"Let me have the berries you picked and I'll put them in the freezer," Mary asked.

There were none. We'd eaten them.

To some extent, successful picnics depend on weather conditions. Since the following day turned out to be warm and sunny we decided to go. Everyone in the family enjoyed these excursions as much as we. But we were firm. These several hours would be for us.

Etymologists aren't sure where the word *picnic* comes from. It may be related to Old French *pigner* ("to pick") and *nique* (a "trifle"). I can justify extrapolating an origin relating to the fact you're "picking" at a "trifling" or "meager" meal rather than a normal full one.

Whatever its origin, Mary and I are picnic lovers.

"What do you think we should take?" I asked.

"We have some nice cheese. There's the herb bread I made yesterday."

"I picked up a bottle of Jadot Bourgogne Blanc, the white burgundy."

"Oh—that's a treat! Put the wine and blanket in your daypack."

"What about dessert?"

"Grapes . . . ?" Mary asked.

"Great . . . Cookies?"

"We have the carob and nut brownies."

Estelle watched us packing. "Can't I go?"

"Who'll take care of the house?" Mary asked.

"Peter and John."

"They're haying at the Kelseys'."

"Celine and Mark are home," Estelle persisted with quiet longing. She had such an eagerness-to-please expression. I nearly relented. The innocent beauty of childhood is without compare.

Mary hugged her. "Another time . . . I promise. But to-day your dad and I really need some time to ourselves. We don't get much of it and we want to talk and think about some things."

"Okay . . ." came the sighing response.

With the day-pack on my back and Mary carrying a basket, we walked down the driveway. Mary's hand felt excitingly warm in mine.

"Just going off for only an hour is like a vacation." She laughed. "Oh, I just *love* getting away with you . . . Where're we going?"

"Don't know. Hadn't thought about it. What do you think?"

"I'll leave it up to you. You know the woods better than anyone."

We ambled along for a few seconds. "What about that spot up the stream . . . You know, where the little plateau is kind of nestled in between the rocks? We can hear and see the water and yet it's *very* private . . . Do you know where I mean?"

"That's my favorite. Let's go there." She squeezed my hand. Perhaps she caught a certain intonation in my voice.

We took our time enjoying the walk along the stream. Sometimes we threw a small stick in it, watching the piece of wood bob out of sight. Water bubbled over the smaller rocks. I stood on larger ones, the water creating ripples around them like glittering, weaving ribbons.

Nature had carved out a niche for us about the size of a small room. A Lilliputian, earth-colored cliff formed the back of our hideaway. Various granite gray rocks made up the other two sides. The fourth formed our entrance. If we lay down, even someone walking along the stream twenty feet or so away couldn't see us.

We spread out the blanket first. We'd learned it's risky to sit directly on the ground. One time all of us sat on a field watching a gigantic harvest moon rising above the woods and fields. We had chigger bites that itched fiercely for weeks. The heads of the insects burrow under the skin.

In the distance we heard Laddie barking. "I'm glad we left

him home. He's such a good watchdog for the children," Mary said.

Chatting desultorily, relishing the rare peace, commenting on and appreciating the different elements of our environment, we ate our food and sipped the wine.

"Do you remember the first spring we were on the farm?" I asked. "Everyone except Peter and John got measles. You were in the house for almost ten days straight . . . Your only entertainment was shopping at the supermarket on the weekend."

She groaned. "How could I forget . . . and Eleanor and Paul kept playing that record . . . How'd it go . . . About the dog." She began to sing, spelling out the words as had the record. "B-I-N-G-O . . . Bingo was his name . . . And then the one Estelle played about Columbus' sailing ships." She sang again. "I'm *Santa Maria* . . . I'm *Niña* . . . I'm the *Pinta*. They drove me crazy. I heard them in my sleep. Talk about the Chinese torture treatment!"

We laughed at the memory.

"And all the blinds were down. It seemed like a cave. You lost your voice because you read to them for hours . . ."

"Well, I couldn't get any sitters. Mrs. McGillian was sick and Tess Snedeker said she'd never had measles and I didn't want her to get them because of her children . . . But dear Tom Richardson . . . How lucky we are to have him as our family doctor. He made *three* house calls! I love that man and his family."

"And then you came down with pneumonia."

"Not my best spring and summer . . . And how I dreamed of something like this." She slipped her warm hand into mine. Her sigh was from contentment. "Nature always makes me feel so natural," she said with an amused smile.

We sat close to one another. Though I'm immersed in words as a professional, I'm quick to acknowledge there are times when they are not only unnecessary, but actually an *impediment*—from the Latin *im* ("in") and *pedis* ("foot"), literally meaning that our feet are tangled up. Words at times can be an impediment to understanding, or expressing profound emotions and feelings.

A touch, a kiss, a look can convey nearly all.

How could words alone express my love for Mary or hers for me?

Our lives and our loves were inextricably intertwined. Though life and love are separate entities in one sense, each has similarities to the other. Each has a certain fragility and can be shattered and blotted out. Yet each can be tenacious, surviving against the most incredible odds. Each can grow and be nourished partly out of self. But the best of each flourishes as a response to the care and concern of another. And then paradoxically, the giver finds himself receiving life and love in abundance, echoing the ancient truth that in giving we receive; in loving we are loved.

I thought of some of these things as I lay beside Mary. And then time and thought lost its way in a light so brilliant all things became one.

7

In the early years of our marriage I took a dreary daily commute back and forth between a suburban community of squeezed-together houses with mini-lawns and New York City. Mary and I felt incarcerated and restive.

Plotting our escape, I read a book called *Five Acres and Independence,* which detailed how to grow everything you need on five acres. We were tempted by the dream of freshly picked fruits and vegetables, with contented farm animals wandering through our Eden.

Here we were, years later, on 110 acres, with 60 of them in open fields. How much real farming could we handle? We didn't want to run a glorified pet ranch.

Mary and I ruminated (an appropriate word, coming from the Latin *ruminare,* "to chew the cud") over possible options. After discussing the situation with our county agent and reading reams of government material, we concluded raising sheep would utilize our land best.

The agent told us that the Johnsons (who lived four or five miles away) sold sheep. Buying some from them would start us on our way.

One afternoon, while Peter and John worked on a neighboring farm, we took Celine, Estelle, Mark, Paul, and Eleanor to buy the sheep. The Johnsons' farm, about fifteen minutes from us, stretched along a valley on the north side of a wooded hill. Their fences, barn, outbuildings, house, and equipment weren't run down exactly. They looked just plain tired.

The muddy driveway ended in the center of a cluster of buildings more or less adjacent to the roof-sagging, paint-stripped house. A brood of chickens fluttered out of our way and then began pecking at the ground again for whatever they hoped to find. A few ducks cleaned themselves as well as they could in brown puddles. A work-battered tractor with a flat tire partially blocked the entrance to the barn.

Mrs. Johnson came around from the back of the house wearing a soiled apron over her blue jeans and a once-white blouse. Take away the sun wrinkles from her face, wash and set her graying hair, dress her in something reasonably fashionable, and she would have been a beauty. Her intelligent, friendly brown eyes warmed when she saw the children.

A huge sow confronted us as we left the car, tiny pink eyes trying to assess us.

"She won't hurt you none," Mrs. Johnson called in a pleasantly modulated voice.

"That's the biggest pig I've ever seen," Mark said amazed, rubbing his hands over his tousled red hair. "Do you just let her walk around? Won't she run away?"

"Pigs are real smart. They know where home is."

Mark, who especially liked to care for animals, cautiously lowered his hand, patting the firm skin as the animal sniffed his hands as though looking for something to eat. "I thought pigs were dirty . . . I mean rolling in the mud and stuff. She's pretty clean."

"Reason they like mud is they don't want to get sunburned," Mrs. Johnson said, obviously pleased with the interest the boy showed.

"Sunburned!" Mark said. "Pigs get *sunburned?"*

"They got real sensitive skin. Mud keeps them cool."

While the children wandered around, we explained to Mrs. Johnson we'd like to buy a dozen sheep.

She shook her head. "Too bad. We're all sold out." She pointed to a flock in the field where small black Hampshire lambs tagged closely after their mothers, occasionally bleating anxiously. "Got a farmer who's taking all of them. Got some other sheep too, but they're sold."

Mary's quiet disappointment showed through, "I never realized how hard they'd be to get."

"Spring lamb's popular." She looked toward the barn, rubbing a strong, rough hand against her cheek. "Well . . . ," she said slowly. "Tell you what. Have a little fellow in there. Mother rejected him. I'm feeding him on a bottle. Kind of a pet of mine."

"His mother *rejected* him . . . ! You mean she didn't want her little baby?" Estelle asked, her face reflecting an imagined empathy of anguish for someone spurned by a parent.

"Sheep do that sometimes . . . Don't rightly know why." She hesitated, as if looking within herself. Then she smiled at Estelle, resting her hand on the child's head, soft with an abundance of shoulder-length blond hair. "He's a cute little feller. Would you want him . . . ? Has to be on a bottle a couple of more weeks."

"Oh wow . . . !" Estelle replied, overwhelmed by the unexpected offer. "But he's *your* pet, isn't he?"

The woman shrugged, a shadow of sadness on her face. "Guess I don't have much time for pets . . . Only thing. Please do watch out for dogs. Just natural for some of them to want to kill sheep. It's a big problem with us."

"I can't believe it . . . A *real* baby lamb . . . Celine! Guess what?" she called to her sister excitedly. "Mrs. Johnson's giving me a real lamb." Estelle so often radiated a glow, as she did now, as if surrounded by a circle of light. Her large blue eyes expressed wondrous joy. Though somewhat small for her age she had a sturdiness to her that was more of an inner quality, for she was neither especially muscular nor overweight.

"What's its name?" she asked.

"Peanuts. That's what I call him because he's kind of small right now . . . Peanuts."

"How thoughtful of you," Mary said. "We really appreciate

that. What fun! And I'll tell you something . . . Estelle will watch over the little fellow as if she were its mother." She adjusted her daughter's hairband, pushing back strands of hair that fell over the child's forehead.

"I could see that when I looked at her. That's why I'm giving her Peanuts," Mrs. Johnson replied.

"How much do we owe you?"

"Don't rightly know," she said heading toward the barn. "Five dollars?"

As we crossed the barnyard, Paul called to me. "Hey Dad . . . Look at that goose."

A regal white bird came from around a corner, stopping to survey us, stretching his long neck upward, lifting his head as some people do when peering over their eyeglasses.

"Hubert's a gander and he lets everyone know it too," Mrs. Johnson said, emphasizing her observations.

I don't know why, but I found him appealing. I liked him immediately. I suppose the same kind of chemistry can happen between us and animals as it does with people. "What a good-looking bird!" I said enthusiastically. "Paul, he's magnificent!"

Mrs. Johnson stopped and looked at me, surprised. "You want that gander?"

I shook my head apologetically. "No . . . We don't want to take another pet away from you."

"Hubert ain't *my* pet," she said, glancing quickly at the house. "Belongs to the old man. He's asleep . . . That bird's a real nuisance to me. Him and me don't get along . . . You can have him for a couple of dollars. Pilgrim geese make good eating."

I had visions of Mr. Johnson careening down the road after us in his truck, accusing me of gandernapping. "What about your husband? I mean if Hubert's his pet . . . ?"

"Him," she said derisively. Moving deftly, she surprised the big bird from behind, scooping him up and putting him in the back of our Volkswagen bus. The act so astonished Hubert he made no sound. He looked around him bewildered. In a few moments, he had a small, bleating lamb to keep him company on the way back to our farm.

Hubert immediately adopted me and Paul as *his* pets. We discovered quickly why Mrs. Johnson wanted to get rid of him. He epitomized male chauvinism, eschewing or attacking all females, human or otherwise.

A number of times Mary repeated Mrs. Johnson's suggestion about pilgrim geese making good eating. I warned Hubert.

To keep Peanuts safe while he grew, we built a pen for him in the nearby garage where we kept our tools and lawn mowers. Estelle took over his care, giving him his bottle, cleaning his area.

"He's so cute," she said. "He's just like one of Eleanor's stuffed toys. But I'm scared something's going to happen to him. There are lots of dogs around." Estelle took responsibility like a sacred trust.

"Laddie's the best watchdog in the world," Mary said. "He's not going to let anything happen. He's part Border collie and they naturally protect sheep."

Estelle's given name was Mary, but we found that two Marys in the same house became confusing, so we began using her middle name. However, whenever we saw her with her four-legged friend, we thought of her as the "Mary" in the rhyme:

> *"Mary had a little lamb,*
> *Its fleece was white as snow.*
> *And everywhere that Mary went,*
> *The lamb was sure to go."*

Whoever wrote those words knew lambs and little girls. Peanuts followed her everywhere. And when she went to school, the lamb bleated forlornly until she came home.

Peanuts flourished under Estelle's loving care and grew into a super-size animal. His sheepskin coat would have been the star feature of any clothing catalog. Sometimes when I looked at him, imagining a large, succulent leg of mutton, I felt pangs of guilt.

No one ever talked of him being anything other than a pet. I realized finally he would never grace a freezer and felt relieved my family made the decision for me. Then, too, he did his share of work keeping our lawn trimmed—*and* fertilized—and at least we were becoming familiar with the ways of sheep even if not commercially.

One hot summer day we visited Mary's parents, taking Peanuts in the back of the car with us.

As we walked across the broad lawn to a swimming pool, our children's cousins saw Peanuts. They squealed and shouted, scrambling out of the pool, running toward him.

Mary's mother, whose reddish hair Mark inherited, always seemed to have an infant grandchild on her lap or in her arms. She laughed jokingly in her easy, spontaneous way as we walked across the lawn. "What kind of a new breed of dog is *that?*"

I'd been prepared for the question. "It's a tame ulotrichous bandersnatch," I joked.

"Now *that's* what I call a mouthful," my father-in-law replied. He spoke loudly so as to be heard over a rapidly urgent commentator's voice from the ever-present, ever-on radio.

"A woolly, imaginary, fierce wild animal," I translated.

"Peanuts is a sheep, Grandpa . . . He's *my* lamb. Daddy's only teasing," Estelle said.

"Well, Estelle, he looks like a sheep to me," her grandmother said. She placed a toddler on the grass. "You better watch her so she won't fall into the pool," she suggested to one of Mary's sunbathing sisters-in-law.

"I'm going to be the first one in," Estelle shouted to her brothers and sisters, running to the pool, springing into the water off the diving board.

When she rose to the surface, a large object hurtled past, landing beside her with a gigantic splash. We pushed Peanuts to the shallow end where we could pull him out more easily.

"Did you see *that!*" Mary's father said with amazed delight. "Why, he'd follow Estelle anywhere!"

"The poor thing almost drowned," Mary's mother added. "You'd better tie him somewhere."

Peanuts obviously enjoyed his plunge into the pool and we realized he must be excruciatingly uncomfortable underneath all his wool in this hot weather. Anxious to help him as quickly as possible, when we arrived home we took one of Mary's large sewing scissors and tried to shear him, thinking we could finish in a half hour or so. Hours later, with blistered fingers and aching hands and arms, we'd rough-cut only about one half of his tough, thick wool.

"But oh how I love getting all this lanolin on my hands from his wool," Mary said, rubbing them back and forth through his coat, savoring the softness. At least this was modest compensation for our empathy.

We didn't have the energy to complete the job at that time. With his black face and sideways-pointing ears he ended up looking like a weird breed of poodle.

Several months earlier, Danny O'Connor, a neighbor, had telephoned us. Apparently our philandering, romantic Laddie had carried on an affair with Danny's German shepherd and she'd delivered a litter of five pups. Danny planned to keep one and would drown the other four unless he could find owners.

Drown Laddie's progeny! Unthinkable! We agreed to take one and managed to persuade friends to take the other three. Being careless about genders when it came to names, we called ours Tammy.

As he grew, we worried about his personality. Though gentle with our family, he snapped and growled at the children who lived in our cottages and nipped Peanuts even though I punished him. Mary and I discussed giving him away several times. But the children thought Tammy would grow used to other people and the farm animals. They found him appealing and fun to have around. Not wanting to disappoint them we agreed to wait and see for a while.

During the winter, Peanuts spent nights in one of several alcoves alongside the barn. Estelle made it snug with thick layers of straw.

Early one morning after a heavy snow storm, she trudged through the drifts to the barn. Today was Estelle and John's turn to feed and water the animals. She went ahead of her brother. Whenever she appeared, Peanuts would bound out to greet her, bleating happily.

As Estelle approached the barn, she saw him standing in front of his sleeping quarters.

"Peanuts . . . ," she called, expecting him to run to her. He didn't move.

She thought he hadn't liked the storm and was waiting for her. But when she came closer she saw blood streaking the snow like shredded sheets of crimson tissue paper. Vicious teeth had torn away most of his wool, ripping off bloody strips of skin, lacerating his face, partly chewing his ear, mangling two of his legs.

The child stared at the gruesome specter, not believing what she saw, expecting it to vanish like a photographic slide in a carousel.

"Peanuts!" she gasped.

Head low, breathing quickly and shallowly through an open mouth, the mutilated animal seemed oblivious of her.

She stumbled toward the house, meeting John on the way. She pointed to the savaged sheep, sobbing.

"What happened?" John asked, plunging through the snow to the suffering animal. "Poor Peanuts! What happened to you?" He touched the sheep's head, his eyes filling with tears. "Poor Peanuts." He raced to his sister waiting by the gate. "Let's get Dad."

I hurried to the barn with them, Tammy and Laddie galloping merrily in front of us, leaping through the drifts.

Examining Peanuts, I nearly wept myself. I didn't see how he could even be standing.

Tammy rushed at him playfully, as if to nip the wounded animal. Peanuts trembled violently.

At that moment I *knew*. Lunging for Tammy, I grabbed him by the scruff of the neck, throwing him on the ground, pummeling his body as hard as I could, yelling at him. The young dog yelped and howled, squirming under my knee. I snatched him off the ground, hurling him from me.

My rage was a senseless and cruel reaction and a poor example for our children. Peanuts had been hurt already. Tammy could not understand the punishment for it came too long a time after his attack. Furthermore, he followed some deeply embedded instinct that drove him to do that as naturally as he would wag his tail. The fault became mine. When I realized months earlier that punishment had no effect on Tammy I should have sent him away immediately. Sometimes we confuse love and sentimentality. They are vastly different qualities.

Because of his size, I couldn't carry Peanuts for any distance, and so John and I slid him down to the house on a toboggan, gently lifting him to the cellar. We persuaded Mary and the others to stay away from him because we knew how upset they'd be if they saw their pet.

I telephoned our veterinarian, Alan Schuller, a lank, tall man needing a haircut, who had a compassionate concern for animals. Carefully examining our pet, he shook his head. "Kindest thing to do is to put him out of his misery right now. He's in shock and doesn't stand a chance . . . By the way, I'd give that dog away."

Before I could find a home for him, Tammy and his mother were killed in a curious accident a few days later. A freight train hit them.

"Why did God let that happen to Peanuts and Tammy?" Estelle asked that night as I tucked her in bed, after she'd said her prayers. As a family, we said grace at meal time and Mary and I prayed with the younger children when we put them to bed. All of them had their own inner responses, but Estelle at a very early age had more of a sense of a relationship with God. Tears covered her cheeks in rivulets. We held hands, her small one intertwined with mine.

No one who is not a parent can ever know the fierce intensity of the feelings you have for a child. Your children's pain becomes yours. Their disappointments yours. Their joys touch your heart with joy.

I sighed unhappily. "It wasn't God's fault. It was mine. I should have given Tammy away a couple of months ago to a family that didn't have sheep."

"But why didn't God tell you to do it?"

"God probably did. I guess I didn't listen."

8

Despite our unfortunate experience with Peanuts, we felt we should experiment with sheep. The county agent encouraged us strongly. The following year we bought a dozen from Mrs. Johnson, intending eventually to breed and sell them ourselves.

We planned to raise them organically. No drugs and chemicals for our sheep. For many years we'd been using so-called health foods. We'd read Adelle Davis and other pioneering individuals assiduously even when they themselves didn't seem robustly healthy. We took vitamin C when doctors smiled at our naiveté. And Mary baked her own bread, long before it became the "in" thing to do, spoiling us with the luscious aroma pervading the whole house.

Our skeptical county agent sent Mary to the Agricultural Department of the state university, who might have the information needed for organic farming.

The professor listened to her with an indulgent smile. Mary has a strong and creative mind and is not easily put off when she feels something is important.

The expert tried to convince her that there was nothing in

organic farming. Chemicals were far better. She persisted. Finally he said he'd check with the *real* expert and telephoned a number. When the party answered, he said in an amused, superior voice, "Joe, I have a young woman sitting here who wants to raise *organic* sheep. What do you think of *that?*" His friend corroborated his sentiments, of course.

We compromised. Because of worms and diseases and the fact we planned to sell them, Dr. Schuller gave them the necessary shots. However, our grain and other feed were without chemicals.

Having sheep meant more fencing and more fencing meant more worries about Jenny, who increased her proficiency as an escape artist.

The little white burro took an immediate and proprietary interest in the sheep. We learned later that ranchers discovered donkeys are better at herding and protecting sheep from wild animals than Border collies.

From my office, I could see Jenny following them across the fields. I think she felt comfortable with them, for they seemed to have the same insatiable appetite. We soon needed another field.

Five o'clock in the morning may sound like a terrible time to dig fence holes in a rocky, shale-studded field. But more than ever before, I seemed to feel part of spring as it flowed north, spreading a diaphanous green veil over our land.

When I paused to look and listen, I could hear the plaintive calls of the black-capped chickadees and the cheerful phoebes. A woodpecker hammered vigorously on a hollow tree, as if trying to chop it down. A symphony of other birds played for this audience of one, and here and there I could pick out the notes of robins and a bobwhite. We had a family of cardinals and I welcomed them back silently.

Over in another field I could see the tips of mustard plants about to blossom. Soon we'd have acres of unbelievably soft, yellow beauty. Along the edges of our trails and in the woods, the yellowish brown dog-toothed violets and amusing white Dutchman's-breeches would be coming up.

When I looked at the sky I could see birds darting between

trees, swooping down on hedgerows, while high above, languorous turkey vultures soared on unseen crests of air.

On good-weather mornings the sky gradually lightened in the east, crowding the darkness over the horizon, bringing me a day seemingly inchoate, as if waiting to be shaped by my dreams, desires, obligations, and realities.

I longed to take in the entire panorama all at once and felt as if I stood on God's shoulders and together we enjoyed our creation. I recalled Emily Dickinson's insight: "Exultation is the going of an inland soul to sea,/Past the houses, past the headlands into deep eternity."

I guess I could justifiably call myself a syntonic person— emotionally touched by my surroundings.

With youthful gusto and humor, Peter and John helped me on weekends to set the wooden posts in the holes for the fencing. They were firmer than the steel ones. First we painted the bottom portions with creosote as a preservative against rotting.

The routine was that two of us put a post in a large bucket filled with the solution, while the third painted along the sides to the depth of the hole.

After a while I noticed that John somehow always managed to hold the posts, while we painted. "How come?" I asked him.

"Well, Dad . . . You keep saying that executives work with their minds, not their bodies. I'm just practicing what you've been telling us. I was wondering how long it'd take you to catch on," he said, grinning at the small joke he'd been playing on us.

"You're learning fast. How about giving us a chance to practice?" I handed him my paintbrush.

Though our blue jeans and work jackets protected our bodies, I kept admonishing my sons to be careful. Creosote, a derivative of coal tar, burns the skin like acid. But I was the one who splashed a drop on my face near my eyes.

John saw. Instantly he took his handkerchief and dabbed the spot away.

"Better wash it off in the house," Peter urged. "It can still burn your skin and it's too close to your eye. You don't want to take any chances. Don't worry, we won't do anything until you get back," he added in his best bantering tone, stretching out on the grass. "However, the hard thing about doing nothing is you never know when you're through."

After the posts were set in the holes and dirt packed hard around them with the flat end of a long iron shale bar, we lopped off the tops on a slant with an old, yellow, annoyingly heavy chain saw. We spent most of our energy trying to start the ornery engine, nicking our fingers as it backfired, painfully yanking the cord out of our hands. I had some trouble with my language. As the day passed, the machine seemed to double in weight, and I'd prop my tired arms awkwardly against my body. Occasionally I'd let Peter or John work with it.

A chain saw can be a lethal tool. The razor-sharp teeth on the chain whirl around with blurring speed. A careless slip can cause a devastating accident like the loss of a finger or hand. Once I nearly severed the tendons in my leg just above the knee. But I wanted the boys to learn to handle equipment correctly for their later protection.

An unexpected benefit of working alongside our children was that occasionally we talked about things that normally might not come up. We built closer relations without even being aware of this in the closeness of the moment. The openness and frankness of the boys gave me a good feeling even when I smarted a bit at their criticism.

"You know, Dad," John said as he watched me hack off the top of a post, "we feel you work too fast sometimes . . . I mean, look at those posts. They're kind of uneven . . . Or the barn door we made. It's clumsy . . . It's so heavy."

"What John means is you always seem in such a hurry to get something done," Peter added.

The cranky chain saw stopped of its own accord and I put it down. My first inclination was to protest. I knew from what Mary said they'd been critical of me. But they had a point. And their criticism made me probe the reasons for my actions.

"Well . . . ," I said, thinking it through. "I guess you're right in one sense. But let me put it this way. Your mother and I are so short of time we try to discriminate where to put our emphasis. Not everything is worth doing to perfection. Sometimes a fairly good job serves the purpose. You have to decide what is and what isn't important. Sure, we could take more time in getting every post absolutely even. But would it really be worthwhile . . . ? They'll shift with thaws anyway. Besides, a little unevenness here and there doesn't matter. What does matter is to make the fencing strong enough so that the animals won't get out."

"I think Jenny has other ideas," Peter said, pointing to the burro. "A new fence always seems like a new challenge to her." While we worked, she stood nearby watching us, daintily, continuously pulling and snipping off the fine blades of new grass. In a month or so her stomach would balloon out into a monstrous, lopsided "grass belly."

"What we're talking about, incidentally, reminds me of a discussion your mother and I had recently about something that's very important concerning both of you."

"Such as . . . ?" Peter asked, seemingly casual.

"Well, you know how much the younger children admire and look up to you . . . Paul and Mark tag after you like puppies. Your actions influence them. Probably far more than you think. It's a big responsibility."

"You're saying that we're not a good influence," Peter asked, continuing with the sloshing of creosote on the post.

"No, I didn't say that . . . I just wanted to have you aware of the fact you have one."

We worked quietly for a while, but since we were not alone often in this way, I wanted to pass along a few other thoughts. "Sometimes we get so active we forget, but one of the reasons we moved here is that we wanted to create a place where we could have a center of family love."

"Your turn, Dad," Peter said, handing me the brush.

I painted, careful not to splash. "Your mother and I want all of us to really grow to have a sense of this center so that we . . ."

"You missed a spot," John said, turning the post.

"So that we can use this love in our community . . . in Lambertville. We want to become a part of the town. And then as each of you leave . . ."

"And this spot too," John said, pointing.

"So you can leave . . . I mean, when you leave you take it out into the world and create your own centers. Love isn't love when it's not shared. We want our family center to be *inclusive*, not *exclusive*. Love is to be shared. You can never run out of it. Your capacity to love is endless. The Jews . . ."

"Here's another post," Peter said, putting it in the pail.

"The Jews . . . One of the reasons the Jews have survived as an ethnic group is because they created a center of faith in each family. At this center . . ."

"Dad, let me have the brush. You aren't concentrating." John took it from me.

". . . is God and so they have their religious traditions. So many of these traditions are celebrated in the home . . . And this is a long way around to say that family has always been at the heart of civilization. So when I say you have an influence, it's not just here . . . It spreads out like ripples and you have no idea of all the different people ultimately you're going to effect."

They said nothing. *Well, at their age I probably wouldn't have responded either.*

Peter must have heard my sigh. His large blue eyes spoke more to me than any words. "As Celine says, 'keep talking. We hear you.'"

"Sometimes . . . ," John added honestly.

Mary and I knew they were gradually trying to pull away from our immediate orbit. They were searching out their own answers. This is what we wanted for them also. Yet the emotions involved sometimes became painful because there would be moments of anger and hurt.

We couldn't help but be a little wistful about their growing out of childhood. For us it was a period of special joys.

The fencing completed, we carried our equipment to the barn.

About five o'clock one morning, a slightly different sound awoke me. Looking out the windows, I saw the gate to the lower field ajar—the field Peter, John, and I had just fenced.

Jumping out of bed and hurrying outside, I couldn't find the sheep. Nor could I find Jenny.

Muttering strong imprecations against that precocious pest, that bête blanche of ours, I ran back to the house, rousing the family. My feverish imagination had them stampeding through the town, with Jenny leading the way. Or they could be huddling in the center of a busy highway while Jenny finished her breakfast on the grass alongside the road.

The children responded sleepily and reluctantly. Yawning, they couldn't see the big deal about rounding them up now.

"Relax, Dad. You're too excited. We'll get them later," John said. "You and Mother go back to bed."

"Later! *You* have to go to school. And *I* have to be in New York. Come on. We don't have time to lollygag around."

"What's lollygag?" Estelle asked.

"A prebreakfast lollypop that makes you gag," Peter teased with a smile.

"Where's my hippopotamus? I want her to go with us," Eleanor said urgently, looking for her stuffed toy.

"Don't you think we should dress?" Mary asked me.

"We don't have time. Who knows where the sheep are?"

"Come on, Celine . . . ," Mary urged. "Put a sweater on over your nightie."

A deep yawn. "I'm not cold."

"You might be. And hurry up. Dad wants to get outside as soon as possible."

Putting on boots or sneakers, whichever happened to be closest at hand, everyone humored their fretting father and stumbled out to try to resolve another Jenny-inspired adventure.

I turned around at one point and couldn't help laughing despite my anxiety. Like a tail on a kite, the children stretched behind me across the damp lawn, dressed in nightgowns, pajamas, with and without sweaters. Mary brought up the rear in a blue jacket grabbed off a hook in the entrance hall. Belonging to one of the children, it only reached to her stomach, and the sleeves part way down her forearms.

"Know what, Dad?" Mark said. He pushed the visor of his

blue, grungy-looking baseball cap away from his face, an odd combination with pajamas. "Know what? I bet she took them to the upper field. That's where she runs away sometimes."

We loved this small field in the center of the woods. Dogwood trees rimmed its edges nearly the entire distance around. Butterfly bushes with pink-purple blossoms clustered at either end. Near the short planked bridge, we'd rescued a large oak tree being strangled by a Japanese honeysuckle.

Hurrying up along the hillside trail, we found them. Without interrupting her breakfast, nonchalantly Jenny watched us approach.

I glanced at my watch. Three quarters of a mile of woods and fields lay between us and the barn. Probably we could have them back within an hour. This would give me time to catch my train.

"We'll make a semicircle and stay northwest of them," I explained to my family. "Move slowly. We don't want to frighten them. Sheep aren't smart."

"Peanuts was," Estelle said firmly, the natural wave in her hair bouncing as she walked.

Every time we drew close to them, Jenny moved away, spooking the sheep, who panicked, running in different directions, separating like pieces of spilled mercury rolling across a floor.

Three hours later the sheep were finally retrieved. The bramble-scratched, tired, pajama-clad shepherds rushed down to the house to prepare for their dash to train, school, and household chores.

During the year, the sheep broke loose a few other times. However, Mary and the children evolved a relatively simple way of getting them back. They'd catch a baby lamb and then use it as a lure. One time, for example, Mark held the bleating lamb while sitting on the open back of the station wagon Mary drove slowly. The lamb's mother followed, trailed by the rest of them and a line of impatient though amused motorists.

There's nothing quite so farmlike or peaceful as seeing sheep grazing your land. "Protected" by Hubert, our male-chauvinist gander, and Jenny, they seemed now to be a perma-

nent part of our landscape. But after the experience with Peanuts, no one treated the sheep as pets. They were accepted as
part of the overall operation of the farm.

We wanted to raise them commercially, selling them to
local meat markets and individuals. If we were successful, we'd
expand our operation to wholesalers.

The following spring we ran advertisements extolling our
organically raised sheep, believing this would attract a special
customer. I arranged for a man to slaughter, prepare, and keep
the animals in his freezer until we sold them. He telephoned me
one day, saying he'd be there the following Sunday. We should
have the sheep penned in the barn ready for him.

On Saturday we rounded them up. We managed to corral
all the sheep fairly easily into the barn, when something unexpectedly alarmed them. About half managed to escape, leaping
and flying past us before we could close the door. After that we
could only get them one by one, usually by driving the animal
into a fence corner and grabbing it as it ran past. The boys were
covered with dirt and scratches, for the large sheep dragged
them along the ground.

Jenny galloped back and forth, hee-hawing, head held high,
kicking sideways at phantoms.

"There has to be an easier way!" Mary panted, exasperated,
dusty, and perspiring as I tackled a sheep we'd trapped.

Right! But we lacked the proper pens and a trained dog.
And we were learning on the job. As in most things, we had to
make do. Next year would be different.

Still holding a bleating sheep and about to get up, I felt
something hard ram against my rear end, poking me repeat-
edly. Startled, I turned around. Hubert, honking angrily and
flapping his wings, arched his long neck as he struck at that
vulnerable part of my body.

Paul grabbed him and took him away from me. "Poor Hubert . . . I think he knows what's going on."

On Sunday Mary and the children went off to church. I
waited for Frank Scubrowsky. Hubert paced up and down in
the front of the barn. Whenever one of the sheep bleated, he'd
answer by a flurry of wings and loud honking.

Reasonably on time, Frank's old blue pickup truck backed up to the barn door. A stocky, pot-bellied man eased out of the cab and landed on the ground with a thump.

"The sheep are kind of skittish," I said. "I'll help you drive them into the truck."

"Ain't no need," he replied, reaching into the cab, taking out a .22 rifle.

"You mean right *here* . . . in the *pens?*" I asked.

"Yeah . . . Easiest way."

"Have something to do down at the house," I murmured, walking away. I closed all the windows against sounds and tried ineffectually to do some work. But the written word held no answers for me that morning. I remembered the story about Saint Francis rescuing the lamb being taken to market.

When the family came home, I didn't tell them what happened.

Completely successful, our advertisement disposed of all the sheep. Several weeks later, however, we received an irate telephone call from a Turkish customer, a rug dealer.

"I ordered *spring* lamb and *not* mutton. That was the toughest piece of meat we've ever eaten," he raged. "What'd you do? Feed them rocks?"

Traditionally, Eastern Orthodox Christians often have baby spring lamb for their Easter feast. We hadn't thought about that aspect and sympathized with our customer's disappointment.

Undoubtedly the countryside escapades with Jenny developed sheep who would excel in running marathons but not necessarily in ovens.

When we added up the score, the venture showed a loss. Though we sold the sheep immediately, naturally a dozen could not possibly offset the costs of our time, feed, medical expenses, mortgage, and the like. We knew that when we started. But we wanted to have first-hand experience to assess the possibilities better.

Talking with ranchers and various experts, we determined that a feeding operation—no breeding—would be economically feasible with five hundred or more sheep. This would necessitate outside help and much more equipment.

We were dissuaded from going ahead when we learned that the market for U.S.-raised lamb is a fragile one. Lamb imported from New Zealand and Australia predominate. Though sheep were right for our land, they were not the best investment for us.

We refunded the Turkish customer his money.

And retired from the sheep business.

9

Little Teddy Miller was lost. The slight, mentally retarded eight-year-old disappeared from home on a Saturday morning.

At the time, I knew nothing about it, for I'd been chauffeuring Celine, Estelle, Mark, and Paul to their various destinations. Annie Miller, Teddy's mother, telephoned Mary to ask if we'd seen him. He'd been gone for about an hour.

The Millers lived a mile or so up Mule Hill Road. What worried Annie and Sam, his father, was that being retarded Teddy might not reply when someone called him.

Adding together the different properties in the area, we had about one thousand acres for someone to wander through. Occasionally even I'd lost my way, so the concern for Teddy was valid.

Mary volunteered to go immediately. In fact, she left in such a hurry she forgot to turn off the appliances and the stove.

When Eleanor and I returned, we found the washing machine thumping vigorously, the dryer whirring, and the two parakeets in the wall cage above the appliances chattering their complaints about the noise. A stew simmered on the stove. An ironing board with a hot upright iron on it crowded the center of the room. We turned off the iron. Mounds of pressed, clean-smelling laundry made a multicolored wall across the top of the kitchen table.

But no Mary!

Licorice, Estelle's black cat with Sybaritic inclinations, ensconced himself comfortably on one of the clean piles of laundry. I scooped him up, dumping him outside the screen door. The door didn't close completely. A deft paw could open it easily. I kept meaning to fix it.

"Daddy . . . You're *so* mean to him," Eleanor said.

"Mean! Listen, you should feel sorry for your mother, *not* the cat. She's spent all this time washing and ironing and he gets it dirty again. Look at all the hairs he's left . . . By the way, do you remember if your mother said anything about going somewhere?" I could see Mary's faded, red VW bus in the driveway. That's what puzzled me. I'd been through the house and outside looking for her.

The blond, healthy five-year-old shook her head back and forth slowly. She carried one of the parakeets on top of it. She touched the almost totally white bird. "Old Kingy loves to go for walks."

"You've really trained him well, but you'd better be careful who else sees him out for a walk." I indicated Licorice, who looked through the screen door with particular interest.

Why hadn't Mary left me a note? I worried about a possible accident. Farms are notorious for mishaps . . . Peter and John said they'd return about this time to help me take the tractor and wagon to bring back a load of hay from a neighboring farm. Could something have happened to either of them? They mentioned they might be in the woods finishing up the tree house they'd been building with Bill Miller, Teddy's older brother. Bill, a tall, strong, sensitive youngster had protean talents when it came to building anything.

I hurried across the driveway, yanking the rope on the old farm bell hanging on a crosspiece. The loud clangs could be heard for nearly a mile. We had a rule that when you heard the bell you answered if you were near enough and always returned home immediately. If Mary was nearby she would hear it and know I was home.

Quickly I checked the barn and then returned to the bell, sounding it again.

As I walked back to the house, our Border collie, Laddie, padded slowly around the corner, panting, tongue lolling out. Mary followed, panting just about as hard as the dog. I wouldn't have been surprised to have seen her tongue hanging out.

"Thank heavens you're home," she said. "I'm *exhausted.*" She told me about Teddy. "I thought I'd look around our lower woods and fields and then you and I can check the rest of our woods if he hasn't turned up. Do you have any news about him?"

"This is the first I've heard . . . I wish you'd left a note."

"I'm sorry. But I could hear how upset Annie felt and I forgot everything else . . . I bet I've walked . . . *run* three miles . . . *At least!* And these aren't running shoes either," she said, looking at her thin sneakers. "I'm dying of thirst."

So was Laddie, who lapped up water from his dish. He flopped on a foot mat, his pink, dripping tongue lolling out of his mouth. For a moment he lay quietly. Then he turned his head, pricking up his ears. He got up stiffly, looking down our driveway, and began to bark.

An old car with pinging valves drove into our driveway. We went out to meet it, recognizing the somewhat plump, small woman driver. The combined impression made by her round face and black, bright eyes reflected a friendly candor. Often I recalled how she and one of her young children helped to put out our celebrated field fire that first week we'd moved to the farm.

Robust, pink-cheeked, white-haired Mrs. McGillian, our baby-sitter, sat beside her. The older woman's eyes were bright behind the granny glasses.

"Hi . . . ," I said.

"Did you hear the news about little Teddy Miller?" Tess asked.

"That he's lost," Mary replied. The whole of her fine-boned face revealed the fear that perhaps he'd been found and the worst had happened.

Tess and Mrs. McGillian nodded. "We thought we might see if he was on the road somewhere."

"I've been looking. Peter and I are going out again."

Tess shook her head. "I sure hope he don't go near the cliffs. You know . . . The ones on the other side of your property."

"We're heading out now and we'll check that area . . . Thanks for stopping by."

Back in the house, Mary picked up Licorice, who'd made himself comfortable again on the pile of clean laundry. *"Look* at those darned hairs . . . And he's left a dirty spot on this sheet." She dropped him outside the door. Unconcerned, he stretched and began cleaning himself.

"Come on, Eleanor . . . Put Kingy back. We're going to see if we can find Teddy."

"Who's he?" She carefully took hold of the bird and returned him to the cage.

Mary explained as we hurried over our lawn.

"Why did he run away?"

"He probably just walked off and forgot how to get back home."

"I wouldn't forget."

"Well, his brain hasn't grown as fast as his body. He probably has a three-year-old brain in an eight-year-old body."

We crossed the adjacent field, carefully closing the gate behind us. Though Jenny couldn't see us from where she grazed near the barn, we knew her uncanny instinct for sensing when we'd been careless with a gate.

We shouted Teddy's name several times and then used a rough stile I'd made to climb the fence so we could search the next field. Standing in the lower part of the overgrown, sloping ten-acre field we felt helpless. Bushes, sumac, small junipers, persimmons, oaks, maples, dogwoods, and a plethora of other small growing trees blocked our view.

I shouted again.

"We wouldn't see him unless we stumbled right over him," Mary sighed. "I feel so sorry for Annie and Sam. I suppose it's happened before with Teddy. But as Marge at the supermarket says, 'What can you do?' You can't keep him locked up all the time."

"I guess it's a chance they have to keep taking."

"I really admire them, keeping him home instead of in an institution. How much better it is for him to have the love of a whole family."

I thought of my Franciscan friend Ken, who also has a retarded son living at home. The youngster could become upset quickly and easily. During a vacation in San Francisco, they rode one of the famous open trolley cars where people stand up, clinging to straps and posts. Somehow their son became separated from them and was on the opposite side of the trolley. Ken could see that he was close to panic. Above the noise of the car, traffic, and voices he shouted a family code word in a cheerful, loud voice—"Love." The child's mother called out *love* also as did the younger brother. Soon others joined in what they thought was a game and lightheartedly called out the word. Ken saw the panic gradually replaced by a happy, reassured smile.

As I looked about the field, I sighed. "I'll have to cut this down soon before it gets completely out of hand."

"But not the blackberry bushes. They're one of our treasures," Mary answered.

Again we shouted Teddy's name.

"Does he talk like a baby?" Eleanor asked.

"Sometimes people can't understand him."

"I could . . . My legs are tired," she added.

I lifted her on my shoulders. "You can be my periscope and look for Teddy."

"What's a periscope?"

I explained.

Mary followed behind us. "I'm so glad you're with me," she said. "I was kind of scared because I don't know the woods the way you do. They say there are wild dogs and sometimes bears around! I don't have much faith in Laddie protecting me. He's getting too old."

If he heard, the dog paid no attention. His tail waved like a panache as he sniffed out various trails of animals. Occasionally he took off in a direction with undaunted enthusiasm, barking excitedly, aging, stiff limbs limiting his pace.

Every time we were outside, the sky held a magnetic attraction for us. That huge expanse, so often in flux, contrasted with the more stolid earth. Today the early March clouds, billowy, tinged with threatening darkness along their edges, jostled and shoved each other rapidly from one far horizon to the other. The winds pushing them reached down to nudge the tops of trees and brushed over our faces.

Mary stopped, looking around. Cupping her hands over her mouth, she shouted in different directions, Eleanor joining her. "Poor child. I'll bet he's confused and frightened. He's probably all scratched from these darn vines and prickles over the ground."

She took my hand. "Let's say a prayer that he'll be found soon and nothing's wrong." We closed our eyes, mentally holding the child in God's protective love and light, asking help in the search.

I tell you, whatever you ask in Prayer, believe that you receive it, and you will.

"I'll bet Peter and John are looking with Bill. He'd be very upset about his little brother," Mary said.

"Is Teddy Bill's *brother?*" Eleanor asked, amazed.

"Right . . ."

"Is *his* brain little?"

"Not Bill. He's very smart and as nice as he's smart."

"You know, Tess mentioned the cliffs and that worries me . . . ," Mary said. "It's the one place he could be killed. What about going there?"

"We can cut across the gully just ahead."

"I want to cross on the swing Bill and Peter and John made," Eleanor said, trying to wriggle off my shoulders.

"Better wait till we get through this underbrush. It's pretty scratchy. Then we'll all swing across."

We came to the wide gully and I took Eleanor off my shoulders. "I feel just as if I've dumped a sack of grain," I laughed, stretching my arms and back.

Eleanor ran to the rope swing, which hung from a high

branch of a gigantic tree, dangling a few feet above the edge of the bank before it dropped off into a sharp slope. The boys had tied a thick knot at the end to sit on as you swung across to the opposite side, a trip of about sixty or more feet. They never told us how they managed to get that rope so high in the tree.

We called Teddy's name several times again, Eleanor joining us. We waited a few seconds for an answer or some kind of signal.

Suddenly we heard a clatter of stones upstream. Five deer, their coats blending in with the russet-colored background, scrambled across and up the opposite side of the bank. Once on top they bounded through the woods with leaps so long and light and graceful they seemed to be pulled along with an invisible wire. Though they moved rapidly, the leaps created an optical illusion of a leisurely, graceful motion. Each time they rose in the air, a short, bushy white tail bobbed up like a quick jack-in-the-box, as if waving a flippant goodby to us.

In the midst of such natural beauty, potential tragedy seemed to be an inconceivable anomaly. I firmly focused back on my trust and our prayer.

We'd been walking along the top of the bank, stopping to call every now and then, when Mary pointed to the stream. We saw a large pool of water, the result of a dam made by the three boys.

"Peter and John have more fun with Bill than any other friend I can remember," Mary observed.

When Peter and John entered school in midterm they were thought of as kids from the soft suburbs who needed a few lessons from "real boys." Peter and John are strong and never back away from a fight. But who wants to be fighting all the time? And so when Bill Miller befriended them, it saved a lot of grubby hassles. Bill was well liked and one of the strongest youngsters in school. With his long arms and strength he'd grab whoever attacked him, holding him at arm's length, laughing in his friendly way, calming his adversary's anger.

Wearing patched jeans and a brown plaid work shirt the first day we met him, Bill stepped down into our living room, ducking his head as he went through the doorway. His head nearly touched the ceiling, which made him seem even taller. He carried an amiable, energetic openness with him, and his thoughtful brown eyes behind the dark-rimmed glasses were alive with the new experience. In his handshake you felt a strength that was more than merely muscular.

"Hey . . . I see you have a piano." His soft voice lifted with excitement. The instrument was one I'd grown up with and we'd placed it in the playroom beyond the hallway. "Mind if I try it?"

"You play the piano?" Mary asked pleased. "We'd love to hear you."

He sat down immediately, bending his head over the keys. Suddenly the music of Chopin, Mozart, and Bach exploded into the playroom, seeming to merge with the sunlight pouring through the windows. Astonished, we looked at each other. These young, powerful hands that could build almost anything, that worked at all kinds of mundane farm chores, were creating beautiful and complicated music. We felt as if through some extraordinary serendipity we'd unearthed a rare treasure.

Every time Bill came to our house he played the piano.

At the time we didn't know that Sam, Bill's father, was an accomplished musician and at one time had been offered a job with one of the well-known big bands. He turned it down because this would entail traveling around the country, leaving his family for months at a time.

One day I mentioned how impressed we were with Bill's talent.

An amused, characteristic smile flickered over Sam's thin, pale face as he reached into a worn coat pocket for a cigarette. Compared with his son, he was relatively small. "He's pretty good, I guess."

"Pretty good! Listen, that youngster of yours is *very* good. I don't know what his plans are after high school, but I do know this. He should be heading for some place like Juilliard in New York or the Academy of Music in Philadelphia."

"We haven't talked much about what he's going to do."

"I know a couple of people who might be helpful."

He lit a cigarette, not replying. I couldn't understand Sam's lack of enthusiasm. He should be doing everything possible to encourage his son. What a tragedy if such a talent ended up in a menial job.

With the cigarette in his mouth, Jack inhaled and then let the smoke drift past his face. Again an amused smile touched the corners of his mouth and his eyes, which squinted from the smoke. "He's having fun," he said pleasantly and left it there.

So much said and unsaid in a few simple words. Whatever he did in life, Bill would always have his music to enjoy. It would never become work.

We thought of all these things as we searched for Teddy, every so often shouting.

I tugged Eleanor's leg. "You're up higher than any of us. Really look hard for anything that seems unusual."

"We've *got* to find him," Mary said in an anger of frustration. "When I think of the Millers and their strong wonderful values compared with so much junk that's being written and shown on TV and in movies . . . People yelling at and hating each other and the violence and the sick sex . . . that can be such a rotten, destructive influence. It's families like the Millers who keep the world going . . . Their values are love in action. *Real* love . . . the kind of love that's caring and responsible. Not the self-love that's always worrying about me, me, me."

How wrong was the Russian writer Tolstoy in his famous dictum at the beginning of his novel *Anna Karenina:* "All happy families resemble one another; every unhappy family is unhappy in its own fashion."

This is one of those pronouncements that sound so profound, but on analysis you find it leaky. Each happy family is happy in its own fashion too. Extreme circumstances aside, the heart of happiness or unhappiness is attitude.

The Millers could have found reasons to be unhappy. They had a mentally retarded child. They lived in very modest circumstances in an age that extolled affluence. Sam didn't feel he could follow his career as a professional musician and became a piano tuner in an area that didn't have many pianos.

They created their own happiness, bringing a cheerful warmth with them. Once they needed an additional small house and they built it themselves. They wanted a sailboat but couldn't afford to buy one and built a thirty-five-foot ferrocement sloop in their backyard. They took Teddy with them wherever they went and never apologized for his sometimes bizarre actions. Annie was endowed with an ample body and she didn't worry about being fashionably thin.

Sometimes Sam and his musical friends got together for a picnic in the back of his property. Beer and jazz flowed until it was too dark to play outside and they moved indoors in their plain farmhouse and continued. Bill usually played with him while his younger brothers, Jack and Teddy, enjoyed the excitement.

Bill experimented with interesting kites, and one of his large model planes could fly over two miles.

Now their Teddy was lost. We ached to find him.

We passed the tree house the boys had built at least fifty feet above the ground. To reach it you shinnied a long section of pipe they'd found in the barn. To construct it they had to use their muscles and ingenuity.

"I hope they're careful," Mary said, as she looked up at the height and then at the rocks surrounding the base of the tree.

Pushing on somewhat more quickly, we crossed through the thick woods, the ground always sloping upward as we neared the cliffs.

Mary stopped, grabbing my arm. "Look at that snake! On the rock!" she whispered, pointing to a large, gray, sunshadowed rock about sixty or seventy steps away.

"That's a stick . . . There *aren't* any snakes around here . . . A half mile north of us on the wildlife property you'll find them. But I've told you before, I've never ever seen one around here."

The stick slithered off the rock, disappearing in the underbrush.

"Sticks can't wriggle, Daddy," Eleanor said from her perch on my shoulders with the emphasis of a five-year-old's sure knowledge.

"Hm'mm . . . ," I murmured. "First time I've seen one in this area."

Mary had the grace to say nothing other than, "We'd better keep our eyes open and make sure we stamp to warn whatever's around."

Every few moments we called Teddy, pausing to listen. Occasionally in the distance we'd hear other voices shouting his name.

The cliffs on the far edge of our property were a tumble of jagged edges, sheer drops, and precipitous slopes strewn with boulders and outcroppings of rocks several hundred feet back from the highway and above it. The river lay just beyond, the water foaming over the rapids.

"Let's rest a few minutes," Mary suggested. "I'm getting tired." She held onto a tree, looking upriver. "Do you know," she said in a tone of amazement, "I can see five church steeples from here. Imagine a little town like this having five churches."

"Six, actually."

"I've come to love this place. It reminds me of a European village," Mary said. "It's so nice to walk downtown and know almost everyone there. People are really friendly. Did I tell you that yesterday at the supermarket I didn't have enough money and Marge . . . You know, the check-out clerk . . . Well, Marge reached into her own purse and handed me ten dollars. 'Pay me tomorrow,' she said. Can you imagine that happening in one of the cities or big towns?"

I agreed. "What about that time we were in the Durky's Deli in the winter and the little girl walked in. She was so cold she was shivering. I can see Mrs. Durky leaning over the counter with a kindly expression in that massive way of hers almost the archetype of a big European grandmother with a mass of gray-streaked hair and those jowls. The girl was doing an errand for her mother.

" 'Where are your gloves, Cynthia?'

" 'Don't have none.'

"And Mrs. Durky walked slowly to the cash register on those heavy, aching legs of hers and gave the child some money. 'Now you go next door and buy yourself some gloves, you hear.' The odd thing was that if I closed my eyes it would almost sound as if she were cross."

"That's only because she wanted to be sure the little girl bought the gloves and didn't take the money back to her parents or whatever."

The best thing that ever happened to Lambertville was when they built the Erie canal system, linking the Delaware River with the Great Lakes, five hundred miles away. The barges, towed by mules, stopped at Lambertville to pick up passengers and cargo. With such a convenient outlet, the farming community thrived.

When the railroad put the canal system out of business, Lambertville still thrived because the Pennsylvania Railroad established the town as a repair center. More money flowed into the area. Big homes were built and farms expanded.

And then, apparently because of the changing times and some dispute forgotten today, the railroad company pulled out. The town went into a depression from which it never really recovered.

Curiously, just across the river was New Hope, a flourishing art and antique center, a town with a completely different character.

"They're arty people," Henry McGillian said to me disdainfully. "Don't hardly ever go across the river to that town."

"Bunch of Philistines," one of the shopkeepers in New Hope said contemptuously, referring to Lambertville.

However, we noticed that when our New Hope friends wanted some good wines, they did their shopping at a well-known store in Lambertville. It's reputed to have the finest wine cellar in the state.

"We better get on with our search . . . ," Mary said with a weary voice.

Carefully and slowly for about half an hour we walked along the edge, peering below, dreading the possibility of finding what we looked for.

"Apparently he hasn't come this far," I said, relieved.

Mary nodded. "I think we should go back home. I just realized we forgot to write a note for Estelle. She'll be returning now any time. She doesn't know where we are. And her friend Wendy will be with her."

"We should probably call Sam and Annie anyway to find out what's happening. If Teddy hasn't been found, I'll go out again myself."

We picked up the trail wending through the woods. Eventually it brought us to a narrow field at the lower part of our driveway. The field was ringed with dogwood trees and in about six weeks the area would become a luminous circle of delicate white and pink magic.

Every time I glimpsed our home from the edge of this field I thrilled. Our narrow, old, white, clapboard two-storied house with the big fieldstone chimneys, surrounded by lawn and shade trees, bounded by gracefully sloping fields with different angles, and beyond them the mysterious woods, created a scene of sheer beauty, of unalloyed romance.

But today the shadow of Teddy's disappearance blighted any feeling of joy.

When we walked into the kitchen, Mary saw the open jars of peanut butter and jelly and the bread crumbs. "I see Estelle is home." She called her name. "Wonder where she and Wendy are?"

The raucous chatter of the parakeets resembled radio static.

"You be quiet, Kingy and Flint," Eleanor ordered. "I want peanut butter and jelly too."

"Why don't you ring the bell . . . I don't see them outside," Mary said to me. "The girls are probably in the barn. But this has been such a strange day. I want to know exactly where they are." She eased down onto one of the straight-backed kitchen chairs, her lean body slumping as if the gravity of fatigue pulled her down, tightening her voice, creasing her face. "And then do you think you could call Annie? I'm so tired I can hardly speak. I feel it all in my throat." She put a hand to her neck, holding it there.

As I opened the door, the two blond eleven-year-olds tore down our driveway. "Daddy . . . ," Estelle shouted. "Mom

. . . The funniest thing. We think there's somebody from Mars in the barn . . ."

"He scared us," her friend Wendy added, laughing nervously, glancing over her shoulder.

"He's almost as big as we are and we found him with his arms around Jenny's neck . . . And he was talking to her in some kind of funny language . . . Wow! Were we scared. We came right back down."

Mary jumped out of her chair. "Oh, thank God! I'll call Annie . . . You go and get him," she said to me.

"Bring him here?" Estelle gasped.

"I'm going to hide," Eleanor said, dropping her partially made sandwich on the table.

"You better call the police," Wendy suggested, backing away from the door. "He's so weird."

I ran to the barn, stopping just before I reached the paddock.

The thin youngster walked around Jenny, patting her, talking to her in a language only they understood. Then Teddy put his head against her back and leaned on her, both hands stroking and patting. He moved to her head, throwing his arms around the burro's neck.

Jenny stood quietly, her ears flicking back and forth. What astonished me was that this perpetual eating machine didn't graze or even nibble at the hay in front of her. I knew it was because she didn't want to do anything to hurt him. Again and again I found she had a remarkable sense of responsibility when it came to children.

I decided to wait for the Millers. Sitting on the edge of the stone wall, I watched the two of them. Jenny had her numerous faults, but today I felt a perceptible gentleness emanating from her.

Love compensates for a multitude of escapades.

10

October . . . October for us became an unhappy though beautiful month.

Unhappy because of the onset of hunting.

Beautiful because of the time of year.

I'd been mowing a field at the highest point of our property. Now I switched off the ignition on the green John Deere two-cylinder tractor. The ear-popping noise stopped abruptly. Within the massive rotary bushwhacker I towed, the whirring sound of the heavy four-foot blade gradually diminished. There's a satisfaction in mowing a field. Your efforts are so visible.

I sat in silence. The stillness of this autumn afternoon enfolded me in its golden light, suffusing me with tranquillity and beauty. I'd been feeling unaccountably tired lately, and now relaxed in the surrounding peace.

There was too much to absorb. I tried to store the details in my memory bank, but much of it overflowed, lost forever. In a way I'm glad, for I like to live fully in the immediate moment. I want to give myself to an unusual experience completely, for it will never come again in the same way.

Everywhere I looked I saw colors of different hues and

intensities. The deeper red of dogwood leaves, the variegated oranges and yellows of maples, the brownish-reds of oaks, the fiery magenta bushes, the diverse colorations of cherry, sumac, walnut trees. In the woods, light poured through the yellow leaves of the sycamores, glancing off the peeling layers of their tan and white barks, the trunks resembling the spotted necks of giraffes. Here and there trees had not fully turned. The different species of our growing Christmas trees with varying shades of green contrasted with the pale fields of grass.

All these disparate colors were unified by the sun and an unblemished blue sky into a soft golden haze permeating everything.

"Thou crownest the year with thy goodness; and thy paths drop fatness. They drop upon the pastures of the wilderness; and the little hills rejoice on every side. The pastures are clothed with flocks; the valleys also are covered over with corn; they shout for joy, they also sing."

We'd moved here to seek beauty and peace. Each of us found these jewels in our own way and in varying degrees. For Mary and me, most of the time our treasure seemed to justify the efforts.

Imperceptibly the colors deepened as the earth turned toward afternoon's end and the shadows of trees crept toward me over the fields. I thought of Emily Dickinson's poem in which she gets at the interior meaning of *presentiment*.

> *"Presentiment* is that long shadow on the lawn
> Indicative that suns go down;
> The notice to the startled grass
> That darkness is about to pass."

Presentiment. I thought of the possible threatening "undertones" within the meaning of the word.

I propped my paperback dictionary on the steering wheel, pulling my glasses from my cotton work shirt, and turned the dog-eared pages, searching for the word.

The word was described as "Apprehension, as of evil. 2. foreboding. Syn. (See *foreboding*)."

I looked it up and read: *"Misgiving, foreboding* and *presentiment* express degrees of expectation, *misgiving* and *foreboding* always, and *presentiment,* almost always of evil. *Misgiving* names a feeling of apprehension and dread about the future. *Foreboding* is more positive in its premonition of evil, and is tinged with the ominous. *Presentiment* is the least definite; a vague suggestion of something unfortunate or unhappy in the air."

Even in the midst of this beauty, I felt the poet's *presentiment*—a vague, shadowy awareness, not of an event, not of something outside of myself, but rather within.

What a waste to have dark thoughts on a day like this. I closed the dictionary and shut them away.

Laddie and our black German shepherd puppy, Donna, lay in the swath of cut grass behind the tractor. They liked to follow me as I mowed, to see what they might uncover.

Two shotgun blasts in rapid succession exploded my reverie. The shots came from the woods.

We dreaded this season because we didn't dare go into the woods except on Sundays. Even then some hunters ignored the law.

We found it a dangerous time. One of our children was nearly hit by a bow and arrow hunter. Three drunken poachers too close to the cottages and barn sullenly held their guns on me while I asked them to get off the property. Someone hired to patrol a neighboring farm was found shot to death. Every year livestock and pets became casualties.

I remembered the four dead doe and a fawn I'd found in a clearing and all neatly placed in a row. When the game warden examined the area he pointed out tire tracks, explaining that undoubtedly someone had been "jack lighting." The deer are mesmerized by headlights or a searchlight and then shot as they stand still in the glare of the lights. Why hadn't the hunter taken them?

The hunting season is a fever that sweeps through rural areas. Our town of five thousand always caught the hunting epidemic.

"Sorry . . . Can't repair your car until next week. My mechanic's out hunting."

Furnace or plumbing problems? "Next week . . . My men are hunting."

Of course, if I was truly against the killing of all animals, I'd be a complete vegetarian. I'm not. So admittedly there's a certain amount of self-deception concerning hunting. What really upsets me is the pleasure some hunters take in the act of killing. It's an atavistic attitude and not too far away from killing people. Paradoxically, I can understand the thrill of successfully stalking wily game.

Jack's Sporting Goods on Main Street became a popular store during the season, selling guns and ammunition. Portly Jack and his "full-figured" wife, Mrs. Jack, explained that "There are more deer in our county today than thirty-five years ago when we first opened our store . . . The poor things starve during winter because with the houses and all, there's not enough food for them to eat . . . They should be thinned out. They're dangerous to cars. People have been hurt."

Mary and I experienced that problem. Three times we had deer crash into our cars as the animals leaped across the roads. Neither deer nor car was killed. But both suffered some painful dents.

During the next few months I became increasingly aware of the mysterious physical malaise that had stalked me throughout the year. It seemed to close in relentlessly. I didn't feel well. Getting up early and writing and studying became more and more difficult. Sometimes when I walked down the stairs, ready to leave for New York, a wave of dizziness overwhelmed me. I had to stop, bracing myself against the wall.

Mary watched me with increasing concern, a foreboding concern, a misgiving, a *presentiment.* "I can't stand seeing you look so tired all the time . . . Let's move to something simple or go out west or anywhere. Forget about your job in New York. I don't care about having things. I don't care where we live. All I care about is you and the children."

In one way or another she kept repeating this idea.

Being fatigued became my normal condition. I wondered if

there'd ever been a time when I'd felt rested. Just walking to the barn put me out of breath. Playing tennis for only a few minutes with my children exhausted me.

"Want to play?" twelve-year-old Mark asked, energetically swishing his racket back and forth.

Even getting out of the chair seemed too much of an effort. "I'm pretty busy," I said, using work as an excuse. "What about Peter or John?"

"They're out with their friends. They didn't want me." Dejected at the refusal, his voice fell off.

"Celine likes to play. She and your mother have the best strokes in the family."

"She's talking to some guy on the telephone and shut the door . . . Estelle says she's going riding and Mother's knee hurts. And Paul and Eleanor don't know how to play . . . What's *wrong* with everybody? No one wants to do anything around here. It's just like school."

The non sequitur puzzled me. "How come?"

"Oh, the teachers are always on me for something."

"Such as?"

"I don't know . . ." He swung his racket. "They say I argue with them."

"Do you?"

"Well, sometimes I know what to do better than they do. They're always telling you to do this and do that . . . And sometimes I like to know why they want me to do it, and sometimes I think they're wrong."

I paused, thinking of my father. One nugget he passed along was that most successful people in business were skilled in human relations. Being bright seldom assured success. "Maybe you aren't handling them right. Hitting people headlong isn't always the best way." I explained my father's observation.

"The teachers just have it in for me," he insisted.

"I don't think you heard me."

He took another swing with his racket. "I heard every word you said."

"You might have *heard* but you didn't listen . . . One of

the meanings of 'listen' is to pay attention and *perhaps* to take the advice."

"I listen."

"If you do, you're about the only one in this family that does. It's not our strong point. And you haven't convinced me you do. In fact, your brothers and sisters say you're bullheaded. But maybe that's because you're a May child—a Taurus." I laughed.

Victoriously. "So are you!"

"Don't take me seriously about *that!* Don't get locked into a personality trait because of astrology. We can always change ourselves. Some people take a silly pride in being stubborn. You hear them say: 'Once I make up my mind to something I *never* change it.' What dummies! That means they won't let anyone else open their eyes to another way of seeing or hearing. Think of all the wonderful things they miss . . . ! So be independent and persevering. But don't be stubborn. There's a difference . . . Anyway, enough of that." I stood up and tousled his curly red hair. "Get my racket. It's in the playroom."

"Great!" he shouted, running off.

As we walked on the court, I explained how I held my racket, sliding the palm of my hand down the handle.

"I know how to hold it," he said impatiently. "You showed me."

"Sometimes it helps to be reminded."

"I don't have to be reminded. I remember. I can remember anything," he said with youthful assurance.

Ten to twelve years old is probably the optimum time to start youngsters off in tennis. Their strength is up to holding a light racket, and they're beginning to be well coordinated. However, beginning players are usually frustrated, for the ball seldom goes where they hope it might.

Mark had the rhythm and the flow of a natural athlete. I stood close to the net so I could place the ball more accurately for him. Also, I found it less tiring for me.

Many of the balls went zinging past me, far outside of the court lines. "Listen, I know you're strong and you have a superabundance of energy, but tennis is a lot like life. Where you put the ball is often just as important as how hard you hit it."

"But I like to hit them hard," he said, belting a ball to the backhand court just beyond my reach. He grinned happily. "See! I can do it."

I smiled at Mark's exuberance. "That was a honey. But the more control you get, the more often you're going to get shots like that."

"Let's play," he urged.

"You'll play better if you practice a while longer."

He hit a few more. "This isn't any fun . . . Let's play."

I explained that fifteen or twenty minutes of practice would be more valuable to him in the future. But the future is hard to see for children. He wanted to play.

We rallied, but the ball seldom went over the net more than once or twice at a time. Being so short of breath, I found it hard to give him shots that he might be able to hit back more easily. He grew angry at himself for bobbling so many of them.

A tennis serve is difficult to learn. Few of his went in and I gave him some tips and then suggested we just rally for a few more minutes.

Finally I lowered my racket. "I've had enough."

"But Dad. We haven't played very long. I'm just getting warmed up."

"I know. But I'm really tired . . . Sorry." I walked to the sidelines, annoyed with myself.

I felt Mark's scrutiny. "Why are you always so tired all the time?"

I shrugged. "That's what Dr. Richardson's trying to find out."

"I hope I'm like him someday . . . I want to be a doctor." He looked at me with what he considered a professional air. "You are pretty skinny and pale. Maybe you should eat more. I've been using Peter's weights. Maybe you should use them . . . Build up your muscles."

I smiled at him. "You sound like a physical fitness ad."

Funks are known for their enthusiasm for the culinary arts, and I am no exception, but now I ate simply to keep up my weight. At the end of the day my stomach sounded as noisy as Humphrey Bogart's in the movie *The African Queen.*

I blamed it on my busy routine and the fact we hadn't had a real vacation in years. My business responsibilities had me on the road half of the time. I pushed hard with my linguistic studies and writing, getting about six hours of sleep a night. And Good Ground Farm immersed us in a continuing heuristic challenge.

One day Mary, dismayed, informed me that our friend Betty Taylor had tears in her eyes when she talked about me. Betty, a hefty about-to-be-retired teacher at the children's small Quaker school said: "Have you *really* looked at Peter lately. He's so thin and he's as white as the chalk I use on my blackboard."

Of course Mary noticed. This is what upset her.

Having been a premedical student in college and at one time an assistant to the medicine editor at *Newsweek*, my tendency is to tell the doctor what's wrong with me. Since I may have a few salient facts handy, sometimes I actually sound as if I know what I'm talking about medically. Unfortunately, a doctor's opinion may be influenced.

I told Tom that probably I had a recurrence of an old duodenal ulcer, giving him my reasons. And so that's the way we treated my omnipresent ailment. As I trudged through the following months, I still felt lousy.

One evening when I arrived home from New York Mary asked me to carry a geranium plant from a place in front of the kitchen door to a spot in the back of the house. "I can't," I said, for the first time in my life refusing such an easy job. "I can't do it now. Wait until tomorrow."

And when I returned from skiing with the children on a nearby hill, I said to her more in hope than belief, "Look at the color in my face."

"What color?" she replied unhappily.

On a damp Saturday afternoon in late November, we'd been inside most of the day except when we had to go out to take care of the farm animals.

"Hey, guys!" John announced. "I have a good idea. Let's have a race. We need some exercise."

Mark jumped up. *"Right!* Let's go."

Enthusiasm boiled through the children, everyone for it. "Where should we run?" Estelle asked.

"Down the driveway . . . The two-mile run." John referred to the course that went down our lower driveway and then more or less followed a local road around the perimeter of our property and Trapper Mountain, the ski hill.

They began leaving the room to change their clothes.

"Come on, Dad. Aren't you going to run? We know Mother has a sore knee and she can't."

"Well . . . ," I hedged. "I'll start you off."

"It's a great day for running. It'll get your blood going."

Mary looked worried. "I think your father should stay right where he is."

"I don't know . . . Maybe it would be good for me to get out. I'll give it a try."

"Don't let them pressure you," she said. "I really wonder . . ."

"They're not pressuring me . . . I think it might be good for me."

"I want to go . . . I want to run too," Eleanor said.

"It's too far, Eleanor. That's a long way. In a couple of years you'll probably be beating all of us," John said in an encouraging, kindly voice.

"I can so do it."

Estelle took her hand. "That's *two whole miles* . . . That's awfully far, and Mom and Dad don't want you on the road alone."

Paul, being the youngest, went first. Then Estelle, Celine, Mark, and I went. John and Peter would follow after a minute or two.

Going down our twisting driveway, I felt fine and glad to be out, happy about John's suggestion. I let gravity pull me, lengthening my stride. On the way down, I noticed that some of the cedar trees needed to have the Japanese honeysuckle vines pulled off.

On the flat stretch to the ski area I overtook Celine and Estelle, but suddenly I felt my energy unwinding like the unraveling spring of a mechanical toy. I'd come even with Paul, but I knew even now I couldn't keep up with my ten-year-old. I gasped for breath.

Paul looked up at me, his expression questioning. Normally I would have slowed my pace to his so we'd finish together. Now I knew I couldn't keep up with him.

Glancing at me again, *he* slowed down. But obviously I was still having problems. He slowed down once more. The girls first, and then John, Peter, and Laddie passed us.

"You okay, Dad?" Peter asked.

"We didn't feel like beating you today," I tried to joke, catching my breath.

They ran up the long hill ahead of us, probably thinking I'd stayed back for Paul. I knew I couldn't make it. As if reading my mind, Paul looked at me, his blue eyes expressing puzzled concern. "I think I'll walk," he said.

That didn't sound like Paul. He could run the two-mile course easily. But I didn't argue. I knew why he stopped. Just to walk home became a major feat. Paul held my hand. We continued without conversation. I had tears in my eyes.

The following week Tom took a blood count. "No wonder you're exhausted. You only have about half the number of red blood cells you should have."

"What about my white cells?" I asked immediately, thinking of leukemia.

"Normal . . . No problem there. We're going to load you up with B_{12}. And I've asked Mary to feed you a lot of liver." He told me also to change my way of life and my crazy schedule. At this point I wanted to but didn't know where to start.

Mary took to heart his advice about giving me liver. We had *liver!* We had chicken livers, beef liver, calf's liver. The children complained. But their cheeks became even rosier than before. They *exuded* red blood cells. My count inched up, but I felt only marginally better.

About that time, an experience alarmed me. Waking up at sunrise one morning and not being able to get back to sleep, I went for a walk along one of the trails in the woods, taking Laddie with me.

The old dog relished such walks. This morning his plumed tail wagged vigorously as his graying nose searched the ground for an interesting odor. Finding one, he veered off the trail, chasing a phantom long gone, barking joyously. He never caught anything. If he'd been so unlucky, I don't know who would have gone into shock first—Laddie or the quarry.

He surprised a deer, however, taking off after it full tilt, his barks echoing among the trees. The deer resembled a ballet figure, its long, high graceful leaps looking effortless, its broad flicking tail a flash of white. Laddie couldn't sustain the pace these days while running after deer. He usually glanced over his shoulder at me when he'd had enough of the chase. We had an understanding. I called him back. Pretending to be reluctant he obeyed, spared the public embarrassment of no longer being able to keep up. He returned to me panting, smiling, waiting for the pat of affection. His tongue lolled out of the corner of his mouth as he shared with me in his own fashion the excitement I missed.

I pulled off my jacket. "Too hot for this today," I said to the dog, who probably wished he wore a coat so easily unzipped. A winter thaw melted away the frigid night air into a light drizzle, and the softened ground squished under my imperfectly waterproofed boots. Rather than the metallic light of morning, we seemed to be walking through a sea of amber. The strange yellow-brown color filled me with an inexplicable anxiety.

Since the phenomenon presaged an imminent downpour, I decided to go home. "Come on, Laddie. We'll cut through the woods to the lower trail." I knew where we were and intended to pass Peter and John's tree house.

Unaccountably I became disoriented. I wasn't sure of my location or which way to go. I couldn't even find the tree. I'd been positive Laddie and I were only a minute or two away from it. This puzzled me, for I knew our 110 acres intimately.

The amber light changed the shape and the look of everything around me. The atmosphere seemed to be transformed into a liquid, the yellow stuff seeping through me, saturating every cell in my body. For a few moments nausea engulfed me. Kneeling, I retched, as if trying to get rid of a poison.

I leaned against a tree, resting. Gradually things reshaped into recognizable forms and I walked home.

The following week, I went to a basketball game with Mark and some other fathers and their children. Though we had a good time, I felt especially fragile. Off and on I experienced considerable pain. At such times I remembered Winston Churchill's comment that most of the world's work is done by people who don't feel well.

Because of my discomfort, that night Mary and I slept apart.

Around four in the morning, pain wakened me. I pressed my hand around the area of the lower abdomen and to my surprise felt a lump. I examined the rest of my abdomen and then came back to that one area. The lump was large and well defined. With my low blood count, weight loss, and fatigue, I knew instantly I had a tumor and almost certainly it would be malignant.

For a while I thought about the possible ramifications. If it was so large that I, a layman could feel it so easily, this meant the disease must be fairly well along. How far? Probably entirely too far. This would not be one of the cases where the doctor would say, "Well, we've caught this nice and early so the prognosis is good."

Edges of fear, like cold water, began to permeate me. I didn't want to think of the possibilities and what they could mean—mean not only to me but to my family. How dark and still and ominous my room seemed. Now I understood the *presentiment*.

I'd become that one-out-of-four statistic! Even when you're aware of the possibilities, you *never* think it's going to happen to you.

Sometimes while driving alone in the car, I memorize verses from the Bible. I remembered one now that Saint Francis of Assisi used when he sent some of his friars out on a dangerous mission. Quoting from Psalm 55, he told them to *Cast your*

burden upon the Lord, and he will sustain you. My burden at
the moment was almost more than I could handle.

"Lord, this is too much for me. I need your help. You know
how much I love Mary and the children. I can't leave them now.
I'd be leaving them in a terrible mess . . . And I still have so
many things I want to do yet." A phrase from the Psalms came
into my prayer. *Lord, do not take me away in the midst of my
days.*

I waited, not knowing what else to do. I was frightened. "I
believe, but help my unbelief," I said, echoing the father who
asked Jesus to heal his child in the Gospel of Mark.

Then another verse slipped into my mind. *You will keep
him in perfect peace, whose mind is stayed on you.* I tried to
think about God and not my illness or fear; that God dwells in
me and I in him.

No great sense of comfort rushed in on me. But like a
mountaineer who finds a small foothold while clinging to the
vertical side of a cliff, momentarily I had something to hold me
up.

As I rested, I recalled a passage from Saint Paul in Philippi-
ans. *Don't worry about anything, but in all your prayers ask
God for what you need, always asking him with a thankful
heart. And God's peace, which is far beyond human understanding, will keep your hearts and minds safe in Christ Jesus.*

There was no way that I could keep from worrying. I
thought if I were spiritually more mature I could probably
follow Saint Paul's advice more faithfully. But now was now,
and I worried. My worries were more about what would happen to Mary and the children if I died rather than my own
feelings about death. But all my feelings were entangled like a
ball of knotted-up string. I couldn't really sort them out.

Yet in the stillness of that black, frigid night I began to
experience the emanations of a certain peace coming from
deep within me.

"Lord, I'm dumping this whole thing in your lap. And I
thank you for helping me discover it, because now I know what
I have to face."

I fell asleep.

When Tom's office opened, I telephoned him and mentioned the lump and that I could come to his office at any time. Being a loving and dedicated doctor, he wouldn't hear of my leaving home and made a house call. From the expression on his face, I knew what he suspected. However, so as not to worry Mary and me—I'd said nothing to her about my own diagnosis —he suggested it might be an intestinal abscess. We both knew better. Though I knew we both hoped we were wrong.

Immediately he arranged for me to be examined by another close friend and an outstanding surgeon, Eric Stevens. After poking around me, Eric told the X-ray department he had an emergency situation and wanted pictures taken Monday. Today was Saturday. In the meanwhile Mary took the children to a movie that, though purporting to be a comedy, depressed her. The father in the film worked desperately hard at a job he didn't like. She cried. Too close to home.

Coming back from the hospital, my car slipped into a ditch at the bottom of our driveway. I walked the half mile up the hill, got the tractor, pulled the car out with the heavy tow chain, brought the tractor back to the barn, walked down to the car again, and drove to the house. I felt wiped out. This hadn't been the best of days.

Anyone who has had a G.I. series knows the routine of castor oil and of going without food the day before the X-rays. It's the castor oil that always gets me. I hate it. I can barely gag it down. And afterward I burp about as often as there are bubbles coming out of an opened bottle of soda water. They say it's good oil for machines. I wouldn't wish it on the crankiest one I had in the barn.

The following day, shifted this way and that on the hard table by the technicians, I said to the radiologist, "Well . . . I'm glad to know what it is."

"You are?" He looked at me, surprised.

"I always like to know what I'm facing."

He didn't reply. I thought this indicated he also believed it to be malignant. Of course, I had an understandable hope he might possibly say, "Nothing to worry about. Just an abscess." But he didn't.

"Know the origin of the word *malignant?*" I asked.

The doctor shook his head, glancing at me warily.

"From Latin *malignare* . . . 'To injure maliciously.' Looked it up yesterday. Seems kind of an appropriate description for a cancer, doesn't it . . . ? I like to know the root of words. It gives me a fuller sense of the meaning . . . Anyway, thought you'd like to know."

He nodded cautiously, looking as if I might be on the verge of doing something strange.

I prayed to myself that the Holy Spirit would guide his skills.

I telephoned my parents. With the way things were going I wasn't surprised at the news they gave me. My mother's doctor had scheduled her for a hip replacement operation in the world-famous Hospital for Special Surgery in New York. My father was being checked out for a suspected stroke.

My mother, who had faith in big hospitals, asked me in dismay, "Why are you having major surgery done in a small country hospital?"

I gave her our reasons. Our surgeon was reputed to be one of the finest in the East. The quality and performance of the trained nurses was especially first rate. The women lived in the area because of their husbands' jobs. And so when their children were old enough, the nurses went back to work. Furthermore, the hospital was run by a rotating committee of three women, one of whom visited every patient, asking for an evaluation of its services.

Being small, the hospital presented us with another advantage. Not bound by the bureaucratic red tape of size, they allowed Mary to spend the first two nights with me in a tiny room.

The number of my room was 103. My operation would take place on February 3. In times of crisis it's natural to look for any favorable omens and signs. The number 3 suggested the Trinity to me—God, Christ, and the Holy Spirit. I liked the feel of the room. Mary and I are not really superstitious. But still . . . Well, there is a certain mysterious rhythm to life and at that point I'd take anything that offered comfort.

We had a relatively cheerful afternoon, watching the bustle of hospital activity. In the evening our minister, Crofton Thompson, came to see me. Crofton was one of our favorites. After my novel *My Six Loves* appeared, he asked me if I'd known anything about his past. At the time the book came out we'd just moved to the area and knew nothing about him. The reason for his question was that in my story a minister, the principal character, is in a car accident. His wife and only child are killed. An almost identical accident happened to Crofton on his way to becoming rector of his first church.

He'd been in advertising for years before he'd entered the ministry. My protagonist had also been a businessman prior to being ordained, a curious coincidence.

A relatively small man with kindly brown eyes and a generous mouth so often on the edge of a quizzical smile, he had a quick, incisive mind. I characterized him as everybody's uncle, for he had the ability to establish a personal relationship and treated you as he would a member of his own family with loving concern and sometimes with disconcerting frankness.

But his tragic accident left interior wounds that never really healed. This affected his relationship with God, which vacillated between deism (God created the universe and then had nothing more to do with it) and theism (having the sense of an immanent, personal God). Understandably, his bias was toward the former.

When Crofton appeared in my room, Mary had gone home to care for the children. She couldn't line up a sitter. I had hoped he would stop by, as I wanted more support.

"Crofton, I want you to lay your hands on me and pray for a complete healing. I'm positive I have cancer."

"*I* can't heal you," he said perturbed.

"I know *you* can't. But you can be a channel of God's healing love and light."

I like Agnes Sanford's definition of prayer. "Prayer is asking God to send His power through the channel of our faith so that His light may shine through us." Sometimes a phrase such as this means more than all dictionary definitions combined. It

could only come from a person who deeply understands healing.

Crofton prayed with me. Reluctantly he recounted an incident concerning a woman who'd been blind. She too asked him
to pray. She recovered her sight.

The following morning, while being wheeled into the operating room, I felt literally as if borne on the wings of prayer. I
knew Mary and others were praying.

Firm hands edged me over on the operating table . . .
Bright lights above were like suns sterilizing the gleaming
white room . . . Solicitous quiet faces surrounded me . . . A
needle in my arm.

And then . . . And then as if in the next moment, a faint
voice heard far away tightly wrapped in darkness calling my
name as if in a dream. I tried to respond, but my mind was
bound and smothered by paralyzing forces as dark as the night.
I struggled to reach a surface of fuller awareness, but nothing
within me could move. I had no control over my body. I realized, as if in a dream, the operation must be over.

But I lived!

Whoever called wanted to help me, to lead me through the
layers of thick, paralyzing, muffled darkness.

A touch on my hand. This time the nurse's kindly voice
seemed more within hearing distance. "Do you know who's
holding your hand?"

"I sure do," I strained to say, knowing my words must be
slurred and indistinct but aware intuitively and instantly that
Mary held my hand; that the power of her love was pulling me
out of this frightening morass of darkness. Where else but in this
little hospital would they let a wife into the recovery room?

During the operation our dear friend and family physician,
Tom, came out to see her. Unable to keep the tears from his
eyes, he told her about the cancer. My chances might be 50/50.
Probably less. Poor doctors. Daily they confront such sadness.

The information stunned Mary. She had no intimation that

I had a malignancy. I'd made a mistake in not telling her what I suspected, for then she would have been better prepared. We try to protect those we love. But this is not always best. Sometimes in sharing we gain strength and are able to make better decisions. *Love* is a complex quality.

A day or so later Eric, my surgeon and also a good friend, said the biopsy confirmed the diagnosis of an advanced cancer. In his opinion, however, the operation seemed to be an unqualified success. Of course, time would tell, but "the operation went off like a *miracle,*" he said. He didn't recommend any other treatment for the moment. Chemotherapy was then in its early stages and not a viable choice. The only alternative would be X-ray; he chose not to use either.

During the next few days, periodically, the reason for my being in the hospital enveloped me in a wave of fearful thoughts. The enormity of our situation appalled me.

To leave Mary with seven children on a farm with not much in the way of other assets . . . To let her bring them up alone in today's violently uncertain world . . . ? Unthinkable! Never! I looked back with a certain fondness on the persistent insurance salesman who sold me the policy. At least she would have some cash in the event the worst did happen.

As I ruminated over those dire possibilities, I was darned if I would die and leave Mary in that mess. I determined to turn my attitude around, trying not to let negative feelings overwhelm me. I would be positive. I visualized every cell in the area of my cancer as being healed. Yes, I was utterly realistic about my situation. But I knew also that the body and self respond to a positive outlook.

I'd been thinking about these things one day while looking through my hospital window at the lawn, the parking lot, sidewalk, and street, when I heard Mary come into the room.

She gave me a kiss and a careful hug. "And what are you watching?"

"Life."

"And what do you think of it?" she asked cheerfully.

"It's good."

Mary looked at me closely, sensing something else. She has an awareness of seeing a person not as she may preconceive but as that person is now. She doesn't project what she *may want* to see in someone, but tries to be sensitive to the need or fears of that individual.

She nodded, draping her coat over a chair, putting the mail she brought on the bed. "Did you have a good sleep? Is everything all right . . . ? Are you in pain or uncomfortable?"

"No, I'm fine."

She didn't accept my answer. We try to be gently honest with one another. She sat on the bed. "Something's bothering you."

"They don't let me jog around the hospital corridors."

Laserlike love pierced my thin armor. "Why don't we talk about whatever it is?"

I shook my head. "No . . . I've resolved it."

"What?"

"What most of us shy away from."

She waited with an intuitive, quiet patience.

I took a long breath. Conversing about death with myself was one thing. Talking with others about it was something else. Yet, in talking, you share, you give, you receive.

"My mortality." How we use euphemisms!

Mary nodded, her lustrous blue eyes filling with her own apprehensions. "I know . . . I think about it too. All the time."

We were silent awhile, each with our thoughts. Again I took a breath. "It's interesting about death. It's such an absolute reality. Death is coming face to face with reality. And it's *your* reality. Someone can't do this for you. . . . When you have an illness like this, it's not much different than an older person who's coming close to death . . . Bit by bit your body's letting you down and there's very little you can do about it."

"Except the way you handle it," Mary said softly.

I saw my smile reflected in her face. "I can't remember the exact words, but the thought's enough. It was something John Quincy Adams said. A friend who met him in the street asked how he felt. He said something to the effect that his old body was ailing in all kinds of ways and wouldn't be long for this world. But that John Quincy Adams himself . . . the real John Quincy Adams, the John Quincy Adams of the mind and spirit, was just fine. The whole sense of the passage was that maybe his body was falling apart but that he himself in his own mind was cheerful and upbeat . . . And that's the way I want to be."

She nodded. "Yes . . . Yes. So do I . . . To face death with dignity and courage . . . And *faith* . . . Death conquers so many people before the end, destroying their spirit. Do you know what I mean? It destroys their spirit just as it does their bodies. It makes me sad to see the spirit of a person undone . . . Some people are so strong and courageous and decisive all their lives . . . And *then* they meet death, the most extreme challenge of all . . . It shatters them. They could whip life but not death . . . Maybe for the first time they've really looked deeply inside of themselves, and what they find doesn't comfort them . . . They become so fearful . . . So terribly fearful. I feel so sorry for them." She paused, looking down at her hands. "I'm glad we have time to think . . . to think about . . ."

She was close to tears. We both were.

I looked out through the window again. Morning shadows from the hospital contrasted with the broad places of sunlight. People walked the sidewalks. Cars moved on the streets. A food delivery truck backed into an unloading area. Two black starlings squabbled on a branch of a nearby tree.

I was looking at the flow of life and I wanted to join it. "I don't ever want my body to become a focus point. Ever! Of course, I want to be healthy. My Lord, I long to be completely well. And sure I fear death. But if it's coming, Lord keep me from turning in on myself so that all I do is think about myself and staying alive! I want to face death with courage and dignity and faith . . . And grace. God's grace . . . I trust in God. I never want to forget that trust. Death is a transformation from one form of existence into another. I know this rationally. I know it intellectually . . . But I want to *feel* it in my guts too, and if I let fear get to me in a way where it begins to take control, I never will. And this is the province of *faith* . . . I can get through it with God's help. And by the way, God help me from becoming a complainer."

Such painful words from us at this time. But gently honest ones needed for our perspective.

"The nurses say you never complain," Mary said with a trace of a smile touching her face.

"I let them know if they forget my pills or whatever . . . Complain! Wonder what the origin is?" I found my glasses and dictionary, flipping through the pages. "Ah. Vulgar Latin *complangere*, 'to beat the breast.' Apparently the *com-* is an intensive and *plangere* means 'to strike.' "

"What's the significance of striking ourselves on the breast?" Mary mused.

We eased into another area of conversation.

During my last blood transfusion, I mentioned to the efficient floor nurse that I had qualms about the blood. The donor must have been living on rubber cement the way it kept clogging up the plastic tube in my arms. I worried about getting hepatitis from it.

"That's a crazy idea," she said impatiently. "It's perfectly good blood. You can't tell anything by looking at it."

And so, in addition to the normal hospital stay to recover from the effects of my operation, I ended up with six weeks of absolute bed rest at home because of a virulent viral hepatitis.

As Marge (the plump, blond check-out clerk in the supermarket) used to say about her unsuccessful attempts to diet, "So what can you do?"

11

I've been thinking about this summer," Mary said, sitting on the edge of my hospital bed. "We have everything at Good Ground to make a sensational day camp."

"Camp? You mean a *real* camp . . . The kind little kids go to in the summer?" I'd thought of our farm as a beauty spot, a refuge from the world, a work-trap, but never as a camp.

"Well, actually I got the idea when Mary and Celine said they wanted to earn money and they thought they might take care of some little children during the day in the summer. And you know who'd end up being responsible. So . . . why not do it right?"

"A summer of that and we'd *both* be in the hospital," I interrupted.

"Let me explain. By having a camp, everything this summer will be centralized around the farm . . . Everything will happen there, and I've cut out all that carting around that would take me away from you. You're the one that needs me the most right now . . . Celine's fifteen and Estelle's thirteen. They'd be restless just staying home and I'd have to drive them to jobs."

"But we don't know anything about running a camp."

"We didn't know anything about running a farm either."

"And look what happened! No farmer in his right mind would have let Jenny near his property . . . Let's face it, darling. There's no way you could run a camp. Good Lord! Who's going to take care of the animals, the fields, fencing, barn, emergencies at the cottages . . . ? I'm out of the act for a while. I won't be much help. And something like that could cost us money we don't have," I added.

She nodded, her face and eyes softening with love and concern. "I want to be with you. That's the main thing. But . . . maybe it could make a little money too."

We decided to explore the feasibility of the idea.

During the period of recovering from the viral hepatitis, I experienced a developing awareness that existed beyond the scope of language to articulate. Like any other tool or instrument, words have a limit beyond which they are no longer effective. There is a particular "truth" we experience at the beginning of life and at the end. My awareness of this was as certain as if it had been put into words. Yet the form of it was wordless. An irony for me!

Now, because of a malignancy, I teetered on the edge of an ending. Or a new beginning? No matter what happened, my life was irrevocably altered. There was not necessarily joy in the knowledge. Yet I discovered an inexplicable, though admittedly frightening kind of satisfaction. I wondered at my new, though very murky, view of the mystery beyond this surface—or the mystery ahead in my life.

I'd always thought of myself as virtually indestructible. I could do all kinds of things that took strength.

Now, I awoke in the darkness of deep night full of unfamiliar doubts.

Something else happened to Mary and me. Gradually, the dross that sometimes is mistaken for "life" began to dry up and shrivel like a pulled weed. Our priorities took on a different order of precedence. The things that really mattered to us became less hazy—like a color slide becoming more sharply focused on the screen. Things and objects faded. People were at the center.

And we thought of our children. If we were to die, what values would we hope to inculcate in them? To love God with all their mind and body and soul. With that they'd never want for anything. They would have strength for all things. And then, to love one another as we love them.

We stood in the doorway of change and chance, not sure what to expect.

I no longer worked for the firm in New York. They explained they were in a transitional period and because of the economy were forced to make changes. However, I suspect my illness was a factor. Anyway, Mary had urged me to quit commuting and to make writing and linguistics a full-time career. Not disappointed at the change, nonetheless I felt apprehensive.

At this time also, my mother and father were both still in the hospital. My sister Joan, who lived at a distance and had the care of her own family, graciously spent a few days with Mary doing all that she could. Sally, my other sister, had married a Dutchman and lived on the Island of Aruba, too far to travel from.

So due to a strange concatenation of events, we fell into a pocket almost devoid of normal care from other family members who could have been helpful. Either they were totally absorbed in their own troublesome situations or were unaware.

Perhaps though, we'd expressed such a positive attitude about our circumstances that no one worried about us. Few could possibly guess the fears that occasionally poured over us when we were alone. Together we bolstered each other and it worked well. We used the miracle of "life" as our offense. We found laughter and humor to be the best kind of anodyne.

Friends decorated our small world with flowers, food, visits, jokes, loving concern. For years I kept a lovely collage a woman made out of dried-up leaves and stalks and other things found in the winter countryside.

Nonetheless we felt alone. "Terribly alone," as Mary said. Our strong and unexpected support came from the four children who were still at home, the oldest being Estelle at thirteen. Peter, a green beret soldier, was in Vietnam, John in college, and Celine away at school.

The younger children cared for Mary when she returned from the hospital each night, making sure she had a warm bath and was in bed early. They answered the telephone and under her direction did most of the cooking.

At the time we didn't tell any of the children about my cancer; only that I'd been very ill. I'm not completely certain why we took this tack. Perhaps we were trying to protect them. If so, we're not sure of the wisdom of that choice. It may have been that we wanted to create a more positive atmosphere. Healing has more of an opportunity under such an environment. Their worry and anger at the possibility of losing a father might have affected us as much as them.

On the other hand, to share our concerns, our realism, our hopes and prayers might have been a maturing experience. Death and life are the opposite sides of the same coin. There are arguments for both approaches.

Celine, having a psychic awareness, knew something was terribly wrong and tried to get information from the hospital. They were noncommittal, of course, and so she contacted her mother. She couldn't be convinced that everything now was all right.

"Anyhow, *your* prayers are answered," Mary said to me mischievously one day. "You wanted to leave your job in New York and spend full time on your word studies and writing. Be thankful the firm in New York dropped you."

"I guess you're right," I said. "But I still think God took a pretty Draconian way of working things out."

I should have been elated. I wasn't. Instead I felt troubled. I wasn't sure I could support us as a writer. How well now I remembered everything I'd read and heard about the life of a full-time professional writer. The arts are a lonely and precarious way of earning a living.

A writer's tools are his brain, energy, and creativity. There's no one to whom to delegate the act of thinking up a story line or of writing. There's no regimen that others in a company have set up. No one tells you to do this or that. No office opens at nine requiring you to be there. No committees to work with. No weekly or monthly salary. No way to estimate future income accurately. After months or even years of work, a project may not pan out and all that effort and time goes down the drain. Reader interest is always in a flux. For various reasons some publishers do not necessarily pay on time.

A job counselor with Princeton University told me once that a writer, more than most people, lives with continual uncertainty.

Furthermore you are alone. Hour after hour alone. And then you not only have the hard chore of writing something as well as you can. You rewrite. The popular author Dean Koontz states that once he figured out that he'd rewritten a book thirty-one times.

As I mulled over these *night thoughts* I recalled the letters from some authors my father showed me once. I think he did this to discourage me from relying on a writing career to earn a living.

At the time I was too young to feel the desperate anguish of those unfortunate people who were broke, who'd used up their advances against royalties, whose books weren't moving, who because of frenetic financial worries couldn't concentrate on what they were writing. All begged for money. They were faced with selling their cars, homes, personal belongings. They had no savings; nothing in reserve. They were despairing men.

I didn't want us trapped in the same situation. Yet, for me, being a writer was the finest thing I could imagine. Even as a child I knew that no matter what else I might have to do, writing was what I wanted. Knowing this, Mary encouraged me and felt it worth taking the risk. Since I worried about jeopardizing the family, I decided to try it for a year. If during this time it didn't work out, I'd look for another job.

Sometimes when I was alone I found it difficult to think about the future.

The end of summer? Next year?

I knew that as yet I had no certainty I'd be around the following spring. When a body's cells go wild there's no guarantee that for the first few years they might not break loose again.

Sometimes negative thoughts slipped around the positive barriers Mary and I erected.

I wanted to live. With every ounce of energy and desire I wanted to live, and I "argued" with God against the possibility I might not. "Argue" isn't really the most precise word to use for my struggle. Who can *argue* against *the* creator? I queried. I tried to understand. I asked for insight. Certainly I asked for help. I was frightened. And I was very angry. How unjust to leave Mary with such overwhelming responsibilities!

I loved her. I loved our children and this life of ours and everything in it—dandelions resembling bright spots of sunlight on our lawn, the green strong stalks of tiger lilies, the small black baby lambs, the melodious early morning songs of birds, buzzards riding the wind, the fragrance of spring blossoms. I loved our parents, the members of all our families, my friends, the world.

One day, after my release from the hospital, as I paced around that bare wood floor in my barn office, I remembered what Jesus said about our lives: "He who finds his life will lose it, and he who loses his life for my sake will find it." A paradox worthy of a Zen koan. Well . . . I was trying to save it. Yes, I knew that at one level he meant that by taking his teachings at face value we end up manifesting the best of ourselves . . . finding our *real* life. Yet, at another level did his words mean I should literally give up my life?

And this is what I argued passionately and agonizingly against.

I saw the different farm animals. How strange to think that they could live longer than I. I almost wished I had the possibility of at least their life spans.

Suddenly and unexpectedly something "broke" in me. In church during communion or the eucharist, there's a point when the minister or priest breaks the wafer representing Christ's body, and you can hear the snap. Metaphorically it is the "breaking" of the Lord's body and by extension the Lord is "breaking" you from the past, from everything that binds you to fear, selfishness, hatred. It is a breaking up of an old life and re-forming it into a new one. We cannot keep love within ourselves and still call it love. Our love must symbolically be broken, as is the bread used in the communion service, so it can be shared with others.

At that terrible moment in the barn I heard the "snap" and I surrendered completely. I can't tell how or why. If God felt that my life could be used better in death than in life, I was willing to let life go. Though the creator's plan was beyond my limited comprehension, I trusted God's love for me and the family. I felt inundated by peace; as if I stood on the edge of a magnificent dawn surrounded by a growing light.

The word *satori* in Zen means enlightenment. Perhaps this had been my experience. In any case, I knew that whatever happened would be all right and that the Lord would take care of all of us.

Leaning my arms on the windowsill, a strange, dark, and narrow cloud configuration caught my attention. It formed across the river, a few miles away. On either side of this rolling, dark mass of clouds the sky was perfectly clear. It was as if the storm tunneled through the air. With lightning and deep reverberating thunder, the clouds and slashing rain swiftly blanketed us.

Within ten minutes the tempest vanished and the sky above was perfectly clear again. I glanced at my watch. Twelve noon. My imagination leaped to the Gospel account of the crucifixion of Jesus and I looked it up in the Bible. "Now from the sixth hour [noon] there was darkness over all the land until the ninth hour."

In no way do I equate this phenomenon with the crucifixion. But whether it was coincidence, or just one of those inexplicable events, made no difference to me. Whatever the cause or reason, I felt it a satisfying and dramatic conclusion to my struggle. I like to think of it as a kind of grand way of God putting an exclamation point to that moment of surrender.

We continued to explore the idea for a camp, and it began to seem *feasible.* I looked up the word. Its meanings include "possible," "workable," "capable" of being accomplished. If something is *workable,* there's no problem in getting it done. However, if a project is *feasible,* you may possibly accomplish it, though perhaps with more difficulty. *Feasible* described our situation.

The infrastructure of our camp—I like that big word for such a tiny operation—included enough land, workrooms in the barn, a playroom for ballet, a pool, and the tennis court. We splurged on the court after *My Six Loves* became a film.

The pool we discovered unexpectedly. The previous owner had filled in an old one he'd built and then no longer used. The mound of earth and brambles covering it looked like an overgrown, neglected garden. We dug it out mostly by hand, patched and painted, and found we had an old-fashioned, straight and narrow forty-foot pool. No fancy, kidney-shaped water hole for us. This one was great for doing laps.

"We can give tennis and swimming lessons," Mary said. "And we have that adorable Irish cart Jenny pulls, which the children can ride in."

"One word of advice . . . Keep Jenny away from the camp. She could be our nemesis."

So in addition to all else, Mary became a camp director. One of our friends happened to be a swimming instructor and we agreed she could bring her three children, one of whom would be a counselor. We had a high school coach to teach tennis. A woman who ran a ballet studio agreed to come over each day for a morning class. We happened to have a large mirror at one end of our playroom. I put in a long railing for the ballet bar.

A state regulation stipulated that someone with a life-saving certificate must be on hand near the pool. So twice a week, for six weeks, Mary took the long drive at night to the nearest YMCA which gave the course.

She returned exhausted. Two other girls in their teens made up the group. The instructor, a large mesomorph, bullied them. During the final exam, when they had to "rescue" her, she thrashed around, giving the teenage girls a difficult time, holding them underwater until they came up gasping. Mary grew tired of this nonsense. When her turn came she grabbed the bully firmly, keeping her underwater until *she* came up gasping and could be "rescued" firmly.

"I never knew I was so strong," Mary said to me. "Imagine . . . I could dive in the deep end and bring up an enormous weight!"

Frustrated by how little I could do to help, I tried to finish a book I'd started earlier. When I'd type for too long, I'd turn as yellow as my Chinese bathrobe from the hepatitis, horrifying my family and visitors.

The camp began to take shape. By May I was out of bed and could be of more help, and decided that the most urgent family project was to get the pool ready. We needed sand as a base for the stone border. My sons and I carefully calculated the amount.

Mary took the figures to the local building supply store, a family run organization, friendly and helpful. We knew the foreman. Sliding his glasses down his nose, he studied the numbers. "Building a beach?"

"We're fixing up our pool."

"Must be a pretty big one," he said with a smile.

"Not so big. It's only about forty by fifteen."

"Going to take us a couple of days to get enough sand."

"A couple of days for only a few bags?"

"According to your figures, you'll need six truckloads."

I forgot to convert inches to feet!

We placed a few descriptive placards in stores and schools, and a small advertisement appeared in the several area newspapers for an introductory visit to the camp.

To our surprise, far more people arrived than we'd expected. Delighted, we conducted them around the farm. Jack Swanson, a local farmer, particularly liked the idea of nature instruction. "I want for Sam, Ed, and Billy to know about nature." His boys were six, seven, and eight. "They like guns and someday they'll be hunting with me."

At this point we were walking through the kitchen. The previous day I'd found a large bird near the barn whose wing had been injured from a gun shot. The unhappy, brown speckled creature, too big even for the parrot cage I'd located, sat huddled on the wooden perch.

Jack Swanson studied the bird.

I pointed to it. "An owl I found near the barn. Soon as the wing's healed, we'll let it go. Kind of interesting, isn't it?" I said, nonchalantly informative.

He stepped back from the cage. "That's no owl. It's a sparrow hawk," he replied with undisguised disdain.

His loud voice silenced the desultory conversation in the crowded kitchen where we offered punch.

"You're right . . . Of course it's a sparrow hawk. Anyway, Mary's the nature expert."

I hoped my laugh sounded relaxed. Later Mary told me I sounded as if I was strangling.

Mary's look said, *let's change the subject.*

Following her advice, I said to Jack, "Have you seen our burro? She's the *pièce de résistance* on our farm."

"Piece of what?" he asked, puzzled.

Mary took over. "She pulls an Irish cart and the children will love her. Let's go to the barn and I'll show you where your children can paint and make things on rainy days."

Like most of us, frequently I come across a word that evokes a characteristic of someone I know, reminding me of that person. With Mary I cherish the words she reminds me of. I thought about writing them down but decided my word portrait would be suspect. The skeptic wouldn't believe such a paragon exists. But she does. I should know. I've been with her longer than anyone else. What a delight to be able to tell people that each year my love and admiration for her grows. She's like a lovely intricate piece of art or poetry or music. Always you find another design, an additional meaning, or a particular melody you somehow missed previously.

But with regard to the camp and Mary specifically, one word hangs in the closet of my mind, flashing like a neon sign— *fortitude. The Doubleday Roget's Thesaurus* lists such synonyms as *courage, grit, pluck, stoutheartedness, heroism, hardi-*

hood, bravery, intrepidity, valor, endurance, strength, mettle, spirit, spunk. Mary has *fortitude!*

Our house resembled a T, with each bar about the same length. In the vertical section we had a small entrance hall, crowded with a wrought-iron circular staircase that wound its way to the boys' "dormitory." The corner between the staircase and the outside wall formed Mary's command post into which she squeezed a child's-size desk. Memos, notes, the daily calendar, government regulations papered the three walls.

Mary had a preconceived notion of what the efficient, well-dressed director should wear. Early in the morning she sat at her cramped desk studying the complicated schedules in a uniform that never varied—white sneakers, long white shorts that drooped lower and lower around her waist day by day (all that exercise!), a white cotton sports shirt, a white sun visor.

Each morning the counselors arrived first, meeting in the playroom just beyond Mary's office. The discussions involved the needs of different children. Some were shy or timid, others frightened of the water. Mary outlined her plan of the day and asked for comments and suggestions.

Our camp reminded me of a miniature circus or an enchanting Dufy drawing. Color and activity surrounded us.

At the pool, sturdy Suzi Taylor put the children through a rigorous training schedule. Groups would come down from other activities for an hour at a time.

On the tennis court, the smaller children bounced tennis balls on the ground or on their rackets, practicing coordination. Later, older ones would try to hit a ball over the net, most of the time their rackets moving in slow motion, completely missing the balls. The instructor had a kindly, imperturbable patience.

The girls taking ballet resembled Degas' graceful, colorful pictures of dancers in only one way—the color. Our dancers were a mélange of sizes and shapes, wearing a variety of clothes. Only a few had any real grace. But that didn't matter. They were learning and having fun. And that's what *did* matter!

Near my office in the barn, Mary and her counselors taught arts and crafts. Years afterward I found different artifacts the children made, or some of the Boy Scout posters we'd sent for, describing different birds and other animals. To my surprise, each of these findings evoked a nostalgic memory.

Mary's nature walks were always instructive—*for Mary*. Usually she had a group of nine or ten children, and they'd wander through the woods and fields, trying to see *nature*. They collected leaves, plants, stones, Mary trying valiantly to identify them.

One day, Billy Swanson yelled to her, "Mrs. Funk . . . Mrs. Funk. We've found something interesting."

Mary hurried to the group intently staring at the ground.

She studied it closely. "Why, I'll bet it's some kind of insect that's going to hatch. Maybe we should take it with us and show the others. I wonder what it is?"

"I know what it is," Billy said solemnly.

"You do! What is it!"

"Deer poop!"

Because the children wandered through the house sometimes, I turned our bedroom into my office. This allowed me the privacy I needed to work, but it also gave me a superb view of many of the camp activities.

Viewing the action on the tennis court, I was pretty sure we'd never have the opportunity of saying sometime in the future as we watched a player winning at Wimbledon, "She got her start at Good Ground Camp!"

Suzi Taylor and her aquanauts splashed around about fifty yards away down the lawn. She demanded the best from the children and they learned to swim well. Water terrorized one seven-year-old youngster. Her astounded parents watched as their child swam the length of the pool by the end of the summer.

Suzi's voice, as strong and muscled as her body, made me feel guilty about taking the time to watch the activities. I returned to the typewriter.

Out of sight, but within hearing, ballet music arose from the playroom.

"Take your positions," the teacher's voice said. "Now listen carefully to the music and imitate me. Relax but be firm."

Good advice at any time!

Sometimes I'd see Mary in her white camp counselor's outfit traipsing across the lower field, leading a straggling, motley collection of dilatory wood elves. I knew that later we'd hear about another nature experience.

During luncheon, Mary gathered the children into small groups, each having a counselor who read to them. This turned out to be a wonderfully peaceful part of the day.

Our daughter Estelle especially seemed to enjoy this assignment. She didn't have to pretend she was a teacher. When Paul and Eleanor were small, she'd beguile them into playing school behind made-up desks, with herself as teacher. Occasionally they'd rebel. However, being bigger she forced them to stay in "school" despite vociferous complaining.

"Paul, you aren't listening," she said to him. "You have to listen to your teacher and do what she says."

"*You* don't listen," he stated with the same direct energy he used in roughhousing with his brothers. "Mom and Dad say that when they talk you look like your mind's got a hundred things going on and you never hear what they say."

"You aren't supposed to talk back to your teacher," she replied with angelic peacefulness.

At other times her foot pounded the floor, her hair flying, her eyes sparking. "Oh . . . You make me so mad," she'd shout, her voice sometimes making a growling *gr'rr*.

Now this neat, trim, long-haired blond thirteen-year-old with the blue eyes that so quickly and openly mirrored the depths of her loving self had her own real "class." She read so expressively that the children, and I who listened through the window, entered into the story with her.

When other activities began again, the youngsters begged her to continue. "Don't stop, Estelle . . . *Please* don't stop. Keep reading. We want to find out what happens next. Can't we stay with you? You're more fun than anyone."

One boy, Tommy Marsh, decided he wanted to finish the

book himself. I heard him grumble to Mary he wasn't going swimming.

"Tommy," Mary replied. "Unless you have a note from your parents, you're supposed to be swimming this period."

"I don't have to go. I'm going to read." He wasn't aware of me in the window above him.

"T-o-m-m-y," I said in a slow, stentorian, rumbling voice. "Get down to the pool *immediately.*"

Never looking up, he took off at a run. God had spoken.

Marvin Yates, a neighbor, specialized in bees as a hobby. A tall, cadaverously thin, quiet-spoken man, he looked the part of a beekeeper. His large hands handled the equipment and insects gently. As a treat, he agreed to give a demonstration of his bees to the entire camp one afternoon. We gathered on the lawn beneath the large trees.

He'd brought several glass frames with him, crowded with bees. "Do any of you like honey?" he asked, looking at the eager young faces. He held up one of the frames.

His question elicited a chorus of enthusiastic Yesses.

"Have any of you ever seen a bee close up?"

"I got stung with one once and it hurt," Billy Swanson said.

"It hurt the bee more than you," Marvin replied.

"Did not," Billy replied, a feisty replica of his father, Jack, who helped to set me straight on sparrow hawks.

"After the honeybee stung you, it died. Honeybees never live after they've stung something." He smiled at the chorus of "Ohs."

Mary leaned over to me, whispering. "Do you think this is safe. Look at all those bees in there. What if they get out?"

"About as safe as walking into the lion house at a zoo with all the animals behind bars . . . It's *safe!*"

"Remember when you thought a snake was just a stick?"

"This is a beehive," Marvin continued, holding up a white boxlike structure with drawers. "This is the kind of house my bees live in. I have four of these at home filled with bees. But there aren't any in this one . . . How many bees do you think can live in this house?"

They waited with the silence of expectancy, knowing he would answer for them.

"Around eighty or ninety thousand."

Eleanor turned to her mother. "Is that a lot?"

"Like a trillion," Paul said.

"It would be just about like all the people from ten towns the size of ours living in one apartment house," Marvin explained.

"Wow!" a child breathed.

He held up the frame again. "There are three kinds of bees . . . the queen bee, the drone, and the worker. The queen bee lays the eggs. Almost two thousand a day."

Mark laughed. "That's a lot more than our chickens do."

"The drones are the male bees . . . They're men, and they fertilize the queen bee."

"What's that mean?" a child asked.

Obviously Marvin hadn't intended to get into the subject of "the birds and the bees." He put down the frame and cleared his throat. "The honeybee is called the worker bee and they work *hard!* They feed everyone in the hive, they guard against the strangers, build the combs, collect pollen and the nectar . . . That little bit of golden dust you see in flowers is the pollen." He passed some flowers around so the children could see. "And the nectar looks like water and is found in flowers too. It's very sweet and the bees use it for making honey."

"Doesn't the pollen stick to the bees and is deposited on other flowers so they're fertilized?" the swimming counselor, Suzi Taylor, asked.

Marvin Yates nodded. "And you know, there's a scent organ on their stomachs that picks up a new fragrance and guides the other bees back to the new source." He held up two jars of honey. "The light-colored one comes from alfalfa and clover and is very mild . . . The other is buckwheat, which is dark and has a stronger taste. How long do you think bees live?"

"A hundred years," some child replied.

"You don't know nothing," Billy Swanson snickered. "They're like a bird. They live as long as a bird."

Marvin smiled. "You're partly right, son. A queen bee may live three years. But a worker only lives about six months in the summer. They die of overwork. Once the queen bee is . . ." He avoided the questionable word. "Once the queen bee can lay eggs, the drones have nothing to do. As a matter of fact, only one bee . . ." He searched for the euphemism ". . . helps. If there's not enough food in the hive, the drones are driven out to starve. They don't work and the other bees feel they're taking a free ride."

He showed the children his "smoker," which looked like an enlarged oil can and poured puffs of smoke to quiet the bees. He put on his helmet, gloves, and the protective netting covering his face and tied at the waist.

Trying to involve the children more directly, he took up the two frames and asked Sam Swanson to hold one and to take it around so the others could see how the bees worked.

But Billy decided that as the oldest and strongest of the three Swanson brothers he should help and not Sam. Spitting on his hands (he always spit on his hands before he did anything), Billy jumped up, grabbing the frame, attempting to pull it out of his brother's hands.

"Hey . . . Be careful, son, that's fragile," Marvin Yates said, reaching for the frame.

Sam lurched forward. The glass frame slipped out of his hands, crashing into the one Marvin held. The glass in both of them shattered. The released bees, confused by their unexpected freedom, hovered for a moment over their broken enclosure. Angry at the disturbance, they fanned out over the group of children and counselors, stinging whoever happened to be in their way. Screaming, everyone scattered, running for the house.

"Get the children inside," Mary shouted.

Marvin Yates, holding the smoke gun, stood bewildered as bees buzzed around his still-netted face. The shattered frame lay at his feet.

Baking soda is a good antidote to relieve the pain of a sting. A paste is made up of a bit of water and the soda. We patted it on the places where children had been stung.

Since bees aren't pets and won't come when called, Mr. Yates ruefully picked up the pieces of his frames and went home to wait for those who survived. He didn't know how many had died from stinging the campers. Some still lurked around our kitchen door. We would, of course, pay for the broken material and buy him new bees.

With their faces, arms, and legs smeared with the white, flaking, dried paste, the children looked like left-over clowns. As parents arrived to take them home, we received a number of questioning looks and narrowed eyes. We explained it as a humorous adventure, for no one had been seriously hurt. But the children sounded like miniature machine guns as they told what had happened, making it seem as if we'd been invaded by the "Killer Bees" of South America.

At the end of this day as at the end of all the camping days, Mary found herself so wiped out she could barely speak. We communicated with her in a kind of sign language.

"Things can't go on like this. We've got to have someone to help us with the housework once in a while. We can't do everything ourselves," I observed.

She signaled a weary *who?*

"We'll ask around Lambertville." In a small town you know proportionately more people than you do in a larger one. Frequently, the local grapevine helps locate the person or thing you were looking for.

And so in a roundabout way through the grapevine and churches a remarkable black woman named Nellie became part of our lives.

When she arrived at our home, Mark happened to be the first person she saw. He introduced himself.

"How old are you?" she asked, giving him her full attention.

He shifted on his feet, rubbing his head. "Twelve."

"Twelve!" she replied, astonished. "Twelve . . . ! Why, I would have bet you'd be fourteen or fifteen. *Twelve* . . . ! And you've got nice red hair too . . ." She lowered her voice. "Do you like apple pie?"

"Sure do."

"I'm going to make you one of my famous apple pies. Everybody in Lambertville knows about Nellie's apple pies."

She loved children and they always responded.

Sometimes we are involved with people who bring you more than you are aware of in the beginning. They leave you with an intangible quality that becomes a permanent influence in your life.

"When Nellie finishes her work," Mary said, "everything is always so fresh and neat. And we have very interesting conversations. It's the *way* she goes about her work that impresses me. Keeping a house in order is important to her. She brings such a cheerful dignity and sense of responsibility to everything she does. She's given me a completely new outlook on housekeeping."

And then she sighed. "How I wish we had her more than one day a week. But you know . . . There is one thing that bothers me about Nellie and I'm determined to do something about it . . ." Mary paused with a smile. "The children like her potato salads and apple pies better than mine and she won't tell me how she makes them."

As the summer drew to an end, we were increasingly grateful our stint of running a camp would soon be over. But one cheerful aspect became apparent. After paying all salaries and expenses, we had a small profit. We could hardly believe the good news. The feedback indicated we had a smash success. Should we continue the following summer?

Many of the parents enthusiastically urged us to enlarge the operation. And so on the last day of camp we held an open house for parents with prospective children.

Everything went so smoothly, even we were impressed.

We scheduled the last event of the day to be a ride in the cart pulled by Jenny. The little burro had become a hands-down favorite with the children. Estelle, holding the lead line, took the flat cart packed with children, heading down the driveway from the barn to our home. More crowded than usual, one of the smaller children began slipping off the cart.

Our daughter momentarily dropped the lead line and went back to make the child more secure. Jenny, sensing relative freedom, spurted forward, trotting rapidly. Estelle lunged for the lead line, but it dragged on the ground just beyond her reach. She stumbled. By the time she recovered, she found herself two or three steps behind the cart. Jenny, always ready to enjoy a chase, broke into a gallop.

Standing with a group of parents, Mary and I, basking in the warmth of our success, watched our white burro appear over the rise in the driveway. Our warmth plummeted. Head held high, Jenny galloped as fast as she could, the cart careening wildly, Estelle dropping farther and farther behind.

Gradually the parents realized what was happening. The visitors grabbed for their children, stepping back.

Our driveway ended in a broad apron beside the kitchen and in front of the former garage we'd turned into a playroom. A line of cedar trees, American boxwood, and gum trees along with a five- or six-inch stone wall bordered the far side of the apron. Between the corner of the playroom and the last gum tree there was a five-foot opening. In front of this, for some unknown reason, the former owner had dug in part of a railroad track, making an annoying and formidable bump.

The apparition clattered toward us, the children gripping desperately the slippery edges of the swaying cart. They stared at their parents and the looming white side of our house, apparently too paralyzed with terror to cry out.

I jumped into the center of the driveway, waving my arms, shouting at Jenny. Maybe she saw me. Maybe she didn't. I scrambled out of the way just in time.

She headed straight for the wall. I shut off my imagination. Suddenly she veered, streaking for the opening. She leaped across the bump. The wheels of the cart slammed against the railroad track. It bounced high in the air, turning sideways as it crashed down. Children flew, rolled, tumbled in all directions, their frozen screams finally released.

Parents flocked to their children. No one was hurt. The

crying subsided, cars drove off, and we were left alone. Jenny, with part of the wagon still attached to her, grazed contentedly on our lawn.

We held an immediate, impromptu family council. We agreed that our daily "circus" had been a surprising success. We'd made enough money to cover all the expenses as well as replacing our worn linoleum floor in the kitchen and installing a new filter for the pool. This had been a comical and enjoyable experience for the entire family. But enough is enough. We voted unanimously—except for Eleanor, who wanted the adventure to continue—that there'd be no more camp.

Mary's side of the bed always seems warmer than mine. Later that night as I moved close to her, putting my arms around her, waking her, I told her what I'd been mulling over for the past few hours.

"I have to admit, this afternoon I was ready to give Jenny away to the nearest dog food factory. But you know what! I'm really grateful to her. I think she saved your life. You never would have lasted through another summer."

Sleepily she rolled over toward me, her soft hand resting against my cheek. "I knew you'd end up feeling the same way I do about her," she murmured sleepily.

"I didn't say that."

"Almost . . ."

12

"Last night I started thinking that our life reminds me of a Jackson Pollock painting," Mary commented with some exasperation one morning at breakfast. "It's as though we have a big paintbrush dripping with ideas and we keep slapping it at the canvas of our life . . ."

"What do you mean?" Paul asked, eating his fifth English muffin.

"A patch quilt has more of a pattern than our lives do. I can see a kind of basic pattern or theme to our lives, but right now it seems almost submerged with too many vivid color activities . . . We have a mass of disparate projects."

"What's *disparate* mean?" Estelle asked.

"Latin *dis-*, 'apart' or 'not,' and *parare*, 'to make equal.' So, it means 'different in kind' . . . 'not alike'," I answered.

"I mean, when I think of all the different things we're doing I get confused. Our life has almost gotten out of hand," Mary continued.

"I feel the same way. Somehow we'll have to try to simplify. We've got to live a simpler life," I agreed.

"A few years ago we had more help. But now Peter's in college in Canada, John's in Princeton, and Celine's in California. We have a lot more to do these days and not as many of you to help out."

Eleanor groaned, slumping in her seat. She was lucky in her looks. She had strong, beautiful features and would grow up to them. "I hate it when you guys talk this way. Something always changes. I bet it's going to have something to do with me," she said glumly.

Since both of us were concerned, we thought we might as well spend the time analyzing the situation right now, taking the farm first and my various career projects in a day or so.

From time to time we weren't always sure we could afford to live here. And were we achieving our original objectives we set up when we moved to the farm, and how could we save money and time on the farm? For example, why did we mow so much lawn? Could I mow the fields once a year instead of twice? How could we keep up with the encroaching honeysuckle that strangled so many of our trees? There were vegetable and flower gardens, and yew trees that were growing out of control. The driveway was cracking and filling with weeds. The barn needed a lot of work. Windows were about to fall out, some asphalt shingles had dropped off, a few drains were clogged, and we had rats. Our rental cottages needed attention. The list grew as we talked. And finally we came to our "tree farm" and the horses.

"Let's do the trees first," Mary said. "The horses are such an emotional issue. Especially for Eleanor. We'd better save that for the last."

Our tree farm was divided into two parts. One involved the ten thousand fir trees (evergreens) we'd planted years before and hoped eventually to sell as Christmas trees.

The other was made up of five thousand deciduous trees. The latter are trees that lose their leaves during winter in contrast to the evergreens that keep theirs throughout the year. We'd been caught up by the enthusiasm of a landscape architect who loved trees as much as we. His plan was to put in a variety, which he would sell to his clients. We had various kinds of oaks, three different types of honey locusts, Norwegian maples, and about a half dozen other species. Being something of a purist, our friend insisted that we dig all the holes by hand so the trees would be planted to perfection. With the help of our children and members of his family we dug our way through the shale rock that plagued our land with shovels, pickaxes, and shale bars. We grew stronger!

But it was the Christmas trees Mary and I wanted to talk about, since many of them were ready to harvest—if it seemed worthwhile. The deciduous trees had a few years to go.

We could almost measure the years we'd been at the farm by the height of some of the firs. Since these trees grow a foot a year, technically they should be roughly nine feet tall. Not many reached this height, however, for during this span of time we had five years of drought.

Twice a year we walked back and forth through the rows of these ten thousand firs, pruning them so they would grow into evenly shaped trees, examining them for harmful insects, sometimes having to spray.

Somehow, it being unpopular work, Mary and I had to corral the children to help us.

"I hate doing it," Estelle said, her strong feelings echoed by her sisters. "My hands get so tired and my arms are all scratched. My hair gets filled with prickles."

As we discussed the trees, Mary smiled. "Remember when Brother Robert came last year?" Mary asked.

We put down our pencils and began reminiscing about him. It was just accidental that he had anything to do with the trees.

A week before Christmas, Brother Robert, a Franciscan friar, had come to visit us and unexpectedly became involved with our tree project. He belonged to a Franciscan Order of men and women existing within the Episcopal church. Over the years Mary and I became associated with this worldwide group. Eventually I helped to create and administer a two-and-a-half-year "training" program for newly admitted lay or secular Franciscans such as Mary and me.

Since our friar friend Brother Robert oversaw this project, from time to time he made working visits. We enjoyed our sessions with him. An Englishman, erudite, witty, and engagingly friendly, he took first-class honors at Cambridge. Later he became an Anglican priest and eventually joined the Society of St. Francis, where he was assigned to the United States province.

Robert joked that whenever he showed up somewhere the unexpected occurred. His jocular prediction proved accurate.

The first evening, Celine telephoned from California to say she had a suspicious lump on her leg. A chilling fear reminded us too clearly of my experience. We talked to her surgeon on the telephone. He felt an urgency about doing an immediate biopsy. We checked his credentials through friends and he appeared to be capable.

Robert prayed with us before and during the operation. His prayers were simple, expressing complete trust in God, and asked the Lord to be in the doctor's mind and hands for healing. His confidence in God's love brought us a relative peace. The tumor turned out to be benign.

Early the next day, a newspaper editor telephoned me long distance. At the time I wrote a daily word feature, which was syndicated to newspapers and which put me under fierce deadline pressures. I worried continually whether we'd proofed the copy accurately.

"Peter, I'm sure you know the difference between *principal* and *principle*," the editor said.

"Of course."

"Well, I hate to tell you this, but you've misused *principle* for *principal*."

I felt a burning in my stomach. Though obviously a typo and not picked up when we read proof, it seemed as though I'd misused a common word, a gaff in the lexical profession resembling an airline pilot flying to the wrong airport.

Brother Robert laughed. "That *is* a howler, isn't it? Well, let's see what we can do about it. Show me the piece you wrote."

Literally, he rolled up his sleeves and together we worked quickly. With his help I devised a letter that turned the mistake into something positive. What seemed to be a minor disaster became a successful coup. I used it to illustrate how toward the end of World War II a misused word changed an entire meaning of a thought with disastrous results.

The Japanese term *mokusatsu* is believed to have brought on the tragedy of Hiroshima and all that followed because it was not accurately translated. Depending on how it is used, the word has two meanings, "to ignore" and "to refrain from comment." Apparently, the emperor and the cabinet were ready to surrender to the ultimatum of the Allies, but they wanted a little more time to talk over the terms. They prepared a press release announcing a policy of *mokusatsu,* with the "no comment" implication that would give them the time they needed. The message was transmitted through Russia to the Allies. Unfortunately, during the process of translating the message, it was passed along as "to ignore."

While Robert and I worked on trying to rectify my mistake, Mary raced in to us, distressed. The washing machine was spewing water all over the kitchen.

Robert quickly discovered a kinked hose that forced the water out through a loose connection. He fixed it.

As we washed the dishes after supper, the drain clogged, and I couldn't find the rubber sunction cup—the "plumber's helper."

"I don't think we really need one," he said as he placed a large hand over the drain, squishing it back and forth. With a cheerful gurgle, the drain unclogged.

During Robert's visit we talked about simplicity. Even then Mary and I had a sense we were overextending ourselves. One of the attributes of a Franciscan life is simplicity and we were cluttered, both in the matters of time and activity. We seemed to have fallen into an overbusy life with too little time for reflection.

"It's really a matter of traveling as lightly as possible through life so as to have the freedom to be of service to others, isn't it?" he suggested. "If we get burdened down with things to do or with what we have, it's more difficult for us to move around easily and to be where we're most needed."

We also told Robert about our fir trees and that we'd just placed an advertisement in the local papers stating that people could pick out their own trees, which we would cut for them. It seemed to be an easy way for Mark and Paul to earn money.

"What a splendid idea," Robert said. "I'm sure it will be a success."

However, the boys didn't agree with us. They didn't think much of the trees and particularly disparaged the Austrian pines. "Who's going to want a funny-looking tree like that for Christmas?"

"What do you mean?" Mary replied spiritedly. "They're not funny looking at all. Besides, the forestry department said that this would be the popular tree of the future."

"They were just trying to dump on you," Paul said.

"Besides, I feel bad for the trees," Mark said. "Why should one be cut down just to dry out and die in somebody's house who doesn't really appreciate it?"

Mark loved the beauty of trees and once when he and I cut down a tall cedar for our Christmas tree, he had tears in his eyes as he looked at the magnificent specimen lying in the snow.

The following day was damp and cold. As an added inducement for the potential buyers we offered doughnuts and hot cocoa. Mary drew up a large sign, which we put near the mailbox.

"Maybe we should tether Jenny out in front. She'd draw attention," Mary suggested.

"I have a strong feeling we'll all be happier if Jenny stays where she is," I counseled.

People stopped by, but no trees were sold.

"We told you so," the boys said, discouraged and ready to give up. They'd finished off the doughnuts and cocoa themselves.

"Show me the trees," Robert said after lunch.

Wearing sandals without socks and a heavy, olive-gray sweater he kept on, inside the house and out, he trudged through the snow with Mark and Paul, surveying our stock. With his kindly face, mellifluous voice and a—since reduced— substantial waist, he reminded us of an unfrocked Santa Claus. "You have some splendid trees," he said. "They'll make fine Christmas trees."

Soon a car drew up and a family asked about the trees.

"What kind are you looking for?" Robert asked.

They described what they thought they would like to have.

Robert thought a bit. "I think we have just what you want." And he led them out among the rows of trees. The people were delighted with what they found.

The boys caught his knack of encouraging customers to describe the kind of tree they wanted and then walking out with them to search for just that tree. The afternoon turned out to be far more successful than Mark or Paul had thought it could be.

As we reviewed our list of activities, at least the Christmas tree operation seemed worth continuing. "Thanks to Brother Robert," Mary added.

And now the horses.

"First of all," Mary said, "I don't like Eleanor riding off by herself. She's away from our property out in the woods on trails we don't know for hours at a time. If she fell off and was hurt, we wouldn't begin to know where to find her."

"We could tell her to stay on the property."

"That'd be a little bit better . . . But we have our woods and trails. Well, let's face it. I just don't like having her riding horses by herself . . . Now I wouldn't worry if she was on Jenny. Jenny can't go fast, and if you fall off you don't have far to drop. We've had too many friends of ours who've been badly hurt from riding. Remember how that horse smashed your ankle."

We discussed the cost of keeping the two horses. From time to time we tried to grow our own hay, but our soil wasn't suited for this. A farmer who grew his corn on our fields for a few years came to the same conclusion. And so we decided our land was best suited for grazing and raising trees.

We found buying hay and grain expensive. There were also veterinarian costs, and the blacksmith, Axel Heyst, came every six weeks, or more often if one of the horses "threw a shoe."

In addition to the care I gave the horses, another drawback was that riding took a great deal of time. You groomed the horse, put on the bridle and saddle, and when you finished your ride you cooled down your horse by walking it, often sponging the animal if it was hot. This is fine if riding is your main hobby. We enjoyed riding, but we simply did not have the time to do it frequently.

Considering all aspects, we decided the sensible thing would be to sell Talla and Babe, though we wanted them to go to a family that would care for them as we had done.

"I knew it . . . I knew it," Eleanor cried out when she heard the news. "I knew that when you two started talking that it would end up having something to do with me."

"I think you're forgetting you're not the only one involved," I said. "There are a few others of us around. We are a family."

"And horses can be dangerous. We worry when you're away for such a long time," Mary added.

"Oh Mother . . . ," the twelve-year-old expostulated. "You're always worrying. I'm perfectly safe on them. They're so slow and calm I can hardly get them going . . . But I knew it would be the horses," she continued. "Why couldn't it be something else like those stupid trees."

"Well, trees aren't dangerous. And trees don't take daily care. And they're not just for pleasure!"

"Dad, we've had Talla and Babe for years," Eleanor said. "They're like family. And you just don't go and dump family."

We felt the same way, but we were determined to find them a good home. That would be something of a problem, for neither could be considered fine examples of horses.

Talla, with a coat matching the color of her large, brown eyes, was placid, round, and lazy. She'd only trot or canter reluctantly with strenuous urging on the part of the rider.

Babe, big, bony, awkward, looked out at the world with a worried, weary expression. He walked gingerly, reminding us of someone with fallen arches. We never knew who called this black gelding, this de-sexed male, *Babe*. But he came with the name and it stuck.

"I have an idea," Mary said. "Let's ask Axel Heyst if he

knows of a family. A blacksmith really gets to see who takes care of horses. And I like him. I bet he'll be able to help us."

Eleanor didn't really surrender. She hoped that something would intervene and the horses would stay.

Knowing that Eleanor enjoyed the experience, I always asked Axel to come in the late afternoon when she'd be home from school. When he arrived several weeks later, Eleanor and I went up to the barn to meet him.

He drove up in that truck of his which looked as if a small hut with a smokestack stuck in the side of it had been dropped on the back. The stack, of course, was for his portable anvil.

He waved to Eleanor and me. Stepping out of the cab, he lighted his pipe, an invariable routine. Once he got it going, he leaned on the fender of his truck, looking at me for a few seconds.

Axel didn't resemble the stereotype blacksmith. He had sandy hair and a fair complexion. His long nose accentuated the length of his narrow face. His brown eyes seemed meditative. His hands and wrists seemed to have acquired muscularity from his work rather than genetically.

He took the pipe from his mouth. "What're you reading these days?"

Axel startled me the first time he asked me that question. I'd thought he was going to ask which horse I wanted done first. I was used to him now. "Well, at the moment I'm rereading *The Meaning of Meaning* and one of John D. MacDonald's novels. There's a tough one by John Lyons, *Semantics.* Also one on Saint Francis of Assisi by Fortini."

He puffed on his pipe, considering the answer. *"Meaning of Meaning* . . . Heard of that. Who's the author?"

I enjoyed this interruption of a work day. "Richards and . . ." I groped for the co-author, my mind a temporary blank. "Ah . . . Richards and Ogden."

"Think I'd like it?"

"If you're interested in the ambiguities of our language."

"Ever read Sidney Hook's *Language and Philosophy?"* He spoke in a curiously drawling way as if he took a good look at each word before it left his mouth.

I said I'd heard of it.

"About the importance of language to philosophy." He puffed on his pipe. "Idea seems to be that Locke's empirical tradition in knowledge is false and the rationalistic tradition of Liebnitz is sound."

I knew by this time that Axel would rather talk philosophically than shoe horses. If he was pulling one upmanship with this latest gambit, he had me. From time to time I've read Will Durant's books and some others, but my knowledge of philosophy is sketchy. I was not in a position to make an informed comment on his remark. "Next time maybe you could bring the book. I'd like to read it."

Jenny came up, sniffing the truck, looking at the dog sitting inside the cab. "You always want to get in on the conversation too, don't you?" Axel said, scratching her crown. She enjoyed that and stayed beside him.

"When you're shoeing the horses she always wants you to do something with her, too. She gets jealous," Eleanor said. "I think she'd rather be a horse."

Axel nodded. "That's human. I guess we've all wished we were somebody else at one time or another." He paused, thinking. "Remember that rhyme?

'Until the donkey tried to clear
The fence, she thought herself a deer.' "

We all looked at Jenny, appreciating her, and laughed.

"By the way, Axel, we're going to sell Talla and Babe," and I explained our reasons. "If you know of a family that would take care of them the way we do, could you let us know?"

A few weeks later, Axel telephoned. He knew of just the kind of people we were looking for. We contacted them and agreed with his estimate. The horses were sold.

On the morning of the day the horses were to leave, I'd gone to the barn intending to get some writing done before breakfast. From my window I saw the horses grazing contentedly. They didn't know this would be their last day on the farm.

My concentration slipped away and I went down and perched myself on the edge of a doorway while the fullness of dawn's beauty gradually enveloped me—the sky, earth, views, colors, animals, sounds.

At such times, you sense the interrelationship between all things, animate and inanimate. You understand how Saint Francis would speak of a Brother Sun and Sister Moon, a Brother Wind and Brother Fire, that when he talked to animals there'd be a response. You and I aren't separated from the rest of nature. That's only an illusion. Everything that exists is a part of original creation and therefore interwoven—all with all, each with each.

I looked down at Laddie, our Border collie, who sat below me. I indicated the two horses. "You're lucky you don't have to make such painful decisions."

The old dog ignored my comment. He read his "morning newspaper," those cool currents of air which he sniffed carefully. He mused over the information he "read" and the possibilities they held for him.

I like that word *muse.* It's a quiet, reflective word coming from Old French *muser,* meaning "to stay with a muzzle in the air." He turned his head in one direction and then another, muzzle held high.

Slowly he stood up, stretching stiff, rheumatic sixteen-year-old limbs. He glanced back at me as if to say, "See you later," and then went off on his morning rounds. His first stop was at a stunted, wild privet Mary planted to hide the cinder-block base at the barn's corner. He lifted his leg over it. No wonder the bush didn't grow!

Our gander, Hubert, honked a few times, and I saw him as almost always, standing next to Babe. Perhaps the name confused him, but whatever, the gander had fallen in love with Babe at first flight.

The black gelding moved to another patch of grass, and our white pilgrim goose followed, limping after him painfully.

We knew he was in pain because by standing so close to Babe, that clumsy, well-meaning horse kept stepping and stamping on poor Hubert's right foot, which became torn and bloody. We put ointment on it and did what we could. But somehow this bird, so intelligent in other respects, didn't have the common sense to move slightly. He suffered real pain in his love.

"I think Babe does it to him on purpose," Celine said. "Who'd want to have somebody hanging around you that way all the time?"

When we fed Babe his grain, Hubert picked up the slobbery bits that fell from the horse's mouth. When we put the horse in a stall, Hubert stood guard in front of the door. This became a nuisance because he'd hiss and threaten anyone who'd walk past. Sometimes he chased the smaller children, trying to nip them and when he caught them, his bites h u r t.

If the children rode Babe away from our farm, Hubert became hysterical, yelling and squawking, flapping his wings, running up and down the fence trying to glimpse his friend. He would have flown over its top had I not clipped his wings.

We decided he needed "goose" company and this year acquired Grace to be his wife, a lovely gray-streaked female. He wasn't interested. She paddled after him in that pigeon-toed walk of geese, puzzled and sad for he paid her no attention. Sometimes in the hysteria of his love for Babe he'd trample over her as if she were a piece of wood.

Grace tried to raise a family, but her eggs were never fertilized. Hubert, either true to another mate in the past or to Babe in the present, wouldn't have connubial relations with her. Geese are monogamous and once "married" never "marry" a second time.

But Grace continued to lay the large, beautifully formed eggs that never hatched. Hoping for the impossible, she sat on them for weeks at a time. Frequently we removed them, for otherwise she would have sat there forever and starved to death. We felt frustrated and sad knowing nothing else to do for her.

Occasionally, Mary put a huge, hard-boiled goose egg into the children's lunch boxes as a joke. A bit strong for individual eating, she found them excellent for baking.

As I watched the two horses and Hubert, I anticipated what

would undoubtedly happen within the next few moments. I'd
seen the sequence of this particular action several times before.

Talla, cropping grass, kept edging closer to Babe. Hubert
stopped jabbing his beak at the ground for bugs, seeds, and
grass. His neck lifted straight up and he stared hard at the mare
as if to warn her to keep her distance, muttering angrily to
himself. Soon the mare stood next to Babe.

Jenny followed Talla, her affections favoring the plump
mare. And why not? After all, they had one major characteristic
in common—gorging. They were true gourmands; authentic
cormorants. Their spreading bellies were evidence of dedica-
tion. As they bit off the grass, Jenny's short, skinny tail flicked
back and forth in quick strokes, while Talla's luxuriant one,
nearly falling to the ground, swished around gracefully.

Favoring his mashed and bloody foot, Hubert surrepti-
tiously limped behind Talla, pretending to be looking for food.
Suddenly his neck stuck out full length, his beak snapping on
Talla's tail like a sprung mousetrap. He jerked hard on it.

Startled, Talla sprang forward, galloping across the field.
Hubert, hanging onto her tail, rose like a kite, neck stretched all
the way forward, wings held out. When she reached the fence
on the far side of the field, Talla skidded to an abrupt stop. But
Hubert's momentum kept him going at full speed. His beak
rammed into Talla's rump. An authentic *goose!* He tumbled to
the ground, still holding the tail. Surprised all over again by the
jab, she wheeled around, bolting back across the field, jerking
the gander up into the air, and he trailed her as before.

The procedure repeated itself until the tail finally slipped
out of Hubert's grip and he crash-landed with a sliding thump.
Shaking his wings angrily, dust spraying from them, he held his
head high, honking at Talla, who'd rejoined Jenny as a safer
friend than Babe. With whatever dignity he had left, Hubert
limped back to Babe's side. The gelding didn't notice the gander's heroic act of devotion.

Later in the day when the new owner came to cart Talla
and Babe away, Mary and I nearly wept. Yet we knew we had to
go through with it because of our concern for Eleanor's safety as

well as trying to remove some of the clutter of activity in our life here. Thoughtful decisions are not always the easiest.

When Babe was led up the boarding ramp to the back of the truck, Hubert became frantic. He ran around the truck, honking, flapping his wide, white wings, trying to reach his adored friend. He hurried back and forth between us and the truck, limping and stumbling, honking excitedly as if pleading with us.

If I'd only thought to put Hubert in the barn while Babe was being taken away!

Mary shut the gate as soon as the truck passed through. I held Hubert so he wouldn't follow. When I released him he partly ran and flew alongside the fence, trying to reach the departing truck. He spent the night and the next few days in the corner of that field, watching and waiting.

Jenny's loneliness surprised us. Her braying reverberated throughout the neighborhood. She'd suck in her breath as if gasping to stay alive and then the curious, high-pitched sound blasted out like a bagpipe gone bonkers, ending in breathless squeaks. While she did this, Hubert in his own misery honked and flapped his wings, reminding us of our supposed treachery. They became the "odd couple," thrown together by circumstances. Adversaries in good times, they commiserated with one another now.

Eleanor missed the two horses as much as Jenny and Hubert. She rode the little white burro, but it would always be bareback. For some reason the shape of the animal's body was such that no matter how tightly you cinched the girth, eventually the saddle slipped forward and loosened, pulling the girth away from the largest part of her rocklike belly. The saddle ended up under her and on the ground.

Eleanor played a game with the older boys who came to take Celine and Estelle on dates.

"Can you ride Jenny?" she'd ask innocently, pointing to the peacefully grazing burro.

What an easy way for the young men to show off before the

girls even if they'd never been on a horse! Their feet would almost reach the ground.

"Sure . . . ," came the confident reply.

Eleanor put on Jenny's bridle and then patted the animal's rump. "You sit back here," she said to the boy. Then Eleanor turned the burro so that rider and animal faced down the slope. She gave Jenny a swat to get her going. The two sisters mischievously watched for the inevitable.

Jenny, annoyed by someone sitting so far back, trotted at a fast pace, lowering her head almost to the ground. Because they were going downhill and the position of her head, the young man began to lose his balance, sliding forward along her back. Suddenly Jenny tucked in her head and bucked, her hind feet shooting out behind her, rump exploding high in the air. The boy catapulted forward over her head, plunging to the ground usually in an embarrassing somersault-type fall. Humility replaced manly pride.

Eleanor loved Jenny, but for equestrian use found her unsatisfactory.

"I feel so silly on her . . . I'm embarrassed. If I ride with anybody else, I'm way down here. It's like being a clown in a circus . . . And Jenny can't keep up when the other horses gallop. Can't I have a horse . . . ? Please, can't I? It's the only thing I want. I dream about it all the time. I wish we hadn't sold Talla and Babe . . . The barn's so empty now."

"I don't think you remember why we sold them," Mary replied.

Eleanor began reading the "Animals for Sale" section in the local newspaper. Her sighs soughed through the house every time she found the ideal horse.

"Neat! That's *just* the one I want . . . Ooohhh . . . I bet it'll be sold . . . Nobody understands me in this house."

Eleanor might be the youngest, but she has the same sense of independence, strength of mind, and resilience found in her six older brothers and sisters.

She was determined to have a horse.

"I've got a great idea that I think you'll like," she said to us one evening. "And *please* listen first and don't say no right away

. . . You're really worried about me riding alone . . . Right? I mean that's the main reason."

"Probably is," Mary replied.

"Well . . . ," she hesitated, fiddling with her hands nervously. "I have a friend in school who lives near us . . . She says the place where she keeps her horse is too far away and she wants to leave it here . . . And she'll take care of it and buy her own hay and grain . . . And if she did, then I'd have somebody to ride with."

Her idea was plausible. We told her that. Actually, she had come up with an answer to our principal objection. Yet Mary and I just weren't sure we wanted the responsibility of caring for horses again. The children can do much of the work. But the ultimate responsibility, of course, would be ours.

Eleanor is persistent. She had one objective in life—to have her own horse. We thought riding lessons might satisfy this longing of hers, and twice a week she rode at an excellent stable and did well. In several shows she won prizes. Obviously Eleanor had talent.

Her campaign, sometimes low key and once in a while forceful, continued.

Like most parents, I suppose Mary and I are more soapstone than granite. Eleanor's pertinacity gradually wore away our resolve. And as most parents, we wanted our children to have a real interest in a worthwhile activity, something they could do well and which gives them confidence. Obviously Eleanor had definite ability with horses.

She promised faithfully that she would *never* ride beyond our fields unless her friend was with her.

With a residue of reluctance remaining, we agreed to look for a new horse.

Mistakes come in different sizes and colors. Ours was a large, strawberry roan with a full mane and a sandy-colored flowing tail. His white face with the ring of brown around the left eye reminded me of someone peeking out from behind a curtain. He had a pleasant personality. And I liked him. But unwittingly he became the catalyst for a project that though we enjoyed, gradually got out of hand.

Reading his description in the paper, Eleanor felt that she'd found her dream horse and we went to see him. I tried him out and he seemed comfortable and did have a certain spirit. I was sure he had some Tennessee walker in him, for his trot was like sitting in a rocking chair. He pulled on the reins too much and I wished he'd walk and not prance.

I tried to determine his age from his mouth. The farther the teeth slant forward, the older the horse. This makes it more difficult for the animal to masticate food. When grinding teeth get out of line or worn down, grain is apt to fall out of its mouth. This is one reason some older horses are thinner. I guessed he was about fifteen years old—the upper side of middle age for a horse. I thought the flecks of white throughout his coat were gray hairs denoting age. Eleanor said they were speckles of silver.

She wanted to buy him immediately. We demurred to have time to think about it.

We planned to surprise her and arranged to have the horse delivered while she was in school.

When Eleanor walked into the house, the kitchen was littered with books and clothes from the other children who'd just piled through the door ahead of her. Everyone was eating, trying to talk over the voices of everyone else. Even the two parakeets couldn't compete.

In the midst of this maelstrom, Mary fixed a casserole for supper. She reminded me of a French juggler I'd seen once. He put a dozen plates, one after the other on tall sticks, spinning them so they'd remain there, turning like tops. By some miracle of dexterity he kept them going by running back and forth giving each one a quick twist at just the time it slowed and wobbled, ready to fall off. After a while he removed them one by one. None dropped or broke. Mary juggled her dozen tasks similarly.

"Did you have a good day at school, Eleanor?" she asked, trying to make everything seem as normal as possible, not hinting at the surprise awaiting her.

"No . . ." An impenetrable gloom had settled over her ever since she'd seen the horse. She spread a thick layer of

peanut butter on a piece of bread, tilting a jar of jelly, scraping out a ball of it with a spatula.

Paul watched the procedure. "Know what, Mom? You *better* get Eleanor a horse. She's been around Jenny too much. Her stomach looks the same way."

"You keep quiet!" Eleanor shouted. "I *hate* boys . . . Especially brothers." She slapped on another piece of bread and took a bite of the massive sandwich.

"Eleanor, could you do me a favor?" Mary asked pleasantly. "I think I left my work jacket in the barn . . . Near the saddles. Could you get it for me, please?"

The bread, peanut butter and jelly, and words mushed together indecipherably. "Whycan'tPaulorMarkgo?"

"Because I asked you. I have them doing something else."

"Can'tIgetitlater?"

"No. I want to do some work in the garden."

She rolled her eyes upward. "Why does it always have to be *me?*" she said opening the door.

Eleanor ambled up the path toward the barn. Our garage and some lacy cedars blocked a view of the paddock. We watched her pick up some tiny pine cones, putting them in her pocket. She liked to use them to make bracelets and necklaces for her friends.

She stopped suddenly, staring intently at the field in front of her. We could just see the tail of a horse. She must have seen it at the same time. This was not Jenny's skinny stick of a tail. This rich, luxurious, sandy-colored one belonged to a horse. She took a tentative step to get a better view.

Eleanor became transfixed. Vicariously we shared the emotions of unbelievable joy that must have been flooding through her.

There, standing on a high part of the pasture was—in *her* eyes—the most magnificent animal in the world. Hearing her gasp, the horse lifted his head, looking at her. She ran to him. "Oh no . . . I can't believe it's *you.*" She threw her arms around his big neck, hugging him and patting him in a burst of love.

Then, putting her two hands on his back, she jumped, and

using the mane pulled herself up on him, sitting bareback without reins or halter rope.

Involuntarily we winced. I remembered how he'd pranced and pulled. We were about to call to her to get off.

She touched his side lightly with her heels. He turned and walked quietly to the barn. The two seemed to move as in perfect harmony. Eleanor had her horse!

We couldn't agree on a name for the horse. For Eleanor, no name would be adequate to fit his warriorlike strength and kingly bearing. But an incident occurred that resolved the problem.

Eleanor was riding in the old fenced-in part of our fields when an abandoned pail caught on the horse's hoof. He was lame for a week.

Peter, home on a visit, thought of another possibility. "Achilles!" he said when he learned what happened.

"What?" Eleanor asked, puzzled.

"Achilles was the bravest of all the Greek warriors in the Trojan War thousands of years ago. But he had one weak spot . . . His heel."

Her face glowed. "I remember the story from school . . . You're a genius. It's perfect." She gave her brother a kiss.

And so a more modern Achilles came into being at Good Ground Farm.

13

"Go get him, Pinkie . . . Get him. Get the ball away from Jeff," robust Dick Jenner shouted to his small six-year-old daughter. He pointed to a six-foot-three middle-aged man charging down the field, expertly directing a soccer ball with his feet. Jeff was the outstanding athlete among us.

"Dick . . . ! What are thee telling her to do? Are thee out of thy mind?" his wife, Katie, said, dismayed. Of Quaker origin she used the old-fashioned forms of the pronouns when excited.

"She can do it," he said, blue eyes alight with inner laughter at such an incongruity, his pretense of seriousness a thin veneer over this moment of amusement. "Get thee back to thy position as goalie, Katie, or Jeff's going to blast the ball right past thee . . . Go after him, Pinkie . . . Get him! Get him!"

We were a group of families playing a Saturday afternoon informal soccer game at the Jenners' farm—little children and big ones, parents, grandparents, teachers.

So as to tell who belonged on what team, Dick gave members of one side a red pinny and the others a yellow.

Pretending for a few seconds that she gave him difficulties in getting past her, Jeff let Pinkie's small foot worry the ball. "Pinkie . . . You're so tough. What am I going to do with you?"

Seeing Paul coming at him a few feet away, the big man's foot suddenly came around. Catching the ball expertly on the instep, Jeff booted it into the goal.

"*Katie* . . . I thought thee were goalie. I told thee to pay attention," Dick groaned. "And Paul, what was wrong with you?"

"Dick . . . Thee forgets Jeff was all-American soccer," Katie admonished. "Paul's only fourteen."

"He can do it. When Paul zeroes in on something, he does it."

Broad shouldered and muscular from farm work, Paul had a runner's build. He gave Dick one of his direct, cheerful looks. "I'll get him next time, Mr. Jenner."

"We need you on defense. Stay back."

Someone passed the ball to Jeff, who again skillfully dribbled it through the forward line.

"Chase him, Mother . . . Run!" Mark shouted, laughing. "You can do it."

Paul watched Jeff, moving to keep in front of him. Then suddenly darting forward, running as fast as he could, he lashed his foot out in front of him to get the ball away from his opponent. Instead he slammed into the man, bouncing off him, flipping over in the air and thudding against the hard autumn ground. Instantly on his feet like a spring, he saw he'd knocked away the ball and scrambled after it. His foot reached it and he dribbled the ball and then suddenly smacked it into the goal.

"Pretty gutsy, Paul," I laughed.

With lots of good-natured joshing and laughter, the motley group ran back and forth across the rough, slanting field, bumping into each other, taking tumbles, shouting advice. The teams were pretty well matched.

After settling the last disputed score in the chilled shadows of the late afternoon, we returned to the Jenners' two hundred-year-old house to have cider and doughnuts in front of a warming and welcome fire.

On the way in, Mark, joking, pushed Eddie, one of his friends, who tripped and fell. Mark stumbled over him, falling also.

The boy started wrestling with him and not being able to put Mark down became angry. But Mark, rangy, relaxed and muscular, couldn't take the scrap seriously and laughing good-naturedly held the boy at arm's length.

"You make me so mad because you don't get mad," the boy shouted.

Mark grinned and let him go running for the house.

Most of the children here went to Buckingham Friends school, a small school in Lahaska, about a half hour from our house.

We were captivated by the total spirit of the school—the principal, teachers, parents, children, the Pennsylvania field-stone buildings. A meeting house was attached.

The situation epitomized for us what a school should be. The tuition was nominal and we felt the children would benefit from this extraordinary opportunity.

And who wouldn't enjoy a school where the principal closed it down on good ice days for part of the day so that everyone could skate on the pond at the foot of the hill?

The Jenners were among many of our friends, who like us moved out of the urban areas searching for a better way of life for their families. In this era of fragile relationships they too wanted to help their children and themselves develop a value system that would form a strong and enduring center.

Family life doesn't have to be the painful, tortured existence so many contemporary writers and sociological commentators portray. It's possible to develop a loving, happy, and close rapport. Naturally, there are periods of frustration and perhaps anger. But that's a part of personal growth, of working out stronger and more honest relationships. In the midst of all the centrifugal forces flinging families apart, we wanted to create a healthy and wholesome way of life.

All of us enjoyed the relaxed excitement of playing these games together. No one cared whether or not you were athletic. If you couldn't run, you didn't run. You did what you could or wanted. In the winter we all played hockey on cold, wind-swept ponds. Some of us had saggy ankles, and sometimes when we'd

take a swipe at a hockey puck, our skates would go out from
beneath us. I returned home often with a bruised bottom.

With delightful exuberance the Jenners created their fun.
Who likes to wash dishes? Not many of us. When Mark and Paul
would visit them, the way they decided who'd clean up the
dinner dishes would be to play a croquet game on a crazy course
that circled around the house. The losing team ended up at the
sink.

I snatched up one last doughnut from the pile on the plate.
Frank Bradley took one too. A slender man, he shook his head,
smiling. "I'll be stiff tomorrow."

"So will I, but our kids won't."

He touched my elbow, his smile disappearing into creases
of tension. "Could I talk to you for a few minutes?"

We walked to a corner of the room. "I'm going to ask a
tremendous favor of you and Mary . . . I don't quite know how
to go about asking . . . Could you take Sandi for a couple of
months until things settle down. It looks like Rose and I will be
splitting and the house is in turmoil."

Frank's real estate firm was one of the largest in the area.
We'd occasionally see one another at parties and school functions.

"I know asking you to take Sandi is an imposition with all
the children you have. But she feels comfortable with Eleanor
. . . I'm sick that our kids are caught in between. It shouldn't
be like that."

I could easily anticipate Mary's answer. "Certainly she can
stay with us. We'd love to have Sandi . . . But maybe you and
Rose can patch things up and you won't have to split."

"Patches in marriage never hold. Once a couple has it in
mind to split, they almost always do. Rose is a frustrated interior
decorator. She's thinking of going back to school . . . You know
how she's always buying things for the house. That's the real
love of her life . . . That and the children."

He also volunteered that Rose had been sleeping with a
local sculptor. Then he admitted that he himself was having a
liaison with a woman in a neighboring town. However, he slid
over that quickly and appeared to blame Rose for the breakup

of their marriage. "She's made a beautiful house, but not a home."

The center does not hold. William Butler Yeats' line from his poem about the disintegration of modern life seems to have become an epitaph for our age.

"How does Rose feel about Sandi staying with us?"

"Like I do . . . That Eleanor and your family could be a kind of haven during this period. It's going to be tough on her."

"We'd love to have her," I reiterated. "She's a very special youngster."

When we arrived home, we found Ellen McGillian, our stalwart, white-haired, pink-cheeked, former babysitter waiting in her car.

"Hi . . . Wondered when you were getting home," she said, her eyes bright and alert behind the steel-rimmed granny glasses.

"Come on in . . . How would you like some tea?"

Though we no longer needed Mrs. McGillian as a babysitter, she kept in touch with us. We had a keen admiration for her. A widow during the Great Depression, she'd brought up her large family alone by baking bread, walking from farm to farm and house to house selling it. Her children grew up with the same sense of courage and sensitivity, an unusual blending of traits. Eventually she married again, to Mr. McGillian, a building contractor who did some work on our cottages.

Mrs. McGillian had an especial fondness for Estelle, who asked her for help in making dresses from patterns. "She likes to do things right. There's nothing halfway about your Estelle. I remember one time when she was getting a dress ready for a dance and she just couldn't get a seam on the collar right. No one would have noticed it, but she was in tears."

Too much of a perfectionist, we said, hoping Estelle would not carry that burden through life.

"Maybe you could help Tess Snedeker," Mrs. McGillian said to Mary, sitting down and getting right to the point. "I never told you before, but her husband's a heavy drinker and a wife beater. He deserted her six months ago and I'm *glad.* He's an awful man. She has the four children to take care of. And you know, Tess didn't graduate from high school. She doesn't have any skills to get a good job. Besides, she couldn't take a full-time one because she wants to be home when the kids come back from school.

"Anyway, Tess is on welfare and they don't help her to get something she can do to earn money . . ." She paused. "My son Otto's been going around with her. Tess thinks they might get married. But she's a Roman Catholic and someone in the church told her she can't get a divorce. Besides, she doesn't know any lawyers . . . They're too expensive anyhow. It's a real mess."

"Can't the Welfare Department find her a lawyer?" Mary asked.

"They're not interested in helping her that way. But it's hard on her children because of the other kids in school . . . Well, they look down on them living that way. I thought maybe you might know something to do."

Mary immediately arranged for Tess to help her around the house occasionally, and found other places for her to do house cleaning. I located a lawyer to handle the divorce, which went through with no problems and virtually without cost.

Tess reminded us of a character in a Charles Dickens' novel. She had that essence of goodness sometimes found in the midst of devastating conditions. By sociological evaluations she should have been a loser. Her alcoholic parents neglected her. Her education was limited. She was impoverished. She'd married a wretch. She had all of her children by the time she was twenty-two and lived in a shack with a dirt floor kitchen.

Tess was kind. She had integrity and courage and an innate sense of taste and propriety. In another era you would say she had the instincts for the best of what it is to be a "lady."

Once in a while, working around the house, she'd become sidetracked polishing something for hours. A rather ordinary bureau in an out-of-the-way corner received more than its share of attention. It glistened in the shadows. Mary thought she felt sorry for it.

Looking a bit like a plump pixie with alert, intelligent eyes, Tess's friendship enriched our lives.

"Are you and Otto getting married?" Mary asked.

She shrugged philosophically. "You know how men are. I'd like to."

"Do you think Otto is . . . Well, I mean is he the right one for you?"

"I guess . . . He likes the children well enough and he seems to like me."

Mary and I thought Otto a pretty basic character. He could have been one of the muscular farm workers in the pictures of Brueghel, a seventeenth-century painter who caught the churlish, earthy personalities of those country people.

From time to time Otto worked with me around the place to the background of loud country music from his portable radio. He recounted his many amorous conquests and barroom brawls. And defiantly he told me that in his entire life he'd *never* worn a tie or "one of those g————d suits where the coats and pants match . . . And I *never* will."

He appeared to be physically fearless. We'd been talking about dogs. I mentioned that sometimes they threatened me when I jogged.

He spit out a squirt of tobacco juice. "Tell you how to handle one of them s— of b——. Had trouble with a big old b—— once. 'Bout as big as that there white burro of yours. S— of a b—— tried to bite me. I grabbed him by the neck and threw him on the ground, and I shoved my knee in his g————d ribs and I choked him . . . Mister, I choked him good until the s— of a b—— went limp. I guess he almost liked to die when I finished him . . . The g————d b——d never bothered me again. Every time I come past he slinks off around the side of the house, his tail down. If he comes at me again I'll kill the s— of a b—— and he knows it too."

That's one way of handling a threatening dog I haven't tried yet.

But Otto turned shy if I mentioned Tess.

Sandi arrived a few days later, melding into our family routine as if she'd always lived with us.

"No wonder she's so smart in school," Eleanor said awed.

"Do you know she gets up at five o'clock and does her homework. I don't even feel like getting up at six when I have to go to the barn."

"But I feel sorry for her," Mary said to me. "She told Eleanor she's positive that Rose is going to come by and pick her up in a couple of days and everything's going to be all right at home." Mary thought about her. "Have you seen her sitting by the window when she reads? That's so she can watch the driveway . . . Who knows? Maybe Sandi's right. Maybe it'll all work out. How I hope it will for her sake!"

A neighboring youngster and a classmate, Vijay Peterson, sometimes rode his pony to our farm. From my barn office, I could see the three youngsters sitting bareback on their animals —Eleanor on Achilles, Sandi on Jenny, and Vijay on the pony he called Muffin. They chatted while their animals waited with relative patience. Then having decided where to go and what to do, they'd ride off together.

Frequently they'd go back to Vijay's house. Indira Peterson, Vijay's mother, was something of an expert in natural foods and Hatha Yoga. She taught them the Yoga way of breathing and of exercising. They struggled to sit in the lotus position. And after the workouts she'd give them carob cookies.

Because Sandi barely knew how to ride, we had a stipulation that she could *never* get on Achilles. The horse meant well. And though he didn't kick, bite, or try to rub you off against a tree, he became skittish very easily. If an animal can lose perspective at the slightest provocation, that was Achilles. He'd shift the bit in his mouth so he could hold it in his teeth. Because of that, the bit couldn't press against the corners of his mouth and you'd have no real control over him. Then he'd take off as if racing the Kentucky Derby, his body slathered with sweat. Curiously, he never tried this with Eleanor and me. We seemed to be the only ones who could talk him out of his silly apprehensions and quirks. Consequently, no one else in the family bothered riding him.

Sometimes when Mary and I became discouraged, we questioned the sanity of our move to Good Ground. We seemed to be spending our lives working. The word *vacation* wasn't a part of our lexicon. Then when we'd try to think of where else we might live, we'd convince ourselves the work was worth it. The children were having a fundamental experience that would add a quality to their lives we felt we couldn't get for them anywhere else. They realized also that we too loved the place and that they were a needed and integral part of a family unit.

"We couldn't have this farm without you," Mary told them. "Your father and mother couldn't possibly run it alone. We can't afford the help." And so it gave a purpose to their young lives. Their work had meaning because in a very real sense they not only worked for themselves but for all of us as a group. They had a shared feeling of responsibility.

If we lived on a kind of island, there were many bridges to the shore of the wider world's realities.

"I've decided I'm never again going to ask about our children's friends," Mary said one day. "I met Jane Lentz shopping. I haven't seen her in a long while and I asked about Larry . . . You remember him. He's about Peter's age. When I saw the anguish on her face after I asked her about him, I thought I'd start crying myself. 'Just don't ask me, *please*,' she said and walked away. I found out later he'll probably be in a mental institution the rest of his life . . . He's destroyed his mind with drugs. Do you realize we've had *three* parents tell us almost the identical thing this year. And this is a *small* town."

All of us, the Jenners, and other like-minded families wanted our children to incorporate into their lives those traditional values that throughout history have proved to be a valid basis for a fulfilling, constructive, happy life—the quality of a mature capacity to love and to have compassion; to have a sense of integrity and responsibility; to be able to have fun and laughter and to enjoy fully the precious gift of life; and finally, to have at the very heart of themselves in a fresh and personal sense an awareness of that central power of creation, the creator of all things, or whatever other words or phrases we care to substitute for the one so many people find hard to use—God.

We found ourselves battling to defend our beliefs against a

deluge of confusing, meretricious, and destructive influences that within a few years saturated the world.

Most of the people who foisted off destructive life-styles on the young were persuasive and articulate. But their minds were skewed, their thoughts shallow. And none mentioned the possible damage that could be done to minds and lives. Most of the time we found them full of what we had to shovel out of the horses' stalls each day.

For Mary and me our refuge was our home. One of our especial delights was that we had a sensational view of the valley and the hills beyond through the leaded windows of our bedroom.

One night, ready for bed, we'd swung open the windows to watch an approaching spring thunderstorm. Far off, lightning danced on the rims of the hills while the drums of thunder faintly rumbled a barely audible accompaniment.

The telephone rang.

Closest to it, Mary answered. "Indira Peterson," she whispered to me. Indira explained to Mary that her husband, Roger, had disappeared. The other day he'd committed himself to a city hospital for psychiatric treatment. This afternoon no one could find him. Somebody said they thought they'd seen him walking along the highway heading for Lambertville.

Both Indira and Roger had been married previously. From Poona, India, she'd worked for the Indian Embassy in New York City. She gave up her job when she married Roger several years ago, happy to spend more time with her children, Vijay and Lydia. Indira had no desire to return to India and took out American citizenship.

"I didn't know Roger was so upset," Mary said.

"He's been in a terrible depression lately."

"But everything's going so well . . . He's *the* astrophysicist. I see him quoted all over in the papers, and last month *The New York Times Magazine* wrote him up. He has everything."

"I know . . ." She paused, again apologetic. "I just hate to bother you and Peter, and I know you have Sandi Bradley with you, but the children are a little scared . . . I guess I am too. Roger can get into awful tempers . . . He's never hurt anybody. I don't want you to think that. But . . . Well, we don't know what he might be like now . . . Could we spend the night with you?"

"Of course you can."

"The children would feel better if you and Peter were here while we get ready . . . I mean if Roger suddenly showed up."

"We'll be right over."

As we drove down our driveway, the impending storm had risen over the horizon. The rumbling thunder reminded me of a night on Okinawa during World War II during an intensive battle for the city of Naha. The bombardments from the opposing armies reverberated in a continuous, ominous, hollow sound. For a fraction of a second I became a Marine again, nauseated with the horror of seeing the mutilated bodies of the dead and wounded.

"Supposing Roger shows up?" Mary asked. "He's such a big, strong man . . . All that work he does with rocks."

Mary's voice dispelled my nightmare.

"He's a very gentle guy."

"When he's normal."

Roger's house seemed to mirror the labyrinths of his mind. In fact, Indira said, when she and her children moved in, he told them, "You're living in my thoughts." Though he said this in jest, she believed their presence constituted, in some odd way, an intrusion.

To reach Roger's house, you crossed over a wooden bridge spanning a moat that formed the backside of the house set in against the hill and constructed in a semicircular design. "A house, like the universe, must curve back on itself," he said.

The massive wooden door opened into a circular stone stairway leading down to the main floor. You became aware of the circular motif again, for this inner room curved and then opened on a glass-enclosed room, also curved in a semicircle. Beyond was a terrace, sweeping gracefully around the house in a curve.

Have you ever drawn semicircles on a piece of paper, one overlapping the other? This was Roger's universe. One universe of the mind intersects with another, and he'd enclosed all of them within a full circle. "We live and die in a closed system," he told us. "There's no escaping it . . . We have to learn how to organize this system so it works and it's being done through science. Science is the only reality . . . The only hope today."

The house gave you a feeling of being in the midst of a riddle or a mysterious secret and that the semicircles would go on and on. I knew what Indira meant. You had the eerie impression you were walking through the corridors of Roger's mind, and he resented your presence.

We waited for Indira in the room off the terrace. The storm reached us now. Lightning scorched the sky, flashing like a pale fluorescent light through the woods. I wouldn't have been surprised to see Roger's imposing figure, illuminated by the lightning, walking toward his house across the small piece of lawn.

I felt a shiver, and my imagination wondered whether he might be out there looking in at us after all. "I think I'll turn off the lights," I said to Mary. Ashamed at my apprehensions, I didn't explain my reasons.

"To save electricity, or are you afraid Roger could see us?"

I didn't know my fears were so transparent, but from Mary's voice I could tell she felt the same way.

Indira said she should leave a note telling Roger they were staying with us. We agreed he should know. It was the only fair thing to do.

Our household expanded by three more. We bedded down the children and offered Indira a drink.

She shook her head. "Mind if I brew some camomile tea? When I'm nervous, it's the only thing I can drink. It calms you."

Mary stood up. "I've got some."

"I brought my own. It's a special brand."

We sat in the kitchen talking to Indira. The girls had their camomile tea. I had a Coke. She told us that Roger came from a stern, humorless, Pennsylvania Dutch family who stressed perfection and success to their only son. These were their twin gods.

"I'm furious at them . . . I never want to see them again. They just told me the other day he'd had two major nervous breakdowns and tried to commit suicide. *Why* didn't they tell

me earlier? Either I wouldn't have married him or maybe I
could have helped him avoid this . . . The doctor told me
something else, too. Roger's afraid I might walk out on him . . .
That's what Elsie did . . . His first wife. She left with another
man."

We remembered.

She then went on to tell us that her former husband had
been a "workaholic" and seldom home. "He never saw the
children." Tears filled her eyes. "Roger's such a nice person
. . . I thought he'd be just the father my children need. Why
did this have to happen now?"

When we went to bed, the stars were out and the air was
washed by the storm. We said a prayer for his peace and safety.

Several days went by with no word about Roger. Indira
didn't know whether to continue staying with us, or to move to
New York to her sister.

Since Indira was a vegetarian, Mary decided it would be
easier to follow her diet. This was not difficult, for Mary usually
served us vegetarian meals several times a week. However,
Indira had gone far beyond the Pritikin low-fat diet.

"I'll get lunch for everyone today," she said. "There's this
woman in Boston, Dr. Keever, who knows more about food
than anybody else in the world. She won't let us cook anything.
Everything's eaten raw. She said the trouble with the world is
that people ruin their bodies by poor eating habits. Dr. Keever
says that really the only foods we need are alfalfa and bean
sprouts and fruit. They have all the proteins, vitamins, and
minerals you could ever want. *How* we eat is absolutely the
most important thing in the world."

Mary and I have always liked the so called natural foods.
But we enjoy a well-prepared "normal" meal too. At the moment a cheeseburger would have been just right for me.

"I think part of Roger's problem is diet," Indira said.

We were eating on the terrace. Toying with my dry salad, I
tended to agree.

I saw Vijay look past me, startled. "Hi, Roger," he said
uncertainly.

With a feeling of dread I stood up, turning around, not

knowing what to expect. He'd been walking along the terrace toward the table and now stopped. Dazed and questioning eyes flicked over us. Unshaved, clothes torn and splotched with mud, he looked like a trained bear mistreated by his original owner. He'd found himself loose in an equally inhospitable world and didn't know whether to continue dancing, or to rage.

His unmistakable torment replaced my fear. I reached my arm up around his burly shoulders. "Roger, we're glad to see you. Thank God you're back."

He nodded and looked at Indira. "Will you and the kids come home with me?" he asked quietly, as if not daring to believe they would.

"Of course we will," she answered, rising from the table. The sun glistened against her dark hair, pulled back tightly into a bun. "I'm so relieved to see you." She stood on her toes and kissed him.

"I found your note. I drove over."

"Let me get some of our things. I'll be with you in a few minutes."

I went inside with her. "Why don't I give you a call in about a half hour to see how things are."

A few days later while Mary and I worked on a new vocabulary builder I was writing, the telephone rang. I recognized Vijay Peterson's frightened voice. "Can you get over here right away? Something's happening to Roger . . . *Please!*"

"Oh my Lord," Mary whispered. "I hope he hasn't gone berserk."

We arrived at the same time as the police car. Roger had committed suicide. While Indira and the children were shopping, he'd shot himself.

We read his note. *"I suffer from psychological entropy. I have no more energy left to carry on life."*

Roger's tragedy shook us and I found it difficult to work creatively. A novel I'd been struggling with wasn't turning out. It refused to gel. So I decided to jettison the whole idea. Six months' effort gone for nothing.

I'd been pacing back and forth in my study in the house. Through the windows I could see the slope of our lawn and the

woods beyond. Still mulling over the ramifications of my decision, I spotted Eleanor emerging from the woods on a dead run.
I'd never seen her move so fast. Sometimes she'd jog with us,
but being the youngest, she found it hard to keep up with her
older brothers and sisters. *She's certainly improving,* I thought
to myself, admiring her sprint across the lawn. Instead of slowing down and walking into the house, I heard the kitchen door
bang open.

"Sandi fell off Achilles. She's not moving," Eleanor sobbed.

"The Rescue Squad," I shouted to Mary, running through
the kitchen. I asked Eleanor where Sandi fell.

"On that first trail . . . Almost near the little field," she
said between sobs.

"We'll drive . . . Better come with me. I want to be sure
where she is."

As we ran to the driveway, a slim, neatly dressed young
man stepped out of a car he'd just parked. "Mr. Funk, I'm
Harvey Ostrander. I called you earlier about the cottage . . ."

His car blocked ours. Seconds counted. "Get it out of
there," I bellowed, pointing at his car. *"Get it out* of there . . .
An emergency." I started the engine in the station wagon, beginning to back up. He leaped for his car, convinced I was going
to bash into it. He jammed his in reverse, tires screeching.

We careened down the narrow, serpentine driveway,
bumped across a field, and roared up the rocky trail.

"There's Jenny . . . She's right near Sandi. There she is,"
Eleanor cried out.

I saw our little white burro standing quietly as if guarding
the child. The youngster sprawled on the ground alongside of
her, a large rock inches from Sandi's head. I was sure she'd
struck it.

Achilles had disappeared. "I shouldn't have let her ride
him, but she wanted to . . . She said she could," Eleanor wept.

The child lay apparently lifeless, her face white. I picked up
her wrist, feeling for her pulse. Thank the Lord I found one.
Pulling off my sweater and placing it over her, we heard the
Rescue Squad's siren. I prayed for the ability to pray. A friend of

ours, thrown from her horse, ended up a paraplegic. If Frank and Rose hadn't been messing up their lives . . . !

"She knew about Achilles. I told her and everything. But she said she wouldn't have any trouble . . . That *dumb, stupid* horse started running and she fell off . . . I *hate* him," Eleanor shouted. "He's so *dumb.*"

Mary raced up and down the hills and through the underbrush leading the men of the Rescue Squad to exactly where we were. Others followed. There's an informal, immediate "grapevine" here and neighbors who can, leave whatever they're doing to follow the Rescue Squad to see if they can help.

Panting, catching her breath, Mary knelt beside Sandi, her eyes searching frantically for any hopeful signs, her hands gently touching her head. The men slid a blanket carefully under the child, lifting her on the stretcher, keeping all movement to a minimum in the event of a broken back.

Sandi stirred. Mary held her hand. "You're going to be all right." She turned to me. "I'll ride in the ambulance with her to the hospital . . . Try to find Frank or Rose."

I backed the car down the trail and drove home while Eleanor took Jenny back to the barn.

The polite, bewildered young man was still there, his glasses reflecting the ambulance's blinking amber light.

"About the cottage . . . ," he began.

"Cottage?"

"You advertised for rent."

"Oh that . . ." Hilda and Juan Gomez were leaving. I sighed, pointing to the activity surrounding us. "How about coming back tomorrow?"

Still bemused, he said he'd try.

I located Frank, who eventually met Mary at the hospital. Fortunately Sandi only had a very slight concussion and could return to us the following day.

When Mary arrived home, the older children took over preparing dinner. I poured us some wine and we went to my study. Mary sat in the chair, closing her eyes, leaning back her head.

There wasn't much we felt like saying to one another. We were depressed and tired, each caught up in unspoken thoughts. Events seemed to have moved us so far and fast from the first days at the farm. As parents, we were having our own desperate moments, our own times of searing anguish, of bewilderment.

Swiss Family Robinson lived on an island removed from the world. They contended only with nature. But all families in this era struggled against forces far more difficult and subtle and in the end much more dangerous. We were not to be immune from such pressures.

Despite our pleadings, Celine had left college and hitchhiked to San Francisco with a friend. For us San Francisco meant Haight-Ashbury—drugs and flower children.

Superficially, Celine fitted the definition of a flower child. She believed in love, beauty, and peace. But there the comparison ended. Celine is a true artist, with a true eye. She not only feels a subject deeply but has the ability to express her ideas with an unusual creative ability. She received one of the few scholarships the art school gave out there, by simply submitting her work.

Furthermore, she's adventurous and wanted to see for herself the place that everyone talked about; where so many of her peers said that a new way of life was happening. As a neophyte artist with potential, she argued that the area would be stimulating to her art.

Like thousands of others who wanted to be "free" and didn't want to fit into what they believed were stereotyped roles, she followed Aquarius' Pied Piper call. Most of them, coming from pleasant and loving middle-class families, were unprepared to cope with the brutal realities of violence and the indifference of people who didn't care whether or not these youngsters might be destroyed. Like Celine they were trusting and not thinking anyone would deliberately try to hurt them.

We knew it was a "bad scene" and worried constantly. We had reason.

Celine found herself in the midst of violence too often.

At one point she rented a room in a house. Her landlord agreed to let her use the two-car garage attached to the house as a studio for her painting. She found this convenient because she had plenty of space. Though small, Celine liked to work on large canvases and sculpture. The inside door of the garage led to the kitchen, handy if she was thirsty or wanted a snack. Because she liked to have as much light as possible, she left the garage doors open. One day she heard footsteps behind her. She turned, finding a large, well-dressed man. He approached her.

"Hey, you're an artist," he said pleasantly. "Let's see your work."

As he moved closer, Celine edged back. Though she wasn't as "paranoid" as some of her friends about strange men, nonetheless she was reasonably wary.

They talked a bit about her art. Being an artist, Celine had good visual memory. She thought she'd seen him driving past in a station wagon with children.

"I'm looking for a place to paint," he said. "What about if I rent the other half from you?"

"It's not mine . . . It's my landlord's."

He nodded. "Think he'd rent it to me?"

She shrugged. "You'd have to talk with him." When painting, she preferred to work alone and didn't want to have anyone else, especially an older man. Yet she knew that her landlord needed the money.

"Is he in?"

"He went out. He'll be back in a couple of hours." Quiet for a few seconds, as if thinking, the man stared at Celine. "Why don't you write down my name and telephone number and give it to him. He can call me if he wants to."

"Okay," she said, turning her back to get a pencil and paper.

Suddenly she felt his arms snap around her waist, squeezing her so tightly she could hardly breathe. Jamming his hand over her mouth, he dragged her to the kitchen door.

Celine struggled and tried to yell. She bit and scratched at his hands, punched his arms, terrified and outraged. For an instant he took his hand away from her mouth as he grabbed for the kitchen door.

Celine screamed. Feeling him go somewhat off balance, her foot kicked back sharply, catching him in his groin.

"You b——," he bellowed, his grip loosening from the unexpected pain.

She twisted around, kneeing him in the same place, screaming for help.

He turned, stumbled, and ran to the sidewalk. Celine followed, chasing him down the street, calling for help. People quickly stepped out of their way. She lost him when he turned down a side street.

She might be small, but she has an inner core of strength and courage. However, she wouldn't leave her room for three days.

We disagreed completely with Celine's move to California and told her so. We tried to explain our position and kept in touch with letters, and telephone calls, and a trip I made to the West Coast. We had confidence in her, but we worried about her situation.

In their own way our other children were also going through various stages of growing pains as they confronted the hazards of these times.

At the moment, however, another family's child colored our thoughts. "Waiting in the hospital with Sandi this afternoon," Mary murmured, "I wondered if we'd made a mistake in moving to Good Ground."

I stood up, walking slowly back and forth in my small office, understanding her uncertainties. I had them sometimes myself.

"Have the children really benefited?" she continued, opening her eyes. "I don't know . . . I just don't know."

I looked out the window at the view sweeping down to the river. "Well . . . Don't judge it by today. It's been a long hard one . . . I hope we made the right decision in moving to Good Ground. I think we did. We've laid a foundation for them to build on. They'll have a little trouble with their architectural designs in the beginning. That's happened with some of them. But that's normal . . . I think the important thing is we've produced strong-minded, self-reliant kids who have a lot of love in them. That's what we wanted, isn't it . . . ? Maybe sometime we'll really know."

The hint of a smile pulled against the tide of weary sadness in her face. "When I got to Sandi this afternoon in the woods, I bet you didn't know I could run so fast."

"You really impressed me . . . Remember the Dalmatian dogs that used to run with old fire wagons? I heard the Rescue Squad's making you an offer."

"I brought them to the *exact* spot."

"You have a nose like Laddie."

"Thanks a lot! I'm not so sure I appreciate the comparison . . ." She sipped her wine. "Oh, by the way, I haven't had a chance to tell you . . . Otto and Tess are getting married . . . And they asked you to be the best man and me the maid of honor! What a compliment! It's so thoughtful of them. Oh, and you know what? Tess said to tell you that Otto's wearing a *three*-piece suit . . . She wants to know if you'll help him pick out a tie."

14

Unfortunately, Eleanor's friend who kept her horse at our farm moved, and so once again Eleanor rode alone. And again we worried about her, stipulating that she absolutely confine her riding to the fields.

One day a neighbor called to say that she had our daughter in her home. She'd been thrown by Achilles and something seemed to be wrong with her ankle. She couldn't walk.

Driving to the house, a mile or so beyond our property, we found Achilles tethered to a lamp post and a chastened daughter inside the house. Apparently the girth holding the saddle broke while they were cantering and Eleanor slid off. The hospital X-ray showed that she'd fractured her ankle.

"I admit I was a little bit off the property, but I was on my way home," Eleanor said contritely later, her vivid coloring reminding us of a portrait by the English painter Lawrence.

"Well, Eleanor . . . We'll have to do a lot of thinking about your riding," I said.

"I'm sorry . . . I was wrong. I promise I'll never go off by myself again. It was so dumb of me."

When Nellie Johnson, Mary's one-day-a-week cleaning woman, learned of Eleanor's accident, she telephoned her.

"Eleanor . . . I'm going to make something special just for you. You know everyone loves Nellie's pies. Well, I'm going to bake you a pear pie. I bet you never ate a pear pie before . . . And don't you let those big brothers of yours eat it all up . . . This is all for you, this pear pie."

"You're going to spoil me," Eleanor said, cheered by the prospect. "Thank you *so* much!"

A few days later after supper while I studied Sam Glucksberg's *Experimental Psycholinguistics* and Mary perused one of her art books, Eleanor's crutches clattered on the floor as she slid into a chair. "I hate them," she said.

"Poor you," Mary said, nodding in agreement. "Dr. Richardson said it won't be much longer."

"Anyway, Mom and Dad, I've thought of a neat idea . . . And I think you'll like it." She paused with shy hope. "I've thought of a way I can get a lot of people to ride with me."

I wondered if we weren't teaching our children to be too resilient and strong minded.

"We have such a big barn and lots of room and fields . . . Instead of just having another friend keep her horse here, and I always have to wait until she shows up, why don't we board a few horses. Then there'd always be somebody around."

"You mean to have people pay for keeping their horses here?" I asked.

"Dad, we have plenty of room. We could have three horses . . . And we can store hay and everything, and you always say that you want to really use the land and not just have it sit around."

Mary and I discussed Eleanor's idea. There seemed to be a certain logic to it. The plan might even produce a slight profit. Good stable facilities were hard to find. We were closer to town than most of them. We could offer a reasonable price, superb riding areas, and a loving, experienced concern for animals. What else could the owner of a horse desire?

More than that, how hard it is to turn away from a child's

enthusiasm when the idea is reasonably creative and when she poured so much of herself into it.

We worked up an advertisement, placing it in several papers.

Answering our advertisement, a Mrs. Merriman telephoned to say she'd visit our farm early Sunday afternoon. She planned to bring her horse and perhaps do a little riding in the fields. Three girls would be coming also, all of whom had horses and might be interested in boarding them at Good Ground Farm.

"I can't *believe* it," Eleanor cried, running to the barn to tell Achilles about the wonderful possibilities.

To our surprise we had a telephone call from Minnesota from a Margaret White with two children, a son and a daughter, plus three horses. She planned to move to our area and a friend sent her our advertisement. This happened to be a felicitous contact, since Rex and Melissa Etherington were moving from their cottage. The Whites were interested in renting the cottage *and* boarding their horses.

We entered Sunday with excitement. While I made pancakes, the children straggled into the kitchen. Eleanor sat on a chair, her hair tousled, her face still more lost in sleep than wakefulness. Nature had painted her in fresh warm colors.

"Eleanor, you're down with everyone else!" Mary observed, pleasantly surprised. "But of course. This is your big day . . . Could you please help me set the table. . . . Paul, why don't you help your father with the pancakes, and Mark, you can take out the sausages and drain them."

The parakeets in the cage above the washing and drying machines, the children talking, the whirring of the kitchen exhaust fan created the usual morning din.

"How could anyone sleep with all this noise," Eleanor commented, stretching. She'd been off her crutches for a week.

"Eleanor, you've got a problem," Paul said.

"What?"

"You've got the people coming to look at the barn today . . . Right?"

She nodded.

"It's a mess up there."

Mark chuckled. "How come you're so interested in neatness all of a sudden, Paul. Have you looked at your room lately . . . ? And your toes are sticking through your sneakers and you have a rip in your shirt."

"This is different," Paul said crisply. "It's like a business deal."

"Paul, with your attention to detail and your love of sports, I thought you'd end up a coach . . . But maybe you'll be the businessman of the family," Mary joshed gently.

Eleanor stretched and yawned noisily. "After they see Achilles, they won't notice anything else. They'll just want their horses with him because he's the greatest one in the world."

"Paul, you have a real point," I said, stacking banana pancakes in the oven to keep them warm.

"It's really grungy up here . . . Cobwebs everywhere . . ."

"Cobwebs are good in a barn," Mark said authoritatively, putting down the sausages, leaning over the fish tank. "They catch flies. Over at the Dillons where I work, the farmer always leaves them. They catch all kinds of things."

"Well, I agree with Paul," I said, getting into the spirit of the moment. "They won't catch customers."

"And there's paper and junk around and the fence posts are lopsided where Jenny's fanny's pushed into them," Paul continued.

"Mark, while you're there, could you feed the fish?"

"I thought that was Paul's job."

"How about you doing it today . . . Let's go back to having chore lists again," I suggested to Mary. "We have so much to remember."

"You mean at sixteen I have to check off if I've brushed my teeth?" Mark laughed.

"By the way," Mary asked me, "are we going to church?"

I looked at the wall clock. "If we're going to clean up the barn area, I don't think we have time, do you? Isn't Mrs. Merriman coming at two?"

"Guess what my horoscope says for Leo today," Eleanor

said, reading from a small booklet. "Try not to burden your family with troubles you may be having, since they probably have enough of their own."

Mary laughed. "That's about the only time I know that a horoscope is one hundred percent accurate."

After breakfast we all worked on cleaning up the barn area. Naturally it took longer than we'd counted on. In fact we missed lunch, finishing just as a station wagon, pulling a horse trailer, parked in our driveway.

A large, dark-haired, good-looking woman glanced around her. The deep color of her face suggested she was very much of an out-of-doors type. "I'm Jane Merriman," she said pleasantly, putting out a strong hand for me to shake. I liked her instantly. "And these are my three young friends, Sally, Anne, and Phoebe."

I tried to remember their salient features to link them with their names. Sally had short sandy hair and wore dark glasses. Would she make a witty remark, a *sally?* Anne, shorter and chubbier, had darker hair. Could she be a portrait of the English Queen Anne? Phoebe, a small, lithe girl had big brown eyes that reminded me of a bird—a phoebe.

"You have a beautiful place here . . . Just spectacular," the woman said.

From where we stood, the view was indeed an unparalleled one. The land dropped off into the valley, and in the distance there were the darker woods and rolling shadowed hills. A golden mist wrapped around the afternoon with a charm that would have been worthy of King Arthur's Camelot.

"Look at that adorable white donkey," Sally said, pointing to Jenny who was doing the thing she could do best—eating!

"Is she in foal?" Anne asked.

I couldn't help smiling. "Afraid not. It's only a grass belly. She's programmed to eat twenty-four hours a day . . . Do you ride much?" I asked.

"Almost every day."

"Ride!" Mrs. Merriman broke in. "These two are real pros." She pointed to Sally and Anne. "They're always coming back

from horse shows with the winning ribbons. Great riders, these kids."

I felt Eleanor's growing insecurity. We'd written "expert care" in the advertisement. After a few minutes with these people we knew who were the experts.

Jane Merriman poked around the barn a bit and nodded to the girls. "It's nice and big, and it has more than one entrance." She turned to me. "Where we have our horses now there's only one way out, and I worry about fire . . . Do you know, I've had my mare twenty-three years. Brought her up and trained her myself."

"Wow!" Eleanor exclaimed. "She must be like a daughter to you."

The woman laughed. "More like a grandmother. She's a great old gal and a marvelous hunter. A bit stiff these days, but she goes."

She had a hearty, cheerful voice full of enthusiasm. I knew she'd handle a horse well.

Eleanor had put Achilles in his stall. Mrs. Merriman and the girls went up to look at him. The horse, however, in one of his awkward moments, turned his back on all of us and put his head in the corner, a favorite position of his. Eleanor said he was smart to do this because it kept the flies away from his face. But he looked silly.

"Over at this other place, they hit my mare with a hammer. The groom was drunk," Sally said.

"I can't believe it," Mary said. "What a terrible thing to do to a poor horse."

As tall as Mary, but heavier, Mrs. Merriman stood with her hands on her hips. "You have stalls for your horse and burro and I see there's one more available."

"Your mare can have the one Achilles is in," I said. "It's a bit larger."

"And you have water," she said, noticing the faucets. "You said there were riding trails?"

"All over," Mary said. "We have our own in the woods. But there are a lot of other ones throughout the entire area."

"What about a blacksmith."

"We use Axel Heyst. He's one of the best. Used to do race horses."

"What do you think, girls?" Mrs. Merriman asked.

"It's great up here," Sally answered in a relaxed voice. "The only thing is I don't see a ring or jumps . . . So I don't know." Except for the swish of Achilles' tail, silence in the barn. "Do you have standards?" Anne asked.

I hesitated. A word like that illustrates the ambiguity of language. Many of our words do double duty. As my mind rummaged through my mental dictionary, for an instant it linked up *standards* with *value systems.* Obviously the context in which she used the word gave it the other meaning—the upright side supports of jumping bars.

"There's no problem in making jumps," I answered. "We could lay them out on the field in any way you want."

They were trying to decide. A few wasps buzzed along the edge of a window. Crows cawed at some intrusion.

Paul broke the silence, feeling something more was needed. He looked at the woman directly, his gray-blue eyes serious. "Dad won the first prize for the Goodhands Cup when he was a boy at the National Horse Show at Madison Square Garden. And he had a beautiful little mare no one else could handle and they won lots of blue ribbons and championships showing. He really knows how to talk to animals. They do what he says. Animals love Mom and Dad. They're very kind to them . . ." He didn't know what else to say.

Jane Merriman smiled. "What a nice thing to say about your parents . . ." Her hands went to her hips. "Well, girls, I don't know about you, but I'm sold. I'm going to leave Glorious Girl here and give it a try."

I was delighted for I liked her.

Sally adjusted her glasses. Like Jane Merriman, she too wore old jodhpurs and boots and a jacket that looked as if it had been on many rides. "I know you'll have to put in additional stalls . . . Would you consider making ones that had Dutch doors?" she asked me.

"So the horses can look out. They get bored," Anne added.

With good carpentry almost anything could be done. "Sure, we could do that. We'll have them facing the south."

"What about a ring?" Anne asked. "It's important for training your horse."

"Well, I guess it's something we could work out."

Mary's expression became more and more doubtful, while Eleanor's transformed into ecstasy.

"That sounds like an awful lot of work," Mary murmured.

"We could help make the jumps and ring," Sally replied.

They asked about hay and the grain mixture, seeming to be satisfied.

"Dutch doors would be nice," Anne mused. "Wildfire gets bored sometimes and this would keep her from jumping the fences. We could leave the door open and she could wander in and out."

"Your horse jumps out . . . ? Out of the field?" Mary asked apprehensively.

"When she gets bored."

"Then what happens?"

"Whoever's around has to bring her in."

"I know you do the *Reader's Digest* 'Word Power' and so I suppose you're around most of the time," Jane Merriman said to me.

I nodded. "If I'm not, Mary or one of the children will be . . . And we may be having someone in that first cottage who'll have three horses here who can help."

Phoebe spoke for the first time. "Maybe if Anne and Sally are here, my mother and father will let me bring my pony, Peppermint."

"I bet they would," the woman said, putting her arm around the child's shoulders.

The two girls talked to one another for a few moments and then came over to me. "How soon could you have the stalls built?" Sally asked.

Without thinking about it I suggested two weeks.

Sally smiled. "We like it here and we'll bring our horses too."

Jane Merriman noticed Eleanor's face. "You'll have some

company up here now, won't you?" she laughed. "We'll all have a lot of fun . . . Why don't you let your horse out and see how yours and mine get along this afternoon."

At last able to show off "the greatest horse in the world," Eleanor led Achilles out of the stall.

"Look . . . he has a white forehead and a white ring around his eye," one of the girls said.

"Like he's peeking out from behind a curtain," the other replied, laughing.

I saw Eleanor flush. She released him in the field surrounding the barn.

As Jane Merriman backed her mare down the trailer's ramp, Mark sauntered out. He'd heard three girls were in the neighborhood.

Glorious Girl, a large light-brown horse, backed down the ramp without fuss and with a certain dignity. Then she looked around, ears forward.

The woman patted her and kissed her on the nose. "That's the girl. This is your new home."

Eleanor whispered to Mary. "See . . . She's not afraid to kiss *her* horse."

"I'll stick to kissing your father and you children."

Achilles, who'd been cropping grass, jerked his head up, his ears forward, body taut. He stared at the new arrival. Jenny lifted her head partway. From a distance she looked like a teacher with glasses partly down her nose, examining her pupils.

"Doesn't he look like a stallion on the prairies guarding his herd from danger?" Eleanor said, referring to Achilles.

Paul laughed, indicating the fat, shaggy burro. "Some herd!"

"Will they fight?" Mark asked.

"Good Lord, I hope not," Mary said as if she were murmuring a prayer.

I opened the gate and Jane Merriman released her mare in the field. Achilles stalked forward threateningly, his ears flat against his head.

"Don't you think you should do something?" Mary asked me.

It was too late. Glorious Girl, feeling threatened, reared and then plunged off across the field toward Jenny. The burro looked up and began running. Her bulging sides resembled the cheeks of a very fat person. With her tail between her legs, ears back, and many small kicks, she zigzagged across the field, surprised and angry.

Achilles joined the chase. There was squealing, starting, stopping, wheeling around in circles, rearing, bolting, running, panting and snorting, bucking, kicking. And no one was touched or hurt!

Glorious Girl bared her teeth with something like a *Zrrrrrr* sound. Achilles pawed the air.

"He won't hurt her, will he?" Jane Merriman worried.

No one replied. The fate of our project depended on the discretion of Achilles.

"Maybe he's trying to protect Jenny," Eleanor suggested in a low voice.

"A gelding won't hurt a mare," I stated with crossed fingers.

For another moment the two horses squared off at one another. Then with a squeal, Glorious Girl lunged toward Achilles, her teeth bared to their roots. She made the terrible *Zrrrrr* sound again. Achilles must have realized she was enraged, for unexpectedly he turned and ran as fast as he could. Now he was the one being chased, and she tried to reach out to bite his flank.

All of us, except Eleanor, laughed. She was mortified.

"Achilles has taken to his *heels,*" Paul punned.

Like the passing of a brief thunderstorm all became serene in a few moments. Apparently Glorious Girl decided to make Jenny her friend. After all, girls should stick together. As long as Achilles maintained his distance everything was fine. Not impressed, Jenny was content to eat undisturbed.

We all helped Jane Merriman unload her gear—saddle, blankets, bridle, brushes, water pails.

Then everyone left. Our first boarder turned out to be a happy surprise.

"Hey . . . I think those girls are pretty nice," Mark said.

Estelle shook her head. *"Boys* . . . You're always thinking about girls."

"Why not?" Mark laughed. "I kind of like Sally."

"She's older than you, I think," Eleanor replied.

"No girls that like horses for me," Paul said. "They get interested in horses and that's all they think about."

"That's *not* true," Eleanor said firmly.

"You ought to hear girls talking about how silly boys are," Estelle added, laughing.

Paul nodded. "Yeah, I hear you talking to your friends on the phone. Glad I'm not one of the guys you're talking about."

"Oh . . . Most of them are okay. The trouble is they're always pawing you or holding your hand or trying to kiss you . . . They're always leaning on you. We laugh about them. They're goofy."

The sense of relaxation and fun withdrew from Mark's face. He put his hands in his pockets, walking off slowly toward the house.

"Guys are more sensitive than you girls think," I said to Estelle and Eleanor. "They act big and bold, but most of them don't have much confidence when it comes to girls. You'd be surprised how many are really shy about it."

That night in bed, Mary said, "Are you awake?"

"I am now."

"I've been thinking."

"Don't. It's dangerous to the mind."

"Who's going to build the stalls and the jumps and the ring?"

"Well . . ." I stretched my feet, flexing my toes. "For the stalls I thought of getting Henry McGillian. He did a good job repairing Rex and Melissa's cottage."

Mary sighed. "What worries me is that I don't want anything interfering with your work . . . Are we taking on too much?"

"I've thought about that. Yet this seems like such a natural thing for us to do . . ."

"And it is a good way to use our land and to have others

enjoy it . . . Eleanor will have friends who have the same interest. I like Jane and the girls so much. But . . ."

We were quiet for a while, listening to the wind brushing through the trees. "I hope Mr. McGillian can do it because carpentry isn't really your forte." She laughed. "Remember the rabbit cage. It was so big you had to take it apart to get it out of the cellar!"

"Don't forget they were the happiest rabbits you've ever known . . ." I paused, thinking about all the horses coming in. "You know what . . . We haven't even included the possibility of Margaret White's three nags from Minnesota. Somehow I think this project is getting a little larger than we anticipated," I worried.

"How do we get into these things?"

"I guess the same way we got seven children. We get carried away by the romantic."

Mary sighed, moving closer to me. "The trouble is I don't get enough headaches."

15

From my barn office I heard the resonant clanging of our farm bell. Like a parent who's learned to discern between different cries of his infant, I'd found that certain tones and rhythms gave me clues as to the urgency of the ring. This clanging had a feel of exigency to it.

Mary usually rang the bell to signal that someone wanted me on the telephone, and so I plugged it in now. Finding no one on, I knew she wanted me at the house. I turned off the lights, covered the typewriter—the dust from the hay penetrated the cracks in the floor and walls—and walked down the long stairway into the hayroom. Looking up the length of the barn, I thought about the coming changes.

I didn't fully realize then just how much things would be changed.

"Fanny Fulbright wants you to call her back," Mary said, looking harassed. The washing machine and the dryer thumped away resolutely and the parakeets chattered. A pile of early apples we'd gathered were on the kitchen table. The warm, spicy fragrance of others simmering in a pot on the stove cooking up to become apple butter smelled more delightful to me than the most expensive French perfume.

"Fanny Fulbright . . . ? Oh, right. Promotion Director."
My new novel, *Love and Consequences,* was being published.

"She has you lined up for some talk shows," Mary continued. "And Margaret White called and said she found our place
ideal. She's planning to come east in two weeks—*with her
horses!*"

Margaret had stopped by earlier in the day.

"That's *six* stalls to build." Mary's voice didn't try to hide
her growing alarm. "How?"

"Henry McGillian."

"He hasn't called you back."

"I know." I felt my equanimity dissolving like a lump of
sugar in water. "I'll try again."

In his laconic way Mr. McGillian said he'd try to see me
later this afternoon. Because of his wife's yapping Welsh corgies,
I had to yell into the phone to make myself heard. After talking
to him I felt better. If he said he'd try, that was tantamount to
saying he'd be there. He was the most dependable man I'd ever
known—and one of the most independent in character.

True to his word, he appeared. We stood in the main section
of the barn. For me he represented the quintessence of an
aspect of traditional America. His was the face that endured the
hardships with Washington during the Revolutionary War. He
was like the pioneers that trekked through the wilderness and
across the plains searching for new land. He was the farmer, the
blacksmith, the rancher, the frontier merchant who'd been the
cornerstone of the American spirit. And he had a prickly candor.

One corner of Mr. McGillian's mouth was larger than the
other. It was there he stored the wad of chewing tobacco. Occasionally his mouth moved to spit the tobacco juice through the
pane of a broken window. His pale blue eyes were clear and
untroubled. He'd look at you for a while with disconcerting
frankness before he'd reply to whatever it was you said. He had
no interest in chitchat.

I'd been explaining to him the way I thought the stalls
might be placed. "We could knock out this partition between
the two sections of the barn and put the stalls in the other room.

But here's the problem. Since the stalls have to be on the south side and ten by ten feet, we'd have to move this post." The dark wooden post set on a block of concrete was fastened to a cross-beam in the ceiling, the floor of the barn's second story. I touched it.

In a vague way I had a plan but wasn't really sure of myself. Any major alteration would become permanent and this worried me.

His clear eyes fixed on me. Seconds went past. "Can't move that post. Supports the floor above." *Splat* went the tobacco juice out the window.

Yes, I could see now that it did. "H'mm . . ." I paused, reorienting my thoughts. "Couldn't we make another post? Farther out, that is . . . I mean, the stalls have to be big enough." Obviously that would entail some careful work I hadn't counted on doing. I certainly didn't want the ceiling crashing down on us.

He looked at me with a long and steady gaze. The tobacco shifted to the other side of his mouth. I felt he could see into the confused paperwork of my mind. *Splat* out the window. "Mistake having horses."

The unexpected remark unnerved me. "What do you mean?"

Another long unwavering look from the pale eyes. "Won't make nothing on them. Lumber costs money. So does my time."

I nodded. "The problem is I've agreed . . . And my daughter . . . Well, a kind of project . . ."

A long pause. *Splat.* "Had horses once. All they did was to cost me money. Always getting into trouble. They take a lot of time, horses. Wouldn't do it if I was you."

His stubborn words disconcerted me. All I wanted were some stalls, two of the six with Dutch doors. "We're kind of experimenting. I mean with all this land . . ." I waved my hand vaguely in the direction of the fields.

The silence was filled in by raucously arguing crows, Achilles' snorts, and Laddie and Donna barking down by the house. Jenny lay on the ground near the barn where it was dusty, trying to roll over. She'd get three quarters of the way wriggling and wagging her tail, but her grass-swollen belly prevented her and she flopped back on her side.

"I'd put pigs on."

I considered his suggestion. "You're undoubtedly right. But I'm stuck with horses."

He studied the room a moment. "How soon do you want them built?"

Relief came in a rush. "Ten days."

Splat. Pause. *Splat.* He never missed the spot where the windowpane had been broken. "Can't do it in that time."

"I could help you."

His face expressed patent doubt.

"I could put in the floors," I said. "If you could lay it out, cut through the wall for the Dutch doors, and put up the partitions in the others, my boys and I could do all the odds and ends."

"Lumber's got to be ordered. That takes time. Has to be cut."

He didn't want to do it. This was clear. Well if he wouldn't, I'd have to try. The only other carpenter I knew in the area had welched in the middle of a job and never completed it even though we'd paid him.

Normally I don't talk to myself in front of other people, but I began muttering. "I guess I *could* do it myself . . . Doesn't look too hard. Just a little careful planning. The Dutch doors might give me some trouble, though. I could use an ax and chop through the wall. Might knock off the asphalt shingles on the outside, but that wouldn't matter . . . Now let's see about the measurements . . . My feet are just about twelve inches." I had a hundred-foot tape measure I used for laying out our tree farm, but it was in the tractor room. I began to put one foot after the other, heel to toe, counting. I walked around the post. "Going to make things pretty tight if I put a stall in on the other side of the post."

The tobacco shifted more quickly from one cheek to the other. *Splat! Splat.*

"My only real problem is this blasted post. If I leave it in, the horses won't be able to squeeze past. It's too tight a fit. Maybe I should take it out. Would the roof fall in?"

Splat! "Don't need ten feet this side."

I looked up at him. "What?"

"Don't need this ten feet. Don't need to make an exact square. Cut an angle. You'd only lose a foot or two in one corner, that's all. Then you don't have to remove the post." *Splat!* Those unnerving eyes of his.

But I understood instantly what he meant. "You're a genius! You've got it! You're absolutely right," I said enthusiastically.

Perhaps Mr. McGillian had been challenged by the vision of what might happen if I worked on this alone. Perhaps he took pity on such a novice. Whatever, his carpenter's ruler came out of his pocket and he slapped it across the floor, measuring. Then he reached into his pocket, taking out a piece of chalk, and outlined the dimensions of the stall. Now I could see it visually.

Splat! He reached into his pocket for a stubby pencil. "Six stalls . . ." He thought for a minute and then wrote down some numbers on a wrinkled piece of paper. "Here's what you need to order." *Splat!*

Nothing else was said. We began work two days later. Off and on I helped him, coming down from my office when he needed something held, or wanted to explain why he was making a slight change.

He finished his part. Now it was up to me. We had three days to put in the floors and to finish off the details.

Laying in a floor would seem to be simple work. For carpenters, or for people with natural skills it is. For us it seemed almost as complicated as a moon shot. First of all, I didn't have the equipment. I needed an electric saw, but didn't feel it was right to ask Mr. McGillian to rent his. Anyway, he was off hunting in Maine. No store in our area had such tools for rent. This meant using my handsaw. After a few tries and seeing the pile of boards to go through, I knew we were in for trouble. My arm ached already.

"But why do we need a wooden floor?" Mary asked. "It seems silly to give them all that luxury."

Eleanor laughed. "Mother . . . ! I'm glad you're asking *me* that question and not somebody like Sally. Cement ruins a horse's legs. It's cold and hard and it's damp."

What would be the simple answer to the problem? What would Mr. McGillian do? He'd probably take the lumber back to the lumberyard and have them cut it to size. And this is what I did.

Even so, frequently I had to trim edges. The work was far more than we could have imagined. The underlying supports had to be measured out and put down. These were strips of wood one inch by one inch, ten feet long. The oak boards were two inches thick and about a foot wide and ten feet long.

A friend of ours who ran a local restaurant heard about the project and brought up a power saw. That helped immeasurably with the trimming.

With Peter, John, and Celine still away, we had four at home. Because of the demands of school and sports none of them could give us any real assistance. Eleanor did what she could.

Mary held the heavy planks while I sawed them. After that we laid the boards on the supports, hammering them in. For each nail, it took her thirty exhausting strokes to my ten.

With one day to go, we had to work late into the night and the children joined us. There was a certain fun and excitement to all this activity as the stalls really began to take on a finished look.

The Indian summer weather brought unexpected heat during the day, but a cooling breeze came through the open Dutch doors in the evening, carrying the soothing sounds of nearby lowing cattle. With blinking lights a jet moved silently through the darkness against a web of bright stars. We heard the wings of the Canada geese as they swept south, their cries stirring a primitive wonder in us. Everything seemed to be connected to everything else and there was a oneness to the moment.

We were happily aware that Eleanor felt almost overcome by joy. Once, unable to contain herself, she threw her arms around each of us. Then she danced in and out of the Dutch doors, making us laugh.

Friday afternoon, the day before the horses were supposed

to arrive, I called Henry McGillian, now back from hunting, to
tell him we'd finished just in time.

"Going to oil the wood?" he asked.

"Oil wood?"

"Horses will start cribbing if you don't creosote."

I noticed that sometimes Achilles nibbled the wood off the
edge of his stall. I never thought of creosote.

He continued. "What you want to do is to mix two-thirds
creosote and one-third crankcase oil. Any old oil from your car
or tractor will do."

Using big paintbrushes, Mary and I painted on the mixture,
being careful not to splash it on our skin, since creosote burns.
The next day, the day of our invasion, the stalls were still wet
and we wiped them down with rags.

I ran extra wire along the tops of the fencing in case Wildfire became bored.

The end of the barn nearest the stalls was made into a tack
room. Since we had none of the fixtures used for bridles, I took
six tin cans, bent the edges of one end out in several places, and
drove nails through these edges, fastening the can firmly on the
wall.

"Great," Eleanor said, hanging Achilles' bridle on one and
Jenny's on another. "Why didn't we do this sooner?"

Jane Merriman's metal saddle holder extended neatly from
the wall. I took two-by-four pieces of wood and built seven
more.

We were amazed by the stalls. To say they were magnificent was no overstatement. Somehow we'd concocted a perfect
blend of oil and creosote and the wood came out the color of
lightly stained mahogany, a shade that would grace a playroom
or library. It appeared too elegant for a stall.

Eleanor could hardly believe the transformation. "They're
better looking than my room. I'm moving up here. And Achilles
definitely should get one."

"Sorry about that," I said. "These are for paying guests
only."

Sally telephoned and said they'd arrive about nine. She
asked if we had enough light in the barn.

"I told her we had a light in each stall," Mary said during supper.

Paul looked thoughtful. "You know what! I just thought of something. You put in new floors, which raises everything about four or five inches. Doesn't that mean the lights will be a lot closer to the horses' heads?"

I put down my fork with a sigh. "You're right. You're absolutely right. Good thinking. That's too close. If the horses are as big as Jane's and they tossed their heads, they could cut themselves."

"What about Mrs. Merriman's horse?" he asked.

"We don't have a light in her stall."

We rushed up to the barn. Why is it that things done at the last moment always seem to be the most difficult? Moving the fixtures to the ceiling outside of the stalls is fussy work. I'd hurt my finger earlier, which hampered me.

Mark eyed my work critically. "Not too good, Pop. You're hurrying too much. Better let me do it," he said with a sixteen-year-old's forthrightness.

"I just want to get it finished in time."

"I can do it . . . You and Mother look really tired."

"My finger does hurt," I admitted. "It's all yours. Thanks." I climbed off the stepladder.

About the time Mark finished moving the last one, we heard the heavy grinding gears and the rumble of a horse van. We looked out the window. Its headlights were like flaming eyes, and as it hit the low branches of our trees lining our driveway the sound resembled that of a huge monster crashing through a forest. The three animals in the barn lifted their heads, ears forward, as they tried to assess the potential danger of the unfamiliar sounds. Hubert honked threateningly but stayed close to Jenny's stall.

"If they're unloading the horses down by our house, they won't have a light," Eleanor said. "I wish we'd told them to come up here."

We ran across the field. "Wait for me," Mary called. "I'm not used to running in the dark."

The massive van stopped. At the house, our driveway en-

circled a small sunken garden of rose bushes and taxus. A low
wall formed the edge. The huge truck couldn't make it around
the circle and stopped to unload where it was. We could hear
the whinnying of horses and the stamping of hooves.

The girls were returning from a show and were still dressed
in their good boots, jodhpurs, and jackets.

Eleanor whispered to me, "Maybe next year I'll be unloading Achilles from a show."

"How did you do?" Mark asked, hands in pockets. He'd
wandered out.

"I got a Reserve Championship and a first and second,"
Sally said. "And Anne won two firsts and a second. Phoebe
didn't go in the show." She held up a silver plate.

"Sally, how exciting," Mary said, giving the girl a hug.

The driver surprised us. I thought he'd be large, but he was
very small. Later Sally told us he'd been a jockey. Clambering
up the sides of the van he threw open the doors. A dim light
inside only dissolved a little of the outside blackness. Then the
driver pushed out a heavy, long ramp.

I felt they were too close to the wall, which dropped off
about three or four feet on the other side.

Jenny answered the whinnying and snorting horses with a
high-pitched, drawn-out braying, ending in something like
choked-off sobs. Hubert added to the cacophony with a blast of
his own.

"I guess they want to know what's going on," Phoebe
laughed.

"I'll take Wildfire out first, because if I don't she's going to
tear your truck apart. Listen to her kicking," Anne said. She
turned to the driver. "Hold Morning Mist until we're away from
the van."

I'd sent Mark for a flashlight. Since the batteries were weak,
however, it didn't help much. I flashed the wavering light on
the low wall.

Suddenly a black form rushed down the ramp at us, drag-
ging Anne along. There was a clatter and the sound of somebody falling. Anne plunged over the wall and Wildfire began to
fall on top of her.

"Oh my Lord," Mary cried out.

I dropped the flashlight and grabbed the halter rope, pulling back on it as hard as I could. Wildfire stumbled to her knees on the wall for an instant and then scrambled backward, yanking me with her. Anne jumped back on the wall and took hold of the rope with me.

"Are you all right?" I asked.

"I'm okay . . . Thanks for holding him. He could have really cut himself up." It was a matter-of-fact reply. No mention of the danger she'd been in. The girl immediately began feeling the mare's knees to see if she was hurt. The safety of her horse had been her first thought, and any cuts or bruises she herself might have could be taken care of later.

"This is *not* a good start," Mary murmured. "I have funny feelings about it."

"Oh, Mother!" Eleanor whispered urgently, fearful the girls would hear.

Morning Mist was a large and handsome dappled gray gelding. In contrast to the excitable Wildfire, he walked down the ramp quietly, sniffed the air, and looked around him peacefully.

"More my style," Mary observed more or less to herself.

Phoebe's pony, Peppermint, followed.

The girls walked their horses to the barn while Mark and Paul hitched the tractor to our wagon and brought it to the truck so we could take up all their gear. There were five trunks, a number of buckets, five or six saddles, many bridles, blankets, boxes.

The tack room now began to really look like one. Each saddle was on its holder. I'd taught Eleanor that a saddle should be either on a horse's back or on the holder. If you have to place it on the floor for a few moments, set the saddle on its front end, upright. It can be damaged by putting it either on its back or its bottom, when it spreads out.

With all the lights blazing, the barn seemed to take on the activity of a basketball game. The horses were stamping and snorting in their stables, the girls rushing back and forth getting their buckets filled with water, placing hay in the stalls, giving them a little grain.

"Do you have a hook we can hang our buckets on?" Anne asked.

"We've been keeping Achilles' and Jenny's on the floor," Mary said.

"Mother!" Eleanor winced. She worried they'd find out too quickly we were not experts.

"It's better for them," the girl explained. "Their throats are so long it makes it harder for them to drink water or to eat grain."

Their buckets were clean and new. Ours were old and tired.

I handed Anne a few hooks I'd found.

"Maybe you could get some bigger and heavier ones tomorrow. The horses will pull these out in no time."

"They will?" Mary said, looking more worried. "I never realized how violent they were."

Eleanor moved away.

Anne had gone to get a blanket and Wildfire decided she would go along too. She leaned briefly against the single strand of rope that Eleanor and Mary had put up earlier in the day. It pulled out immediately. The big horse trotted past Mary, snorting, looking from side to side, giving the impression of being unpredictable.

"Good grief!" Mary said. "Eleanor, watch out!"

Anne turned around. "Hey you . . . ! Get back in that stall," she yelled in a surprisingly rough voice. "What're you doing out?" She grabbed her halter and hit her.

The horse jerked her head up.

We may not be experts, but we don't hit our horses, I thought to myself.

"We need a web," Sally said. "Do you have one?"

Built out of pieces of canvas, a web is like a net stronger than a gate or rope. Four big bolts are screwed into the wood to hold each corner. It has a slide hook to fasten and unfasten it.

"We'll get some." I sighed, looking at Mary. As usual at such times, we could read each other's mind.

Blankets were put on the horses. We seldom put one on Achilles unless the weather was freezing. Furthermore, we never bound his legs. All three of these horses had neat bandages around their ankles. Wildfire's were green, which made a nice color contrast with her dark coat. Morning Mist's were blue, a complement to gray.

"Are you going to let them all out together tomorrow?" Phoebe asked.

"I think so. They'll probably mix it up a bit with Glorious Girl and Achilles, but I find horses really don't hurt one another unless they're mean. Your two horses get along, don't they?" I asked Sally and Anne.

"They're in love with each other," Anne replied.

At that point her horse squealed, lifted her head high, and bit one of the boards separating the stalls, tearing a big chunk out of it. Morning Mist, used to her friend's antics, continued eating.

"That's love?" Mary asked.

The creosote burned Wildfire's mouth. Served her right for marring our beautiful job! The mare licked her lips, flattened her ears against her head, and with another squeal turned around and kicked the boards viciously. Chips of wood flew in the air.

"Cut it out," Anne yelled, threatening the horse with her arm. "She's pretty high-strung. At the other stable she was always kicking out the stalls."

"Kicking them out!" Mary said, eyes wide. "Then what happens?"

"They have to be rebuilt."

"So will I after this project," I heard her mutter.

"Oh, I forgot," Sally said. "Wildfire gets six quarts of grain in the morning and Morning Mist five. Peppermint gets two, doesn't she Phoebe?" The pony was in Jenny's old stall and Jenny was where we'd kept the chickens.

Phoebe nodded. "And then some hay."

"Right . . . Give them a couple of sections of a bale. The grass doesn't have as many vitamins and minerals at this time of year." A bale of hay is pressed into six or seven sections.

"I forgot something else," Anne said apologetically. "The

blankets should come off in the morning. You take them both off and then put the outer one back on."

With a squeal, Wildfire belted the sides of the stall again. More chips of wood flew up.

Mary jumped apprehensively. "I don't want you going in there," she said to Eleanor.

"Oh, Mother!"

"Oh Mother, nothing."

"Eleanor and I figured you'd like to do it," I teased Mary. "Thanks."

Anne laughed. "Don't worry. If she looks like she's going to kick, just yell at her."

"What happens if you lose your voice?" Mary said.

Eleanor rolled up her eyes.

"One more thing," Sally said. "Could you get wood shavings instead of straw?"

I had quite a bit of straw on hand. "Wood shavings?"

"They're so much easier to handle. Straw gets bulky. The shavings absorb the dirt and moisture better. It's more expensive, but it's worth it."

I felt Mary looking at me. "I'll check it out."

"They come in bags."

"Fine."

"It's better for their feet."

I was beginning to wonder what was better for our pocketbook.

After the girls were satisfied that their animals were comfortably ensconced in their new quarters, we went back to the van. The girls planned to ride home in it.

"Understand somebody wanted to buy Morning Mist today," the driver said to Sally.

"If I sold him, what would I ride?"

"Heard you were offered twenty thousand."

Mary stumbled.

"How come Wildfire didn't have an offer?" the driver teased Anne.

"They'd have to talk about twenty-five thousand before I'd even consider it."

I wondered why they weren't entirely wrapped in cotton and rubber padding. I knew what was going to happen. Every time they'd snort, I'd be rushing out of my office to see if they were all right.

The van drove off.

"I think I'm going to check out the barn. I'm not sure if I locked the feed room," I said. "All we'd need is to have them break in, overeat, and die of colic."

"I'll go with you," Mary said.

Eleanor wanted to come along.

"Those girls seem like intrepid youngsters," I said.

"What's that mean?" Eleanor asked.

Just inside the barn I pulled on the light, took out my dictionary, and fumbled for my glasses, slapping at my pockets.

Eleanor looked at her mother with an amused glance. "Why don't you just tell me, Daddy?"

"I don't have an unabridged mental dictionary . . ." I looked at the page. "Interesting. This has a good little essay . . . Bold. Fearless . . . Essentially it means not afraid, from Latin *in*, 'not,' and *trepidus*, 'alarmed.' "

Wildfire squealed and kicked.

"I'm *trepidus*," Mary murmured.

I read from the dictionary. "Intrepid implies absolute fearlessness and especially suggests dauntlessness in facing the new and the unknown."

"Our perennial situation on Good Ground Farm," Mary nodded.

But Eleanor wasn't listening. She saw the trunks. "They aren't locked. Do you think it's all right if I take a look?"

"I don't see why not," Mary replied.

Gingerly she lifted the top of one and looked into it. There were other blankets, several halters, different kinds of bits, saddle pads, riding crops, lead reins, lunge lines.

But it was the next two trunks that caused her to catch her breath. They were like giant cosmetic cases containing jars of vitamins and special powders whose names she couldn't pronounce. There was Vaseline, water-resistant protection stuff for lesions, vapor rub, liniment, Epsom salts, beeswax, special sprays, hoof dressing, saddle soap, complexion creams that even Eleanor and Mary found they used. She discovered iodine, boric acid, alcohol, woven bandages for the legs, cotton, Q-tips. There was a huge electric shaver.

"I don't believe it," Eleanor gasped. "It's practically like something a movie star would use . . . Poor Achilles. He doesn't have anything. I have a couple of brushes. Look at all the ones they have. They have eleven, and six metal curry combs and a metal scraper. I have a hoof pick."

I joined Mary on a bale of hay as Eleanor looked through the equipment. "We have enough grain for about two days."

"Margaret White will be here with her horses in two days."

We heard a loud squeal and then the crash of steel hooves against wood.

Mary and I looked at each other. We were embarked on another "interesting" project!

"I wish we didn't think about money and everything so I could have the kind of equipment they do," Eleanor said.

"What would it change?" Mary asked.

Eleanor didn't understand.

"I mean what difference would it really make with Achilles or Jenny?"

"All those beautiful blankets and vitamins and soap . . . And did you see the combs and brushes . . . ?"

"I'm still asking you, what difference would it make for your horse?" Mary said.

"He'd be so beautiful and handsome . . ."

I took Eleanor by the hand. "I want to show you something. Take a good look at those two horses, Wildfire and Morning Mist . . . See their tails for example. Okay?" We walked to the next section, turning on the light. "Now look at your love. What do you think of his tail. See how long and luxurious it is. A tail is one of the signs of health in a horse and his is just as beautiful as theirs. That's what your mother means . . . And he doesn't bite or kick and you don't have to yell at him."

"He'd faint if I yelled."

"It's the love and basic care you give that counts. It's never just because you have a lot of things. It's what you give. Achilles is a good example of what you've given him."

She smiled. "I understand, Dad." Then she looked at the tack room wistfully. "But it would be a lot of fun."

We turned off the lights and walked toward the house. Mary and I stopped, looking around us. We could just barely see where the fields ended and the trees began. In the far distance were the outlines of hills, just a few shades darker than the sky. To our right the land rose gently, and beyond the hedgerow and fields a hill encircled a part of our farm.

Mary looked up. "Sometimes I like to think that the sky is really just a piece of cloth and that the stars are really holes letting in light from heaven."

"Remember that old song, 'Pennies From Heaven'? I wish some of them would slip through the holes . . . Our problem is we're too attached to this place."

We heard a squeal and a thud from the barn.

Mary squeezed my hand. "I like *our kind* of love!"

16

A half mile from our bedroom window, against the black background of a night pregnant with a feeling of snow, Trappers Mountain Ski Area, with lights flashing like Fourth of July sparklers, resembled an elaborate glittering Christmas toy.

The lights sprinkled the spotless snow with a coruscating brilliance. The branches of trees, trembling to wind puffs and weaving back and forth in front of the lights, seemed to set everything in motion. The outline of two tow ropes and the chair lift towers were just visible.

Anticipating a snowfall of several inches, the growling snow tractors attacked the lumpy moguls, flattening them decisively to the level of the ski slope.

"It's too beautiful to stay inside," Mary rhapsodized. "We've got to go out for a walk before we go to bed. Let's go past the ski slope."

Our lower driveway took us to an old dirt road, laid hundreds of years ago, paralleling the river, going from town to city. Crusts of snow crunched in dry, squeaking sounds under our feet. Except for the occasional puffs of wind, the night was still —as weightless as a powder puff, while tiny flakes of snow spun around us in whirling dances.

For a while we watched the noisy tractors making the slope ready for skiers. Once in a while a man in a bulky gray parka walked across the lighted snowscape looking as if he were an astronaut exploring the moon. The cold touched our faces like icy fingers.

"All the horses are in, but when I tried to get Jenny, the silly thing kept running away from me . . . She's got to be the most perverse creature I know. Eleanor could do it, but I don't like to have her around the barn after dark. I'll try to get Jenny when we get back. It's too cold for her to stay out," I said. Mark and Paul were at the movies with friends, Celine away with friends, and Estelle visiting her grandmother.

We walked up Mule Hill Road to our driveway. Mary continued to the house and I went looking for Jenny. Tramping across the field, I found her with her hindquarters to a fence which bordered a patch of trees only slightly breaking the breeze. Her tail was tucked between her legs, her head down. I knew the thick, shaggy winter coat would keep her warm for a while, but not enough for the full night.

She didn't acknowledge me at first. As I approached, however, she walked slowly away, always keeping just beyond the reach of my hand. She headed down the hill of the next field and I guessed she was intending to stay near the stream at the bottom. Sometimes she'd take shelter there since it was low and protected from the wind.

"Jenny, I'm trying to help you," I shouted after her. "How can you be so obtuse . . . Sometimes you're the most obtuse creature I've ever known. Okay . . . If you want to stay out, stay out."

I trudged through the snow to the house.

Our bedroom faced northwest and took the brunt of the weather. The winds seeped through the window frames. Because the windows were the kind that opened outward rather than up, I found it almost impossible to close them tightly enough to make them windproof. The compound you can buy to fill in cracks helped somewhat. Usually by morning our room was about as cool as the outside temperature. Except for the problem of stepping out of a warm bed and into a gelid room, we rather liked the experience.

As I lay in bed, I thought about the word *obtuse* I'd used to describe Jenny. Was it the correct usage? I didn't think so.

Earlier in the day I'd written about the word. I find it entertaining to trace the history of words that begin their careers as practical descriptions of concrete objects or situations. Generations later they end up figuratively portraying a human quality.

Obtuse, I learned, comes from the Latin *obtundere* and means "to beat on," or "to make dull as the edge of an ax or knife." Anyone who's mowed lawns knows that at the end of a season of cutting grass and inadvertently striking stones and the like, the blade of your lawnmower becomes dull.

Figuratively, that's the way it is with *obtuse* people. Their minds have a dull edge and have difficulty "cutting" through to anything that takes a reasonable amount of thought or sensitivity. They don't have the emotional and intellectual capacity to respond, which makes them seem slow or stupid.

I'd used the wrong word on Jenny. She was neither slow nor stupid. She was obstinate. Willful. Even so, I loved and appreciated her though she never held an equivalent affection for me, or for that matter for any male adult. We conjectured a man must have treated her brutally. She could never forget whatever it was that had happened.

Yet with children, she was invariably gentle and protective.

Though I tend to be anthropomorphic about animals, getting along with almost all I come across, I learned early on you must never completely trust them. They are not reasoning human beings.

Therefore, when we were first getting to know one another, I noticed that sometimes she'd hunch herself as if preparing to kick me. I worried she might seriously hurt someone. Horses act that way before they lash out with their hooves. At the time, I didn't realize this would be totally out of character for Jenny. She never injured a living thing . . . except me. Once I leaned across her back while talking to someone. Unexpectedly she jerked upward quickly.

I broke a rib.

Another time, she'd lost her halter somewhere in the field, and I was attempting to get her back to the barn. I had one arm around her neck and my other hand squeezed her nose, an acceptable method to control a horse. She was balky, having no intention of going into the barn. She pushed against a small tree. A branch poked my eye. I went to the emergency clinic.

She stepped on my foot and broke my little toe.

Thinking about her antics, I fell asleep.

About midnight I awoke. The rising wind made whistling sounds through the window cracks. I knew by the feel of the air the temperature had dropped—probably far below freezing.

We'd acquired Jenny when she'd been middle-aged and now she'd joined the Senior Citizen category. She was still tough. No question as to that. On the other hand, the weather was bitterly cold and the wind intensified the situation. Perhaps now her stall in the barn would be enticing.

However, this meant my getting out of a delightfully warm bed, dressing, putting on boots, sweater, parka, gloves. I'd be fully awake by then and would have trouble getting back to sleep.

Yet I knew if I didn't go I'd lie here worrying about her and wouldn't be able to get to sleep anyway. Occasionally, conscience makes us minor martyrs to duty.

My flashlight swept the field nearest the barn, penetrating the mist of falling snow, illuminating the individual swirling flakes. I walked around the perimeter.

Since I couldn't find her, she was probably where I'd last seen her, near the stream. Standing halfway down the slope, I moved my flashlight slowly back and forth, growing anxious.

Going down the steep incline, I walked along the tree line close to the stream.

"Jenny . . ."

She'd never answer, but it made me feel as if I was doing something a bit more. "Jenny," I shouted, shining the light around me.

The beam shown on a cedar tree and an irregular bush alongside of it. I flashed the light beyond and then brought it back because I wondered if I'd seen something move. Suddenly I realized the irregular bush was Jenny. When I called she twitched an ear, apparently the only thing she could move.

I hurried to her. Covered with snow, she looked like one of the ice statues at winter carnivals. Brushing the snow off her, I gave the burro a pat. "Come on, old girl, we'd better get you in."

I tugged on the halter. She remained in the same spot. I thought this was just the same old stubbornness and pulled again, encouraging her with visions of a warm stall. Perhaps if I could get her to move her legs. Bending over, I tried to lift one. I couldn't budge it. Now I understood the problem. Her feet were frozen in the ground and she was too cold and stiff to exert the force needed to pull them out.

Scooping the snow away from each delicately shaped foot, I used a stone to loosen the ground. Pulling upward again carefully I freed them, scraping away the frozen clumps of dirt fastened to the hooves.

When I tried to lead her again, she still wouldn't or couldn't move.

"Now what's wrong?" I asked. "Maybe you're a masochist, but I'm not. Let's go home."

Her eyelids were frosted over and I wasn't sure she could even see me. She probably had an ice cube in each ear. "Jenny, you've got to make an effort. If you don't get home soon, you're going to be in big trouble. You will have *had* it . . . and I'll feel guilty the rest of my life. *Move!*"

Getting behind her, I pushed, though not too hard because if she fell down, I wasn't sure what we could do. Mary, the children, and I probably couldn't get her back to the barn. If she'd only take one step! I pushed again, and she swayed. I kept shoving. One leg moved.

Quickly I took the halter and pulled. She needed my help, for she stumbled frequently. The barn was no more than a quarter of a mile away, yet a five-minute walk took us half an hour.

What a relief to open the heavy door, to be out of the

burning wind, to feel and smell the warmth of the other animals, to hear their snorts and stamping feet.

In the passageway I used a brush to get the snow off. Her body quivered from the cold. Putting her in the stall, I took two of the pony's extra blankets and covered Jenny.

Hurrying to the house, I heated water, bringing it to the barn, making a warm mash for her out of the grain. I held the bucket in front of her.

To my consternation, she looked at it without interest. Jenny not interested in eating was like the sun not rising in the morning.

"It's the best meal you've probably ever had or will have. Come on. *Eat!*"

She pushed her nose forward a bit as I lifted the bucket closer. "It'll warm you up. You'll feel like a new burro."

She nibbled, at first tentatively and then with increasing enthusiasm. I sighed. All was well at Good Ground Farm.

The following day, Sunday, came up ideal for skiers—powder snow on a base, no wind, and a cerulean sky.

Home from church we decided to go skiing after feeding the animals. Trapper's Mountain was already packed with skiers, the hill looking as crowded as a honeycomb discovered by a colony of ants.

Happily Jenny seemed as normal as the hay she munched, with no signs of ill effects of the night before, and so we let her out with the horses.

I don't know how it happened. Apparently someone left the gate either open or unlatched because soon after we saw Jenny walking down the driveway in the direction of Mule Hill Road. Fortunately none of the horses were with her this time.

A number of words bubbled up in my mind as to how I felt about her after last evening's episode—ungrateful, thankless, unappreciative, ill-mannered, boorish, unaware, selfish.

Mark, Paul, and Eleanor tried to corral her. She evaded them with her usual cagey tactics. Always before when she'd reached Mule Hill Road, she'd turn left, going to one of the other farms, or to Vijay Peterson's house.

Today, for some obscure reason deep in her donkeyish

mind, she turned right. This didn't trouble me until I remembered that Mule Hill joined the road leading to the ski area. Today it would be thick with cars.

I dashed into the house to get Mary.

She gasped when I explained. "That could be a disaster."

"I think our best chance is to go through the woods to Ski Hill Road. If she's coming in that direction we can intercept her . . . Maybe."

After tramping through our woods we stood on a crest with a good view of the road and slope. Both of the ski ropes and the chair lift were operating, with people waiting their turn. A line of cars moved slowly heading toward the parking area.

Mary pointed. "Oh my Lord! Here she comes!"

Jenny trotted along the road, unaware of the commotion she caused. She zigzagged in front and behind the cars, holding her head high, looking from side to side. The vehicles slammed on brakes, blew horns, barely avoiding her and each other. Mark and Paul were about two or three cars behind her. Not able to keep up with her brothers, Eleanor cut across the fields.

We rushed down the side of the hill.

"What's your plan now?" Mary panted, tripping and sliding on the field grass, slippery because of the snow.

"Get to the other side of the road. Maybe we can drive her back in this direction. At least she'd be in our woods."

"Is there a better way?" Mary fell on her fanny, bumping along for a few feet.

"Can you think of one?"

"Moving into an apartment with no pets . . . What happens if she's the cause of an accident."

"Stop thinking negatively." *But what would happen?* I should have let her remain an ice sculpture.

Just as we reached the road, Jenny broke into her choppy gallop, veering toward the ski slope.

We darted across the road, almost causing our own accident with a car.

"We've got to get over those bales and on the slope," I shouted, pointing to the barrier of hay that kept skiers from plunging off the bank and onto the road.

"I'm exhausted . . . I can't," Mary cried.

"You've got to," I exhorted. "Here, I'll give you a boost." I joined my hands together and pushed her upward. She sprawled over the bales. I scrambled up, pulling her to her feet. People stared.

This was Jenny's time and she knew it. She cantered across the beginner's area, head held high, the small stiff tail going in circles.

The slope was crowded with children and novice adults, some hanging onto the tow rope, others practicing snow plows or skiing downhill on the gentle slope.

She barreled through them, tripping over the tow rope. The skiers dropped as if they'd been machine-gunned. Frightened, many of the children cried and women screamed.

A chair lift operated just beyond. She scooted in front of one of the chairs and it hit her side. Her heels flew out harmlessly. The occupant scrunched down in his chair. The operator cut the switch abruptly. The chairs rocked back and forth.

Since the main slope is extremely precipitous, people tend to go across from one side to the other, often reaching high speeds as they slash their skis around in sharp turns, sending sprays of snow. Today there were three or four hundred crowded together on this relatively small slope, testing their skills.

Exhilarated by her success, Jenny sallied back and forth over the snow, creating wild havoc. We'd chase her in one direction and then she'd plunge around and run in another. To avoid her, people spun out of control, fell, slid down the slope, slammed into each other. Some ran into her, flipping over her back or sliding under her belly.

Bodies lay strewn over the hill.

After a few more harrowing moments of this melee, she decided to leave. The rapidly moving tow rope, with one strand higher than the other, must have seemed like one of the broken fences she was used to squeezing through.

She ran into it. The upper rope slapped hard against her back. The lower one hit her belly. Startled and angry she kicked at them and they slapped against her legs. Letting out a long, sobbing bray that someone said later sounded like a roar from a strange, terrifying beast, she charged down the tow rope.

Seeing this apparition bearing down on them, panicked skiers let go of the moving rope, spilling off in both directions, flopping and sliding down the hills, skis askew, yelling and swearing.

Galloping, she crossed the road in a burst of speed, her feet kicking out at the cars. Tires squealed as drivers jammed on brakes. One car skidded around in a circle. Running along the old road adjacent to our property, Jenny disappeared from view.

Mary was one of those spread-eagled on the snow. "I can't move," she whispered. "I've never been so wiped out."

I gasped for breath, my own legs as heavy as if I were wearing my ankle weights. I helped her up.

Eleanor doubled over laughing. "If I'd only brought my camera. People wouldn't believe it!"

I had visions of lawsuits running through my head. "Let's get out of here."

For a few moments we stood on the edge of the road, inconspicuously melding in with the astonished crowd. We wanted to be certain no one was seriously injured.

"She yours?" a man chuckled.

"Never saw her before."

"You all were chasing her hard enough . . . What were you going to do if you caught her?"

"Ever try burro burgers?"

We watched the ski patrol check the slopes, helping people up, recovering skis that had come off. Three people were brought to the medical hut for further observation. Another one came on a toboggan guided by two members of the ski patrol. One of them raised his hand to us, grinning. "Hi, Mr. Funk."

I recognized Bill Miller, Peter and John's friend.

"Some excitement she caused," he laughed.

I raised a finger to my lips and went over to him. "Bill, was anyone hurt? I feel responsible."

"Nah . . . It was good practice. Most of them don't know how to ski anyway." He smiled. "Don't worry."

An hour later Mark and Paul came into the house, cheeks bright red from the cold and their exertions.

"She ran another couple of miles . . . Mark caught her when she was so tired she couldn't go any farther."

Over hot cocoa, sitting in front of a fire, we compared our experiences and what we'd seen, laughing at what had become an indelible family memory.

17

You wouldn't think a potato salad could reveal a secret that affected many lives. But Nellie Johnson's did, though it took a funeral for us to discover this.

She helped Mary clean the house once a week. During holidays she'd telephone us. "I've made some potato salad for you. You can pick it up after four." We discovered her potato salad a delightful treat.

Nellie, black, in her upper sixties, used her voice expressively. We had no problem recognizing her when she telephoned us during one Easter season.

"Who's going with me to pick up Nellie's salad?" I asked.

"I'll go," sixteen-year-old Mark said.

"How come your potato salad doesn't taste as good as hers, Mother?" Eleanor asked.

"I don't know. I can't figure out what she does with it."

"Have you ever asked her?" Estelle wondered.

"Yes, but she just smiles and changes the subject."

"It wouldn't be the same kind of holiday without Nellie's potato salad. Can we have it tonight, Mom?"

Nellie lived at the end of a side street in a small, two-storied gray, asphalt shingled house.

We rang the doorbell. In a moment she opened the door, welcoming us with a wide warm smile. Her happy expression, tinged with surprise at the good fortune of having you drop in, came from a generous, gracious heart. "Oh, Mark!" she said, her eyes brightening. "I didn't know you was coming too . . . Come in . . . Come on in."

The door closed behind us. Her living room reminded me of a doll house on exhibition. It couldn't hold much in the way of furniture—a stuffed chair, a Victorian love seat, a low bureau, several hard-backed chairs. The room had been slightly larger before she'd split a third of it off into a tiny parlor, separated from the living room by a waist-high wall with four posts reaching to the ceiling. On the surface of the wall she'd placed various knickknacks. What I recall most clearly about these rooms and her house is that everything was meticulously neat. I'd never been in a home that was neater or cleaner than hers.

"Mark," her voice softened in a musical intimacy. "Mark, I haven't seen you in a *long* while. You're always at school when I'm at your house. My, look at that red hair and ain't you growed though. You're going to be a bigger man than your daddy," she laughed.

My memory of Nellie is of a handsome woman, immaculately turned out, not a wrinkle in the dress covering her ample torso. The seams of the stockings on her thin legs always ran straight up and down. She kept her hair, somewhat thinning, carefully groomed, close to her head.

"Come on and see my kitchen," she said, waving her hand, turning her head. "I just had it finished. My children gave me some money to do it."

She'd taken an ordinary house with no particular personality and year by year transformed it until it was truly reflective of her tastes—tidy, feminine, attractive.

"All these cabinets are new." She opened some of the doors. "And I have everything in them *just so* . . . Do you like the white counters?"

We did and said so.

She held up an enormous bowl. "I peeled so many potatoes for this salad . . . Oh, my hands. They ached like something."

"That's too much work for you, Nellie," Mark said, concerned.

"That's all right. I know you like it."

"We sure do," he grinned, leaning his weight from one foot to the other, hands in his pockets. "Mom's going to have it for supper tonight . . . How do you get it to taste so good?"

"Yes. What's your secret ingredient, Nellie?" I added, hoping she'd slip and reveal it.

She smiled. "And Mark, you look here now. I made an apple pie for you, too. I know you like apple pie."

"Nellie, that's so nice of you . . . You're so nice."

Years later I thought of how nice she was as I sat in Mount Zion Church at her funeral.

Three days previously, one of her sons telephoned, his voice a low, shy monotone. "Mamma died last night." He told me when and where the funeral would be held.

The small Baptist church, unadorned, needing paint, lopsided with age, was squeezed in between two modest-sized homes. A hearse and two limousines were parked in front.

The door creaked when we opened it, and some of the people already there turned to look at us. Though fifteen minutes early I wondered if I'd misheard the time, since the old black minister was already preaching.

A woman in a white uniform—the dress of some women's order—showed us to a pew, handing us a leaflet listing the different parts of the simple service. Beneath a penciled drawing of a cross were the words: *The Going Home of Sis. Nellie Johnson.* Not *in memory of* or *a testimony to,* but a "going home." *Home!* What a comforting word. So redolent of warmth, shelter, comfort, protection.

Nellie was going home.

Her family sat in front of us. The men wore conservative dark suits, the women subdued, tailored clothes and traditional hats. One of the hats, made of black straw with a crown and a broad brim, glistened in the mellow light.

A high platform with steps on the left side formed the chancel, with a lectern in the center and a smaller one near the steps. To the right of the chancel eight women and a man sat in choir stalls, forming the choir. Five of the women wore yellow robes with a deep, red V around the neck. The man and the other three women were dressed in white robes. The children of a young, pretty woman at the far end of the choir periodically climbed on their mother's lap. During some of the hymns, she rocked her daughter back and forth. The children seemed content to be a natural part of this happening.

Centered against the chancel, Sister Nellie Johnson's metallic-gray casket formed a focal point. The spray of flowers behind the casket rose as high as the lectern, almost hiding short Pastor Hayes as he spoke.

A few seconds after we were seated, he glanced at his watch, mentioning the formal service would not begin for fifteen minutes. But he talked a bit about Nellie and quoted a few verses from the Bible. During this period the choir spontaneously and quietly began singing, just low enough so that the music did not intrude on the minister's voice.

Mary and I were keenly aware of the contrast between this tiny wooden structure and the magnificence of the cathedrals in Europe and even the other churches in town with their stained-glass windows, tall spires, and sense of permanency.

When not preaching, Pastor Hayes sat in the middle chair of a group of three massive ones, whose tall backs were set close to the rear wall.

After a few moments, Pastor Hayes stated that anyone who would like to honor Sister Nellie Johnson by viewing her body could do so. He ordered Missionary Ruth and Deacon Walter to stand by at either end of her casket.

The young deacon rose from his bench nearest the chancel and took his position. Missionary Ruth, an older, heavy woman, came down from the choir.

No one got up.

The family, of course, had already "viewed" her, and we supposed that those who'd arrived earlier had done so also. Mary and I glanced at each other, agreeing to "honor" Nellie.

Because of her illness, the effect of death, and the "artistry" of the undertaker, this wasn't the Nellie we knew so well. Yet there was a soft beauty to her, for her family and friends dressed her in a delicately beautiful pink dress. Even in death, her neatness and her ladylike qualities continued, as in a recurring theme of music.

Memories of Nellie circled my mind.

One day, as Mary walked through the kitchen preparing to do her shopping in town, Nellie looked up from her work.

"You going out without stockings on?" she had asked, surprised.

"Oh . . . Well . . . Yes, I guess so," Mary replied uncertainly.

"That's not being neat as you should. You should always go out as neat as you can be. I want people to know I work in a real nice house so I can be proud of my work." She paused. "I get dressed up when I come here," she added with pointed emphasis, speaking more as a mother instructing her daughter than an employee to an employer. "When you walk into a store, you want the clerk to say to hisself, 'This is a real lady. I can tell by the way she looks.' "

Another time she watched Mary laboring over a pile of ironing. "You're making too much work for yourself. Here's a real easy way you can do a shirt without turning it over." She sat at the ironing board, her hands moving the iron deftly. She passed along to Mary many old-time domestic skills. "I like housekeeping," she said.

Pastor Hayes collected my wandering thoughts when he began praying. He thanked God for Sister Nellie Johnson's presence in their lives, for her influence on the congregation, for being such a fine Christian. During this prayer, the little girl in the choir seat snuggled in her mother's arms.

After two short lessons from the Old Testament and the New Testament, he announced the choir would sing a hymn. Taking a few measures to get their voices together, they sang movingly without a piano or organ.

The pastor turned to the young mother. "Sister Harriet, would you come and read the cards, telegrams, and letters from all Sister Nellie Johnson's friends and relations." Placing her child aside, Sister Harriet walked to the chancel, reading clearly.

When she'd finished, Pastor Hayes stood up again. "Sister Nellie Johnson always liked to hear young people singing. We don't have many of them here today, but those we have are going to sing her favorite song."

Three young women stepped down from the choir to the main floor of the church, joined by Deacon Walter. One of the girls, with unusually large, shining eyes, signaled to a youngster just behind us to join them. He looked like her younger brother. I can't recall the name of the hymn, but it pointed out that "I'm going to you Lord, and I will make my account with you in person. Nobody else can say anything about me that counts. You're the only one Lord that knows what's in my heart."

During the song one of the girls began to cry.

The girl with the luminous eyes went to the podium to give the "obituary," telling where and when Sister Nellie was born, the fact she has two daughters, a son, and four grandchildren. She began to cry and couldn't continue. Pastor Hayes stepped forward, telling a bit more about Nellie, emphasizing her goodness to everyone.

On the way to the funeral Mary said, "I always liked having Nellie in the house because I knew she loved children. She always asked about them, where they were, what they were doing. She actually worried about them. She really cared about the people she worked for."

Nellie also worried about the world. She'd say something like "What do you think about what the President said?" Mary learned that this was an introduction for Nellie to give her views, which she did. And she'd listen respectfully to Mary's.

During the fall we gave apples to Nellie, and she made her famous pies for many families. Once, when our trees were through bearing for the season, Mary suggested she bring apples home from a neighbor for whom she worked also. They had a fuller orchard than we. Nellie didn't reply. We found out later that the neighbor had once magnanimously offered her a few spoiled apples. Dozens and dozens of better ones were lying on the ground. I wasn't surprised. These were the same people who paid Peter and John a munificent twenty-five cents for an afternoon's work of rounding up their scattered sheep.

Another memory fleetingly touched my mind—that of Nellie frequently taking care of a chronically ill youngster, treating her as lovingly as she would her own child.

My attention returned to the church when young Deacon Walter walked up the steps to the podium. I noticed that when he sang, he closed his eyes, his body moving gracefully in time to the music. His job was now to represent Mount Zion's whole congregation.

He spoke quietly and personally.

"When Mr. Johnson was alive, he and Sister Nellie used to have a little candy store in their house . . . I remember when I was real small and sometimes I'd go there with only a nickel because that's all I had, she'd give me thirty cents worth of candy.

"That's always the way Sister Nellie was. Always giving to somebody. And when I grew up, I used to stop in and see her. We'd laugh a lot together and she'd always make you feel so good.

"That's the way she was with people. Always trying to make them feel good. Even at the end when she was sometimes so sick she could hardly walk, she'd be out visiting other sick people and pray with them."

He wiped his eyes. "We're going to miss her. Everyone around here is going to miss Sister Nellie."

Pastor Hayes took over, giving what he called the "eulogy." Barely able to see through the spray of flowers, he continually came back to her goodness, her sense of responsibility to people and to the church. She always fulfilled her financial pledge even if during the last few years she couldn't always attend.

"And sick as she was, she kept on doing the Lord's work of visiting those who couldn't get out of their homes. Sometimes she was so sick she staggered down the street like someone drunk. She had to hold onto lamp posts so she could rest. She'd have to sit down on the gutter because she couldn't walk. But she'd go on. And when she left a house, the person she was with was always happier. Even when she couldn't afford a taxi, she'd take one to the hospitals to visit the sick . . . That was Sister Nellie."

During this recitation people from the choir and congregation would murmur in agreement.

Gradually Pastor Hayes became more and more caught up in the spirit of the funeral and he preached to his congregation.

"You know what's wrong with you . . . What's wrong with all of us? We're greedy. That's right. We're greedy. We're always trying to get this or that from someone. And we're always out hurting each other.

"We come into the world with an open mouth and clenched fists and we go out of here as an old man with our hands folded across our chests. I'm telling you now, while you can, you better bend your knees in prayer, because someday they're going to be stiff and they won't bend at all and then it's too late."

I'd never heard *a hell fire and damnation* sermon before. His voice and body and thoughts all moved in a unified cadence.

He talked about the Biblical Lazarus, covered with sores and sitting at the rich man's gate. And when the rich man came out he didn't even notice Lazarus. Walked right by him. Lazarus didn't want money or things from the rich man. What he wanted was medicine to cure his sores. But that rich man didn't even look at him. And then the dogs came by and licked Lazarus' sores.

"Then God said to Lazarus, 'Come to me . . . Leave that old body of yours and come to me.' And that's what Lazarus did. He went to the Lord just like Sister Nellie done. Later when the rich man died and found himself in hell, he begged Lazarus to dip his finger in the cool water and to reach across the gulf and touch his burning lips."

Pastor Hayes' voice rose shrilly as he imitated the rich man's voice agonizing in hell. "Help me Lazarus . . . My throat's burning . . . I can't stand it . . . Drop some of that cool water on my lips . . . Help me, man!"

He lowered his voice. "But God said Lazarus in heaven couldn't do it because he couldn't reach across that *gulf* . . . and the rich man in hell couldn't do it because he couldn't reach across that *gulf.*"

Mary commented later he seemed to be looking right at her. I'd been sure he was looking at me.

He then talked about little Christians and big Christians. The little Christians don't pay any attention to God and what God wants us to do. He stressed that Sister Nellie was a big Christian, and then as if paraphrasing her, he said, "Thank you for your suffering, for it brought me closer to you, Lord."

Toward the end of his sermon, just underlying his words, the choir began singing spontaneously the rhythmic hymn, "And I talk with you, and I walk with you."

If ever anyone could sense the presence of the Holy Spirit, it would be here in the simplicity and emotions of this event.

"Sister Nellie is gone from us now. We can't do any more for her. If we didn't thank her, we can't do it now . . . If we didn't help her, we can't do it now . . . If we didn't ask her forgiveness, we can't do it now. It's too late."

I wondered if we'd done all we could have for Nellie. I could think of too many things now.

Then he announced there'd be a last viewing of the deceased. The family more or less congregated around the bier.

One of the daughters broke down, racked with sobs. "Oh, Mamma . . . I didn't mean the things I did . . . I didn't mean the things I said. I did the best I could. I'm sorry, Mamma . . . I'm sorry."

Two of the men helped her to her seat while she continued to weep. The young woman who'd wept before started crying again. The little girl went to her, leaning on her as if to comfort.

During the viewing the choir sang softly, while some of the older ones wiped their eyes. The male member guided Nellie's other weeping daughter back to her pew. Tears ran down his face.

Pastor Hayes looked toward the door. "Undertakers . . ."

The three men walked respectfully down the aisle and closed the casket, while the minister read Saint John's famous words, beginning, "In my house there are many mansions . . ." and Saint Paul's, beginning with "O death where is thy sting . . ." He repeated the Twenty-third Psalm as he followed the coffin being wheeled slowly down the nave toward the door.

The casket was moved from the church.

We shook hands with various people we knew.

Driving back to the house, we were quiet. "That's the way I want to go out," I said finally. "When I *go home* I hope my church gives me a going away party like that. The trouble is most churches have such a sterile burial service . . . We're embarrassed to cry in public and to let people know how much we love and miss the one who's gone."

Mary didn't reply. At last she nodded and smiled. "I finally figured out what Nellie's secret was with her potato salad . . . Do you remember when that young Buddhist visited us and he made bread? He told our children that if they mixed the ingredients with love, the bread would always turn out all right. *That* was Nellie's secret ingredient . . . *love*. She mixed the potato salad and everything else in her life with love."

18

You don't always know where your next challenge is coming from.

This new one accosted me unexpectedly while watching the local news on TV. A college student, a star athlete, was being interviewed. Cancer had sidelined him, though at this point his recovery was pretty well assured.

"But I'll never be able to play competitive athletics again," he stated.

"In college or for the rest of your life?" the interviewer asked.

"Both. I know I'm through as an athlete," he replied despondently.

Mary looked at me. "You had cancer. You're a good tennis player. You ride and swim. You run. I think of all the people watching this who'll be discouraged and lose hope. I think it's a shame. I wish they could see you."

I'd never said anything to her about a notion that sometimes daydreamed on the screen of my mind. I didn't take it seriously. The idea seemed a chimera, the challenge beyond me.

I picked up my dictionary, going through it rapidly. *"That's* the word I want," I said eagerly. *"Transmute!"*

From Latin *trans,* "across," and *mutare,* "change." The word suggests a fundamental change as from a lower to a higher state. Its synonyms also have to do with change, but as with most synonyms there are subtle differences between the words. *Transform* means a basic change of the character of something. *Metamorphose* indicates a fundamental change in structure, though almost a magically induced one. *Transfigure* is similar to *transform* but has the added element of a supernatural or religious feeling, usually in a positive or joyous sense. And *transmogrify* means changing drastically into something ugly or grotesque.

"You've lost me," Mary said.

"That poor youngster and your observation *transmuted* my notion from a private fantasy into a possible reality."

"I'm still lost in your tangle of words."

"I'm thinking about running a marathon."

"A *marathon!* You mean twenty-six miles?"

"Exactly . . . The Penn Relays are about six months off, which would give me time to train."

"You aren't serious?"

"Absolutely."

"But darling, do you think you should? I mean, that distance . . . Would that be good for you after having cancer? I mean it's an awfully long way."

Anyone who's been critically ill is apt to be sensitive ever after to symptoms—a pain that never worried you before; a slight alteration in your bodily functions; tiredness that in most people would seem to be normal. You try not to be anxious. You know holistically that much of illness and health is mind related. You may pray. You try to think positively. There are times when it's prudent to go to the doctor. Mary and I have lived through fear and relief—for both of us.

Generally, I've kept in good shape. I haven't smoked in years, and my drinking habits now are modest. But after the operation I realized I had a lot of work to do to rebuild my strength and set goals. A walk around Mary's rose garden. The next day a stroll to the barn. Then out to the end of the drive-way. I avoided Jenny. I didn't need the burro's capricious spirit at that time. I walked a mile and one day began jogging a little.

A classmate of mine, Josh Minor, has been responsible for the Outward Bound camps in America. These are wilderness camps where youngsters test themselves mentally as well as physically. They climb cliffs with mountaineering techniques, learn to survive alone in the open, handle white water in a canoe, and face similar hard challenges. From this experience they come away with a new perception of themselves and their capabilities.

Sometimes I'd pretend a neighbor would ask me why I jogged, and in my fantasy I'd reply I was getting in shape for a marathon. I didn't believe for a second I'd ever do one. They were for younger people and superb athletes.

Now, after talking with Mary, I could see this as my Out-ward Bound. If I could complete a marathon within four hours, it would be a symbol of total recovery.

In college, because of a sinus condition, I switched from swimming to cross-country. The change made me wonder why I'd spent so many hours swimming back and forth in a pool. I reveled in the changing seasons, the fragrances, the country-side. Subsequently I kept up jogging to a limited degree, run-ning two miles or so three or four times a week.

As a Marine, my jogging nearly jeopardized a part of the campaign for Okinawa during World War II. I persuaded a general and some of his key staff officers they needed more exercise. To make it more interesting, I mapped out a run as if it were a sightseeing tour. My route took us past famous ancestral burial caves—and inadvertently behind the enemy lines. When the colonel in charge of intelligence realized where we were, we sprinted home faster than I believed any of us could run.

Several days later, Japanese snipers were discovered hiding in the caves. The soldiers must have been so unnerved at seeing the enemy unarmed, in casual clothes, and jogging by noncha-lantly, they probably forgot to take pot shots at us.

The general categorically refused to go running with me again.

In built-up suburbia, I'd run early in the morning before commuting to work in New York. Passengers in buses made faces at me. Dogs barked, waking up their irritated owners, who slammed down open windows. Running wasn't popular.

When we moved to the farm, the county had a prison several miles from us. The prisoners often worked on the roads. A large, white *P* was painted on their uniforms. One day I wore an old Princeton University sweat shirt and pants. A large *P* was emblazoned on them. As I ran past a truck full of prisoners, they cheered and laughed.

"Hey man, you'll make it! Keep running! Head for the woods."

The guards took their cries seriously. The truck jolted to a stop. "Hey you . . . Prisoner . . . Halt . . . We'll shoot." A shot was fired in the air.

I halted.

To train for any major event involves an arduous routine. For a marathon this means getting in a substantial weekly mileage of running—for me forty to fifty miles. World class runners do over one hundred miles. There are stretching and muscle-building exercises, and certain foods are better for you than others. At that time running had only begun to be interesting. Except for the Boston Marathon, running twenty-six miles and 380 yards was a relatively rare event.

I found running brought me a variety of new experiences.

I had several different routes through the woods and on the roads. On the trails, rattlesnakes and copperheads were a potential hazard, but the earth trembled with my steps, warning the reptiles in time. One time Mark and I surprised a fawn, tiny and beautiful, clothed in pastel browns and whites. We thought it might need help and considered taking it home, when it cried out. We heard the mother nearby and left quickly. People have been killed by deer. The mildest of mothers becomes ferocious when protecting her young.

Once in a while we surprised lovers who indiscreetly bedded down on trails. They never seemed to have discovered

Mary's and my trysting places. *Tryst* is a word from Old French, and my father, with an amused smile in his pen, wrote that "At some time in a love affair there can be a clandestine meeting. But when two lovers promise each other to keep a *tryst* they are using a most unromantic word, for *tryst* first signified an appointed hunting station where the huntsman lay in wait for his prey."

But I never thought of it as unromantic. For me the word implies a secret place, a waiting for something special.

When I'd run on the roads, sometimes Mary would ride along on her bicycle. One of my routes passed a small cinderblock house where old Matt Dirk and his sister lived. In fine weather Matt, usually with a two- or three-day beard, would sit on the front stoop watching life on the sparsely traveled country road.

One day running by his house I happened to see him sitting on his stoop. Because Mary walked her bicycle part way up the hill, temporarily she lagged behind me. As I passed the grizzled old fellow I shouted, pointing behind me. "She's after me, Matt! She's after me!"

He looked puzzled until he spied Mary. He sprang up, waving vigorously to me. "For the love of God, man, run faster . . . She's gaining on you."

We wondered what he told his sister that evening.

Another time while on a hilltop trail in the thick of the woods, I heard a low, threatening growl—one that meant business.

I stopped, feeling a tingling along my back. Remaining motionless, my eyes picked out a nearby tree with limbs low enough for me to grab if necessary.

Nature camouflages well, and it took a few seconds to locate where the snarling came from. About fifteen feet away I saw a dog so thin his bones showed, his stomach looking like a narrow tunnel. He crouched behind a fallen tree, teeth bared, poised, ready to spring. Behind the log I could see another one lying down and realized they were wild. Apparently the bitch had just given birth to a litter and couldn't run away when I approached.

Keeping my eyes fixed on the snarling animal, I talked softly. Slowly, very very slowly, an inch at a time, I backed away. "Sorry . . . Didn't mean to surprise you . . . *You* stay here and *I'll* go." Gradually I pulled away and the snarling ceased.

Since wild dogs can be dangerous to an area, I telephoned the game warden. He said he had reports of packs attacking sheep and people in the open. He'd do what he could to hunt them down.

Often I'd take Laddie and Donna with me on the trails. For them this was the big event of the day. Laddie, however, being an elderly gentleman, quickly fell behind. I could discern his embarrassment. Finally I found a way to save his face.

I always made sure to loop back on the same trail, knowing I'd meet him. When I found him gamely plodding along, I'd stop for a few minutes, pretending to rest, patting and talking with him while he recovered his wind. Thinking I was tired, he didn't feel quite so left out and contentedly followed us on our way home, his sable plume wagging cheerfully.

Somewhere Mary read that runners doing more than ten miles a day tended to become narcissistic.

"How narcissistic are you today?" she'd ask.

"You tease me. But you don't realized that an ache in the knee is a major event in my life now. And you'll be glad to know that my normal pulse is about fifty-five."

I think she was glad to know.

A friend suggested I run in a local half marathon. "If you can run six miles in training, your adrenaline will carry you the 13.2 miles . . . But for heaven's sake, throw those old work sneakers out and get a pair of running shoes."

Peter and John, our law students in Boston, both of whom had run marathons, sent me a dark-blue jogging suit with a white stripe down the side. No more blue jeans and khaki.

The race was on a Sunday. This was Thursday. Knowing little about training, I decided to try the course to see if I could go the distance. Undoubtedly some friends would be watching. I didn't want to make a complete fool of myself. As the saying goes, *there's no fool like an old fool.* Or was my family mumbling those words?

I made the trial run, but now I know I ought not to have done that distance so close to race day. My feet were sore and my legs stiff. Between then and Sunday I felt the tension mounting and found sleeping difficult. The circles under my sunken eyes looked like smudges of soot. And those hemorrhoids!

"You look awful. I thought running was supposed to make you healthy," Eleanor said.

On that Sunday morning we crowded the YMCA, picking up our numbers. Though geared up, we tried to look cool. At one point I talked with a gray-haired contestant standing calmly with his wife. I mentioned this was my first race since college and said I just hoped to make it. That was all. Just to come in. Couldn't care less about the time. *Liar!*

"Besides, I promised my wife I wouldn't be competitive," I said, preparing an excuse for a poor showing.

"I promise my wife the same thing, don't I, dear?" he said, giving me a patronizing smile. "And it works okay when an older guy passes you. But feller, just wait until a little old gray-haired lady in running shoes goes by. Let's see what happens to your competitive spirit then."

During the run all kinds of people passed me—young, old, skinny, tall, short. But fortunately, no gray-haired lady. I did fairly well. The race was fun and I was hooked. I actually looked forward to the marathon.

"That's good, Dad," John said. "But you have to remember, though, that almost anyone in good shape can run thirteen miles or even twenty. It's those last six that really get you. That's when you hit The Wall."

The Wall! The Wall! I kept hearing about The Wall everyone dreaded. The Wall is a physiological phenomenon. Your body stores the equivalent of two thousand calories. You burn one hundred calories a mile. Theoretically, therefore, at the end of twenty miles you've used up your reserves. You have no more glycogen to supply your muscles with the energy they need. You're depleted. Washed out. Exhausted.

"Nothing new to me," Mary said. "I hit The Wall at the end of each day."

The marathon day arrived. Since the race began at eleven,

we ate breakfast at seven. There are various theories about
eating before a run. A friend with whom we would drive to the
race prefers to eat nothing. I get hungry and stoke myself with
solid, though easily digestible carbohydrates and fats—toasted
cheese sandwiches and peanut butter.

In comparison with today's marathons in numbers of people, that first one of mine was minuscule. There were only about
five hundred of us, no match for New York's sixteen thousand.

We crammed into the small room to pick up our numbers,
which are pinned on the front part of your shirt so the computer
can list them as you cross the line. At least the computer had
confidence in me.

The longest lines in the building were to the bathrooms.
Many people, having done what they had to do, went back to
the end of the line again. Nerves!

I saw people on the lawn stretching, bending, rolling their
feet over their heads and touching the grass with their toes.
Since they seemed to know what they were doing, I thought I
should do the same. On the other hand, that seemed a waste of
energy and so I lay on the grass and closed my eyes.

I felt reasonably calm until Mary came back from the la-
dies' room.

"She's there," Mary said, smiling.

"Who?"

"A little old gray-haired lady in running shoes."

My quadriceps knotted. "What's she like?"

"Small. Thin. Agile looking . . . And she's taking Kaopectate . . . She says that before every marathon she takes Kaopectate."

Before every marathon! Sounds like a pro. Maybe she knows
something I don't. Should I send Mary out for a bottle of Kaopectate? There wasn't time.

I tried to put her out of my mind, relaxing, looking at the
sky, knowing that by this time tomorrow it would all be a memory. But what kind of a memory? That's what worried me.

There's a friendly ambience to a marathon. Old friends
greet one another, people talk about other races and injuries.
There's laughter and joking.

Naturally, the front runners are competitive, but the rest of us are really competing against ourselves, against the time we believe we can complete the course.

As we milled around at the start, I found myself bobbing in a sea of color. Blue, yellow, green, red, black, white running shorts. Mine were an orange-red. The T-shirts were not only in a variety of colors, but some displayed slogans, logos, statements. I wore a white one with orange and black rings around the collar, Princeton University colors. Peter and John gave it to me, affixing the year of my graduation on the back. Perhaps they hoped it might create some kind of respect for age and I wouldn't be trampled in the rush.

The starting gun surprised me. The mass of humanity surged forward and we were launched on our way, resembling the late afternoon subway rush in New York City. Since we were jammed together at first, I wanted to be sure not to trip. In the half marathon someone in front of me fell, and I heard the snap of the leg bone as it broke and the runner's disgusted expletive, "_____!"

Like grapes on a vine we fell into bunches and then gradually began to string out. I resisted the temptation to increase my speed as people passed me. I knew that inexperienced runners usually start off too fast and wear themselves out before the end of the race. There's a balance between your body's ability to utilize oxygen, the glycogen (sugar) in the muscles, and your speed. My anticipated pace would be an eight-minute mile or so, bringing me home in about three hours and forty-five minutes.

Off and on in races you find yourself with running companions. Sometimes they leave you behind. Sometimes it's the reverse. You tend to talk less as the race goes on.

After the first two miles, an official called out the time. "Fourteen minutes, ten seconds."

"Whew!" a young man whistled beside me. "That's too fast for me . . . That's a seven-minute mile."

I agreed. We chatted a bit. This was his second marathon and he was determined to finish. He'd hit The Wall on the first try and dropped out.

Mary finds watching a race entertaining. Delicate small girls paddle along with a wobbly stride, passing larger men who look as though they're going faster. And though most long-distance runners are nearly always slender, there's an infinite number of body builds and running styles. A tall Chinese gentleman glided past me in what seemed to be an effortless shuffle. I expected him to be wearing a pair of straw sandals.

Our course took us along a river for six miles, across a bridge, and then a return to the start, repeating the course, and a bit extra. The first six miles seemed to take longer than I'd expected—and to be harder. The quadricep muscles in my left leg began to ache slightly. Not a good sign. You monitor yourself the way a racing driver does his car on the Indy 500.

Some Marines were standing along the course, cheering on one of their own men. I called out and said I'd been in the Corps. They shouted "C'mon Tiger! You can do it!" Also, I heard a refrain for the first time that's become a staple among race watchers. "You're lookin' good . . . You're lookin' real good."

Suddenly you feel better. Somebody out there appreciates the fact you're trying.

I passed Mary at about the ten-mile mark and she held out a glass of pineapple juice. I drank it hurriedly. She kissed me. "How're you doing?"

"Great!"

"You're lookin' good."

She had it right.

Thus refreshed and with renewed spirit, the knight charged off to do foolish battle again.

A youngster pulled alongside. "Is that the date you were born?" he said, referring to the numbers on my back designating my college class. After a quick glance at me as he passed, he shook his head and laughed, saying emphatically, "I guess *not!*"

At a tired thirteen miles I didn't need that.

Then it happened. *She* passed me. Silently. Hardly seeming to breathe. Mary had described her accurately. Tiny. Lithe. Gray-haired. She wore a white muscle shirt and blue track pants. A white cap with a peak kept the sun off her face. I expected her to tip a bottle of Kaopectate to her mouth. The specter was real. The little old lady had appeared.

As she slipped past, I thought of the warning the fellow had given me in my first race.

What to do? I was running about an eight-minute mile and felt that I could probably complete the marathon at this pace. Should I speed up and try to overtake her. I had to weigh carefully the bruised male ego against reality.

I opted for reality. Let her go. I sighed. "Oh well . . . Who cares?" But I did care.

She drew ahead of me slowly, widening the gap between us by about a quarter of a mile. She had a good stride, light and quick. As I watched her, gradually my attitude changed. Perhaps this is the mysterious affinity existing between many marathon runners.

My admiration grew. After all, she was probably my age or older. I knew she also would have put in thousands of miles of road work. I felt certain, too, that something was undoubtedly hurting her now—a knee, a sore muscle, a foot, possibly an incipient cramp. And she'd be aware also of that sense of growing weariness, the feeling that an invisible monster leech is gradually sucking away your body's energy. You know you're on an inevitable collision course with exhaustion.

"Well," I finally said to myself. "Let's look at it this way. If she's up there ahead of me, she deserves it. Good luck to her."

But then at the sixteen-mile mark unexpectedly she pulled aside, slowed to a staggering walk, and was reclaimed by friends who helped her to a chair.

The specter vanished. I was on my own again. I felt sorry for her, wondering why she hadn't paced herself better. Why was she taking Kaopectate?

Another stop for a shot of Mary's pineapple juice. Most marathons have water stations every three miles. I take advantage of all of them, for liquid is absolutely essential to the body. On hot days you can sweat gallons.

"How are you?" Mary asked, this time a more searching look on her face.

"Okay . . . I guess." A less enthusiastic answer.

"Only eight more miles."

"Is that all?" I tried to make it sound like a quip. Only eight miles! It might as well be eight hundred or eight thousand.

By this time my quadriceps were really hurting and stiffening. Maybe The Wall was beginning to close in on me. Increasingly I found it hard to move, as if my feet were running through deep mud; as if a tidal wave were rolling in after me and I knew I had to go faster, but I could only move in slow motion. I felt drained, surprisingly depleted. My body warned my "gas tank" was empty and it was going to stop even if I wanted to go on.

Others were having their problems too. Many walked. They'd walk and then jog again and then walk. Some pulled off the path and stopped, sitting, head in their hands.

There is no feeling like it. You are totally, agonizingly devoid of energy. There's nothing left. You've used it all up. You have nothing inside of you now but will power. And even that begins to seep away.

"Why am I doing something so stupid?" I asked myself. "It's not worth it."

It was a question I used to ask Jenny after one of her annoying escapades. I thought of the little burro now, recalling her resilience, her tenacity and ingenuity. If she were here, she'd finish with her tail flicking about in little twists. Thinking of her cheered me for a few minutes and I forgot the devastating weariness.

Until now I'd been noticing the other runners, the river, cars, trees, people strolling. Now my awareness shifted, the concentration solely on me. I had one objective—to keep going.

I no longer heard or noticed the spectators or runners. I had to hoard my mental energy. Without it I couldn't finish. My body and mind became one.

The blue magic marker sign told me I had a mile to go. Glancing at my wristwatch, I saw I'd been running for three hours and thirty-seven minutes. That left thirteen minutes if I wanted to meet my goal of finishing within four hours.

I began to realize with a growing sense of elation I could do it. Every step brought me a few feet closer—twenty-six miles and 380 yards! I thought in wonder of those days in the hospital when we weren't sure, when walking the length of the hall became an achievement. Twenty-six miles!

The finish line. I could see it. Sheer relief and joy carried me. My tiredness evaporated in a euphoria.

Two runners darted out from among the spectators. I heard a scuffling behind me. Suddenly a limp figure, propelled by the two men, pushed past me. "You can do it," one of them said to the exhausted runner they literally dragged along.

Well . . . If it meant that much to him, let him go. I wasn't racing now. I was home. The clock said three hours, forty-eight minutes, and eight seconds.

I crossed the line.

"Keep moving down the chutes," officials called. "Keep moving." Chutes are lanes. You move along so as not to block other following runners.

A hug and a kiss from Mary, who led me over to the car where I sat on the hood, rubbing stiffening legs. I know better now. I should have walked for a while.

A pleasant-looking man wearing a mustache approached me. "Peter Funk?" he asked. "I'm Bob Savett of the *Evening Bulletin* . . . Too tired to talk?"

Too tired to talk! No Funk is ever too tired to talk. And especially not this one now. Except for the stiffness in my legs, I actually felt surprisingly well.

He queried me about the race, why I'd run in it, my work, and a myriad of other questions.

The following day, friends told us that Bob Savett had written a piece about me and we bought the paper, turned to the sports section, and saw the headline:

HE'S OUTRUN CANCER SO WHAT'S A MARATHON?

It was cancer and they operated on his intestines and they told him to prepare to meet his maker. [A bit dramatic, but he got the gist of it.]

A transfusion added viral hepatitis—as well as blood—to his system and Peter Funk became weaker still. The same Peter Funk who finished 216th in yesterday's Penn Relays marathon.

"It's a sense of being alive—doing something like this," the writer from Lambertville was saying, a yellow sweat stain on his Old Nassau T shirt and a radiant glow on his face. "Each of us tries to make an achievement in his own way. At my age, having had cancer and not expected to live . . . I think it's encouraging to people to know you can do it.

"It's past the five-year mark [since the cancer was discovered] now. I'm home free. People say, 'Did will power make a lot of difference?' Well, I had a lot of people praying for me. And good doctors. I'm just grateful to be here. You don't care about the unimportant things anymore."

The piece continued in a most gracious manner, more complimentary than was warranted. Mary and I hoped that others would be encouraged to find their own "Outward Bound" challenges.

A week or so later as we were getting ready for bed, Mary said, "Since you haven't been running any distances lately, Matt Dirk probably wonders what happened to you. I bet he thinks I caught you and *that was that!*"

"We should have let you catch up with me, and then you could have given him something *really* to remember. What would you have done?"

"I'd have thrown you on the lawn in front of his house," she said pushing me on the bed. "And kissed you . . . *Like this!*"

"Like *that?*"

"Well . . . Maybe not quite like that."

Our hushed laugh held the intimacy of lovers.

"I'm glad Matt isn't around," I sighed finally.

19

As we finished an early morning coffee, Mary suddenly looked at me. "Do you know what I just realized?" When she resolves a problem, she tends to look directly at you, as does Paul, often tapping her finger on the table or against the air in time with her words. "We see more of Alan Schuller, our vet, and our blacksmith than our closest friends. We're always working."

Her declaration might have been something of an exaggeration, but she pointed out a failing in our life. We hadn't taken a real vacation in years, and ninety-nine percent of the time it seemed we were working.

"We haven't entertained anyone for at least six months," Mary continued. "I think we should give a party. We owe so many people, I'm embarrassed. And it would be good for us. I miss our friends."

We set a date for several weeks from then.

On the day of our party, Mary went into high gear, cooking, cleaning, setting the table. Estelle and Eleanor helped her. Later in the day I took care of odds and ends.

"When everyone finishes taking care of their horses," I said to Eleanor, "please be sure everything's picked up, the heating coil around the pipes and anything else you see that needs to be done. And the last thing to do is make certain the door to the feed room is latched."

A hearth with a low-burning fire, friends chatting lightly or in more serious discussions, Vivaldi on the record player, hot hors d'oeuvres, a drink.

An *oasis.*

We were weary of working and it was time to play. A time to dress up.

Mary had on a combination three-quarter length warm cotton dress with a hood and matching pants. Its lines were simple and classic, the print of a subtle combination of fleur-de-lis and shell-like patterns in light pastel browns, interspersed with orange and white spaces.

She wore her hair neck length, the ends turning up in soft, loose waves and one side slightly falling over her forehead. Hairdressers tell her she's lucky because her hair is so full and healthy.

From time to time I glimpsed her animated, finely sculptured face, blue eyes happy, alert with quick intelligence. She has strong, well-shaped hands, and her gestures are often as expressive as her words.

We have a friend who's critical of the way we use our hands when we talk. "Speak with words, not hands," he tells us. He's a lawyer, and lawyers tend to cool their emotions in public.

On the other hand, I believe gestures help to emphasize, to bring words to more of a fullness of specific meaning and intent. A shrug, a lifting of the hand, a tilt of the head, can intensify a meaning.

I sat beside Mona, a young teacher from Lebanon, and we talked about language.

"The right word summarizes a whole situation," she said. *"Procrustean'*s a word that summarizes some of the governments where I live . . . Your father had such a good description of the word's origin in his book . . . *Word Origins?"*

"Word Origins and Their Romantic Stories," I said. "I think it's my favorite book of his."

"That story of that old Greek robber Procrustes who tied his victims to a bed and then altered them so they'd fit . . . If they were too long, he'd hack off their limbs, and if they were too short, he stretched them . . . It reminds me of those totalitarian states . . ."

Mary told us dinner was ready. Her culinary speciality at the time of the party was veal blanquette, and I enjoyed it now. The plates were nicely warm. I like them that way, a crotchet of mine. A hostess or host works hard at creating a delectable dinner that's meant to be served warm, and then the plates turn out to be cold, which lessens the effect.

Paul came up to me, speaking in a low voice. "Hey, Pop . . . ! I was going to practice some hockey shots in the barn and I saw Peppermint acting in a peculiar way. I thought you should know."

"What's he doing?"

"Well, he's lying on his side outside his stall . . . And he's breathing in a funny way and his legs are twitching."

Mary saw Paul talking to me. Her expression asked what was wrong.

Excusing myself from Mona, I put down my glass of white wine and crossed the room. "Paul says Peppermint seems to be acting strangely. I'd better check him out. It may be nothing, but I don't like the sounds of it. I'll probably be back in a few minutes."

Her look mirrored my annoyance.

Coming from the warm house, I felt the dank winter air sift easily through my sports jacket. We ran over the crunchy snow, lumpy from being trodden on by the horses. A light Paul left on in the barn made an elongated yellow rectangle over the ground, partially illuminating our way.

"I closed the door to the feed room. Someone left it open."

"Well, that's the answer then." I felt certain of the diagnosis. We had a problem. "Eleanor told me she checked out everything."

He shrugged. "I don't know. It was open and so was Peppermint's stall door."

"Wildfire kicked the stall last week and hit the latch. It's loose, so I can understand how Peppermint got out. And once out, all she'd have to do is to follow the sweet smell of molasses to the feed room."

Our barn was long, and between the area for the horses and the place where I kept the tractor I'd made a room where we stored the feed and hay. Though we took the horses out the main door, the shortest way for us to get from one end of the barn to the other was to walk through it, which meant passing through the feed area.

"You were really observing," I said, trying to compliment him on his sense of responsibility.

He pointed to the animal lying on the cement floor, its sides heaving in quick breaths, legs jerking, body stiff. He couldn't help laughing at my comment. *"Observing . . . Pop! How could I miss?"*

I raced up the stairs to my office, directly overhead, to telephone Alan Schuller. His wife, Peggy, answered. Unfortunately, he was out on another emergency and she thought he'd be back in an hour or so. She'd try to locate him immediately. His two associates were away for the weekend.

"I agree it sounds like colic," she said, "especially when you mentioned the feed room. You've got to get him on his feet and walk him. I know that's what Alan would tell you. Don't let him lie down. It could be fatal. Get him up right away and walking."

Very sound advice. But how do you get a creature on his feet who weighs seven hundred or eight hundred pounds? After discussing different options, Paul and I decided he would take the halter rope and pull as hard as he could and I'd get behind and shove and lift.

Another thought troubled me. Peppermint was Phoebe's joy and love. I didn't want a sadness tonight for either her or us.

The suffering animal couldn't understand what we were doing to him. He didn't want to move. I remembered reading about a man who communicated with his dog by forming pictures in his mind of what he wanted his pet to do. I tried this with Peppermint—visualizing him walking, having him feel the agonizing pain abating, the swollen grain moving out of his stomach, relieving the pressure. Paul and I talked to him, explaining what we wanted him to do.

Finally he lurched to his feet. "Keep him walking . . . Pull on the rope."

"I hope he doesn't try to lie down again," Paul said, towing him through the barn.

"I hope not," I agreed. "You'd better tell your mother what's happening. I may be up here a couple of hours if Dr. Schuller's delayed. And while you're at it, how about bringing up my heavy coat, gloves, and boots . . . ? I'm freezing."

Paul returned with my clothes. "Mom said she'd keep your food warm . . . Want me to walk him and you can go down to eat? You have all your friends down there."

Acts of love don't have to be heroic. More often than not they show up in the small, mundane things of life like Paul's offer.

"Thanks. I'd better stay here. This fellow's in pretty bad shape and I'm the one who has to take the responsibility."

"Mother's not very happy."

"I bet she's not."

"I'm going upstairs and practice some of my slap shots. I think I left a hockey stick up here," Paul said.

"Tonight? Now?"

"Sure . . . I want to make the team."

In a few minutes I heard the tough, loud, banging crack of the hard hockey puck smashing against the barn wall. The impact reverberated throughout the barn. He'd reinforced the wall and made a goal cage to practice his slap shots. When I worked in my office and Paul practiced, my concentration made a lot of stops and starts.

With football, hockey, and lacrosse, Paul concentrated too much on sports and not enough on studies. We thought about curtailing his sports program or working out a penalty system based on grades. But obviously he took such sheer pleasure in his sports and he was so good at them that we held back. He was "goal" oriented. We rationalized that a large part of our education is acquired outside of the schoolroom. This was one of the reasons, of course, that we had the farm.

As he slapped the puck around that evening, Peppermint and I walked back and forth, from the pony's stall to the feed room and back, his hooves clicking on the cement. Each time we passed Wildfire, the rascal would lay back her ears, stretching her head toward us, trying to nip Peppermint. Sometimes in frustration she kicked the walls.

My experience with horses taught me that their memories are long, and they are not naturally vicious. Most of the time, if they turn out to be mean, it's because they were badly treated as colts. Even though this probably happened to Wildfire and we were sympathetic, she was a pain to have around.

Who left the door unlatched? Someone must have come along after Eleanor, and in going through the feed room forgot to lock it. I felt sure it wasn't an oversight of Eleanor's because we were meticulous about this after Jenny had pushed the door open a few times. She gorged. Fortunately it didn't hurt our white burro. Her innards must have been held together by rubber bands that kept stretching.

Paul came down from his practice. "I was trying to shoot from the right side . . . I don't know why it's so hard . . . I think I'll go on down to the house. See you later," he said, closing the door behind him.

"What in the name of h— is going on?" I heard Amory Neilson saying, our neighbor who had his office in the barn. "I'm trying to work out some architectural problems and I hear that kid of yours slamming the hockey puck . . . Then you're mumbling to some dumb animal, pacing back and forth . . ."

"I'm sitting up with a sick horse."

"Likely story. You're all nuts in your family."

"Like it or not, it's the truth. If I wasn't afraid he'd lie down on the job, I'd let you do it."

He eyed me critically. "You always get dressed up for a sick horse?"

I jerked my thumb toward the house. "Party."

"Ah . . . Too bad. Well, I suppose you have a word for it?"

"Easily. It stinks."

"Good old Anglo-Saxon word. Remember the story about Samuel Johnson . . . Wasn't he at a theater and the woman sitting next to him said, 'Dr. Johnson, you smell.' And he looked at her and said, 'Nay, madam. *You* smell. *I* stink.' Well, haven't seen much of you lately . . . We're all so busy. Let's get together soon . . . Anyway, I've got to get back to work."

Left alone, I tried not to let my disappointment at missing the party annoy me too much.

Mary and I learned from my cancer to try to keep our priorities in the right order. Sometimes we forget and then have to remind ourselves. The interruption of a party wasn't a cataclysm. We would have other ones.

And there was a satisfaction in being helpful to the pony in deep pain. Zen teaches you to live in this moment; in this instant. Not yesterday. Not tomorrow. Now. Live this instant fully, with all your senses. I was with the pony and would try to be fully aware of him.

With that approach as a restorative, I didn't mind being Peppermint's first-aid kit on a night I was meant to be host. But this incident reminded me acutely that Mary and I once again would have to rethink our priorities and to see where and if and how the farm fit into our current lives.

Alan Schuller finally arrived. After examining Peppermint and giving him a sedative, he said the pony would be all right. He left some medicine for the following day.

By the time I returned to the house with the fragrance of horses following me, some guests were already leaving.

The following morning early, Eleanor and I, both wishing we were still in bed, pushed through the snow to the barn for our daily chores. We always did them together. The horses were essentially Eleanor's project. Paul, Mark, and Estelle, of course, helped us in other ways.

Peppermint appeared to be fully recovered. We gave him his medicine and went about our routines.

Sometimes the chores were tough, especially on the days when the water froze in the buckets. Then Eleanor and I chipped out the ice, banging our hands against the sides of the buckets. Occasionally the pipes froze, and then we'd make a half-dozen trips back and forth to the house to get water.

On the cold winter days, Eleanor and I made it more fun by trying to anticipate what Mary planned for breakfast.

"I'd like a nice big cheese omelet," she might say longingly.

"Sounds good. What about muffins?"

"With lots of honey."

"Maybe some Kasha?"

She turned up her nose. "For *breakfast?*" She laughed. "I'd rather have this molasses grain mixture. It smells pretty good to me. Maybe I'll take some down and have Mother cook it up."

Mary might not serve up exactly what we'd been talking about, but she never disappointed us as we walked into the window-steamed fragrant kitchen. And she didn't today.

"Guess what?" Eleanor said at breakfast. "Phoebe's letting me ride Peppermint today."

"You'll be coming home from school about three o'clock then?" Mary asked.

On most afternoons the barn burst into a flurry of life about that time when Sally, Anne, Phoebe, Jane Merriman, and some other boarders arrived. My office, being located directly above and not having the benefit of insulation, caught all the noise of the cheerful hubbub, a condition not conducive to concentration.

The meticulous care they lavished on their horses fascinated Eleanor. She learned to run her fingers through Achilles' coat against the natural lay of hair and to press them against the skin to find out if he was groomed properly. If not, flakes of dandruff and gray lines showed up on his coat. Her fingers would be covered with scurf, a scaly kind of stuff.

The brushing and currying took at least half an hour. She'd get inside the forelegs and in the bends of the knees and hocks, under the crown piece of the halter, below his ears, and under the belly.

I heard the splashing water as Anne and Sally washed their horses, and the buzz of electric clippers as they shaved them. The girls dressed up the tails and manes with braids of colored ribbons.

Hooves were carefully examined and picked and painted to prevent cracking. Sore spots on the body received Vaseline, and if a scratch was found or a raw wound, Gentian Violet would be used, which is an antiseptic as well as a healing agent. If they thought a horse had a runny nose, whatever parents gave children usually applied here. Q-tips removed dirt from ears and mucus from around eyes.

During this ritual the horses fretted, pawing with their hooves, shaking their heads. The girls took longer to prepare their horses for a show than they would to get themselves ready for a date.

We enjoyed watching the three girls and Jane work their animals. They walked them first to limber up muscles that might be stiff from standing. I do the same before I go out running! Then there'd be a session of trotting. Finally they'd canter—not gallop—around the various fields. This regimen lasted an hour, sometimes longer. After that came practice jumping.

Sally reminded me I'd promised to build some jumps and suggested different kinds—post and rail, chicken coop, brush, maybe one with barrels.

All of us in the family worked on these, and at the same time we made a small riding ring. From a distance the jumps added a satisfying pictorial quality, for they were like interesting pieces of sculpture. For my birthday, Mary painted a delightful picture of a portion of the field, with barrels used as side posts painted red and white and lengths of wood in the form of an X between them. Excited about her painting again, I hoped this might be the catalyst to reawaken her interest. But she said there was already a plethora of artists in the world. Besides, she was too busy. She's an excellent artist and I was sure she'd paint again someday.

As Phoebe promised, she let Eleanor ride Peppermint while she rode Achilles. As I watched from my office, I could see so clearly the faults in Eleanor's horse. He shook his head nervously, pranced instead of walked, pulling on the reins. He would have nothing to do with jumps, running through them instead of going over the barriers. I'd already come to the conclusion he was kind of neurotic and was sorry we'd succumbed to his inherent gentleness and élan.

Late that afternoon, Sally, Anne, and Phoebe came to the house to wait for one of their mothers to pick them up.

"Do you have an aspirin?" Sally asked Mary, smiling.

"Certainly. I'll get the bottle. Do you have a headache?"

"No . . . I think I broke my arm when I fell on a jump."

"You did *what?*"

"It seems broken. I can't move it." She held her arm.

"How awful! When did it happen?"

"About an hour ago."

"Why didn't you come right down here so I could call your mother?"

"I wanted to finish taking care of Morning Mist. His stall was pretty grungy." Though nonchalant, Sally was obviously in pain.

Later that evening Mary was telling her mother over the telephone how much she admired Sally. "That girl has real courage . . . She has guts. We found out she really did break her arm. I think all of the boarders are a real inspiration to us. I *love* those girls."

Because of her broken arm, Sally couldn't ride. Consequently, she let someone else take Morning Mist in a show. The individual rode him too hard and unfortunately the horse became lame. They spoke fearfully of a bowed tendon, most of the time an incurable situation. Sally became frantic.

I telephoned our veterinarian, Alan Schuller. Since late winter is the time for a physical checkup, we thought he could go over the rest of the horses as well as Morning Mist.

Tall and lanky, the doctor wore sideburns. His wife probably cut his shaggy uncombed hair and he tucked his pants into high, waterproof boots. His green eyes, slightly mocking and skeptical, reflected an agile mind. He walked into the barn with a long stride and a natural, relaxed confidence.

He'd taken care of our sheep, geese, Jenny, the other horses, our small animals. I came down from my office and we greeted one another.

"Alan, you vets are the only doctors left making house calls."

"If we didn't, our waiting room would be pretty crowded with ten horses and a burro," he smiled.

Fortunately only the girls and Jane were here at the moment. The owners of the other horses we boarded probably would arrive later.

I saw him glance at Achilles. Eleanor winced involuntarily, as though expecting some kind of joke at her love's expense. The girls judged Achilles by show-horse standards and consequently didn't think he was worth keeping around. Eleanor, loyal to the love of her life, was hurt by their not recognizing what she believed were his other sterling qualities, which more than offset whatever else he lacked.

"Is this the horse selling for twenty thousand dollars? . . . The one with the injured tendon?" Alan winked at me.

Stunned silence in the barn. Sally had been grooming the docile Morning Mist, preparing him for the doctor. Her brush clattered on the floor.

Eleanor swallowed, barely able to speak. "This is Achilles . . . My horse."

Alan nodded. "Right. I forgot. He's a fine-looking animal, by the way." He patted the horse, looking at her. "I like him."

Incredulous, she stared at him. "You do?"

"Sure. Don't you?" A corner of his mouth smiled as the young face transformed into an ecstasy.

She couldn't contain the giggle. "Sure . . . Yeah . . . I mean, well, *I've* always thought he was the greatest."

"He may not be the *greatest,* but he's a good horse . . ." He turned to me. "I think I'll give all the other horses a physical checkup and worm them and save Morning Mist to the last so I can concentrate on him . . . I'm getting some things from the car. I'll be back in a minute. Want to help me carry them in, Eleanor?"

When he walked out of the barn, the stunned silence turned into an angry one. Anne had just hooked Wildfire to the other cross ties, planning to clean the mare's hooves. She threw the small cleaning pick on the floor and walked over to Sally. Bits of muttering reached me. "Stupid . . . Ridiculous . . . How could he make such a mistake . . . Ignorant . . ."

When Alan finished worming Achilles, the doctor went over him carefully, ending his examination by checking the mouth.

"Is he in good shape for an old horse?" Eleanor asked.

The doctor studied the horse's teeth. "Who says he's old?"

"I guess about everybody." She glanced at me.

"He's probably between ten and twelve."

"Is that all?" Eleanor gasped. "You've *got* to be kidding."

He laughed at her reaction. "So you thought you were stuck with an old nag?"

"I didn't care . . . But I'm really glad. See. I told you, Dad."

After taking care of the other horses, Alan spent a long time examining Morning Mist, running his hand up and down the injured leg, pausing at certain points. His diagnosis confirmed the bowed tendon. Sally began to cry.

He put his arm around her shoulders. "There's a new treatment and we're going to try it. You've got a great horse here. He's a real beauty. Too good to lose . . . So don't give up. He's got a chance."

At supper, Eleanor thought about Sally. "I feel so sorry for her . . . I know just the way I'd feel if anything happened to my baby."

"I like horses, but I don't look at them as if they are babies," Mary said laughing.

"That's because you never had a horse like Achilles."

A few days later a frightening experience with one of the horses stood as an isolated event until gradually we began to see it as a subtle turning point in the context of our lives—the beginning of a realistic reassessment of the farm. As when a ball is thrown into the air, what is that instant, that one fraction of a second when the apex is reached: the exact moment the ball starts to fall?

Concerns about several of the children and dissatisfaction with a piece of writing had me awake early. Since I knew I probably wouldn't go back to sleep again, I went to my office in the barn.

The horses thought I'd come to feed them. Excited, they

whinnied, nickered, banged their legs against the stall doors, stretching their heads toward me, pawing. Wildfire flattened her ears and let go a terrific kick against the boards separating her from peaceful Morning Mist, spraying chips of wood in the air.

Breath rose from their nostrils like steam from a boiling pot. The warm smell of their bodies, an acrid hint of ammonia from urine, the dry, dusty sweet fragrance of alfalfa from the loft above, mingled together in a distinctive aroma I found enjoyably satisfying. It had the smell of vibrant, earthy life, a scent we never experienced in suburbia or cities.

Ten horses and a braying burro can create an awful hub-bub. No chance to concentrate on work with that racket. I decided to feed them now. Most of the time Eleanor and I fed them at 6 A.M.

On cold days like this the wind blew through every possible crack. It skimmed over the cement floor, leaving miniature frozen rivers and lakes from spilled water. Your fingers ached in your gloves.

Hoisting a garbage can filled with the molasses mixture on a wheelbarrow, I stopped at each stall, scooping out the required amount into the feed bucket. Done with the feeding, I watered the animals.

But I did everything by rote, my mind mostly in a creative mist, unraveling the complex tangle of ideas into simple threads so I could reweave them into a new, harmonious whole.

Automatically I went from stall to stall, removing the blankets, folding them neatly. Vaguely I recall going into Wildfire's stall, unlatching the green blanket's buckle around the chest, folding the cloth over her back. I have a dim awareness of moving toward her rump, my hand on her haunches feeling her gather her massive body into tightness, her back rising as I started behind her to pull off the blanket.

"Darling . . . ," Mary called, out of breath, anxious.

I stopped when I heard her voice. At that second the steel-shod hooves lashed past me, ripping into the wood. The stall trembled. She tried to nip me. I jabbed my elbow in her nose and she pulled away.

Running down the passsageway, Mary threw her arms around me. "I'm *so* relieved you're all right . . . You don't know. I had this terrible feeling."

"All I can say is that you know the right time to show up."

"Let me tell you what happened. It was the strangest thing," she said, pushing back stray strands of blond hair beneath the red ski cap.

"I was sleeping when suddenly I heard a voice *Mary Funk* . . . It woke me up. And then I heard it again just as plainly as I hear yours now . . . *Mary Funk*. And it was so insistent . . . So commanding . . . As though something was terribly urgent. And it wasn't a dream, because when I heard it the second time I was sitting up . . . I mean I was really awake when I heard the voice.

"I saw you weren't there and so I went downstairs. I know you like to work early sometimes. And then when I didn't find you I began to worry. I decided you were probably in the barn. I pulled on the boots over my slippers and this jacket over my bathrobe and ran as fast as I could through the snow . . ." She looked at me, her eyes filled with love and anxiety . . . If I'd been a second late . . . Just one second . . . Even a fraction of a second later." She sighed, her arms going around me again, holding me tightly. "Oh, my darling . . ."

I took her hands. "How could I be so stupid? . . . Unbelievably stupid. All the years I've spent with horses . . . And to do that with one like Wildfire?"

"I hate that animal . . . She's vicious."

"It's funny. I was in a kind of dream thinking about my work. I just wasn't aware of what I was doing."

"You're a *writer* . . . You're a *linguist* . . . You're not a farmer," she said passionately. "I'm sorry we took the horses on. I just don't want them anymore after this. I'll be worrying about Eleanor all the time now."

"Well . . . It's going to make us more careful."

"I'm usually the spacey one." She put her arms around me again. "I don't know how to explain it, but thank God! Thank God!"

How many times in a month, in a week, in a day, do I

realize how much I love her? There's an inner essence to the person you love that in a mysterious way is revealed only to you. It's as if you and you alone had the secret combination to the lock to open the other's inner self. And the love we find within is transformed for us to the whole person.

A woman told me, "I'm losing my looks. I'm losing my figure . . . I'm growing old."

But age peels away the superficial, allowing the inner beauty of a loving person to suffuse the outer. This is the light of a permanent beauty. The one that lasts. You don't need Oil of Olay to keep that.

"I'm getting cold," Mary said. "Let's go down to the house."

"Let me check to see if I latched the door to the feed room. I don't want any more colic in this barn."

"It would serve that black horror right," Mary said with feeling.

We turned off the lights. She stuck one of her cold hands in my pocket and we walked down to the house in the grayness of nascent dawn.

Over cups of coffee in the dinette we watched the rising of the day. Outside the window, sparrows pushed aside from the feeder by jays flittered excitedly in the branches of the trees and on the ground, trying to pick up birdseed. The blackcap chickadees jackhammered their stubby beaks into suet swinging from a branch.

"I wonder what it was?" Mary asked. "Don't you think it's strange? I've never heard voices before."

"Maybe ESP . . . ? You and I are always reading each other's mind."

"But this was a *voice* . . . It wasn't a hunch or a feeling. It was a *real* voice."

"Well, remember Julian Jaynes' book about the bicameral mind and that in ancient times people heard voices, but it was the right side of their brain speaking to them."

"This wasn't any right side of my brain . . . This was a real voice with vocal cords and all."

We read each other's mind now, both wanting to believe it must have been an interception by God.

"Maybe an angel . . . ?" Mary offered.

I sipped my coffee, savoring its aroma and taste. *Whom have I in heaven but you . . . You hold me by my right hand.*

"The mysteries of God," Mary murmured.

"And maybe a clear sign," I replied.

She looked at me, questioning.

"It took a cancer to get me out of that job into doing something I really enjoy . . . writing and linguistics. I don't want a horse to kick me into thinking clearly. I feel we're still a canvas painting with too many activities splashed on it . . . The horses and other projects do cut into my work time . . . Another thing. We haven't taken a vacation in six or seven years."

We looked out the window across to the rim of distant hills, tinted a pale blush by nature's cosmetic, the rising sun.

Mary nodded. "I know we love Good Ground . . . ," she began.

Neither of us finished her thought aloud.

20

Like clouds gradually covering a summer sky, an unspoken sadness shadowed our lives. Without exactly saying so to one another, during the past year a growing feeling in each of us adumbrated a change—a feeling we could not remain on our farm much longer, that we would have to let it go. More accurately perhaps, it would have to let us go.

"We're here for the rest of our lives," we'd told each other exuberantly when we bought Good Ground Farm. "Here is where we'll live and die." Now we weren't so positive. The whirling wheel of change carried us to a different time.

There were cogent reasons for our sentiments. Economic predictions were ominous. Peter and John were in law school, and Celine, Estelle, and Mark in college. Though each always worked, helping to earn tuition money, nonetheless over the years we carried heavy educational and other expenses.

I had a gut reaction we'd be placing ourselves in financial jeopardy if we hung around here too long. Local taxes were on an escalator. Within several years we would have to put money into the cottages and barn to keep them in good condition.

Most important of all, our overall situation had changed. Only Paul and Eleanor were home on a daily basis. The scholas-

tic pressures of college preparatory courses in high school and
school activities preempted most of their time. The sheep had
gone. There were no more chickens. Peerless Laddie was put
down at the age of seventeen. No parakeets. No gerbils. No
hamster. No fish. Two German shepherds, one cat, Achilles, and
Hubert comprised our family of pets.

And Jenny. But like the toy animal in the song "Puff the
Magic Dragon," no one now had the time to pay attention to
her.

However, we boarded eight horses, and Jenny still managed to break out and lead them toward her reverie of a never-
never land of greener grass and tasty oats. The relatively large
tree farm needed a certain amount of seasonal care. Fields had
to be mowed. My skills at carpentry might be basic, but they
were constantly being tested to their utmost because of the
wear the horses and their owners gave the barn.

Nature didn't help. Several times during downpours, Margaret White, now living in Rex and Melissa's cottage, called us
for help. Water flooded her cellar, and her utilities were in
danger. Our family and theirs would form a chain as we passed
up buckets of water. Later I'd slosh around trying to unclog the
drain. The other cottages had their problems.

The same thing happened at the barn, threatening to soak
the lower bales of hay while I looked for and then cleared out its
drain.

Why do things happen late at night? Like toothaches on
weekends.

We ought to have let our lawn go, but we didn't. Somehow
the beauty of a sweeping lawn beguiled us into senseless mowing. We had a vegetable garden and some flower gardens to
tend; bushes to keep trimmed; patching up an aging pool. And,
of course, there was the maintenance on our home, more than
two hundred years old.

A large family necessitates a major investment in time. Not
only did we have our own immediate one but also brothers,
sisters, and parents. We had commitments to the community
and church.

Now most of the farm chores devolved on Mary and me. I

found my writing and studying interrupted with dismaying frequency.

Also, Mary had begun to work with me in linguistics and other areas, something we'd always looked forward to, and we had a raft of exciting, possible projects. I'd hoped she'd be able to begin her painting again. Yet her life was consumed with an endless array of detail, precluding real development in any of these areas.

But we loved this place with a passion. We loved it too much. Thinking we might have to part with it awoke me at night. Couldn't we find a way to keep the farm? Was there another approach that perhaps I'd missed?

Continually we were drawn into its beauty—the streams of water pouring over the rocks in cascades of froth; the early morning shadows stretching over lawn and fields; the contrast of the green of yet-unturned leaves in the fall with the glowing golden orange of sun-illuminated trees; the dark rolling clouds of a storm; the broad sea of sky curving down to rest on a gently undulating horizon of hills and trees; half-hidden paths winding through the woods with patches of light filtering through the cover of wilderness flora; the birds and wildflowers; the knife-edged winter winds and the drifting mounds of pure snow; the incomparable serenity of grazing beasts; the peacefulness—this island of peace, this treasure of tranquillity so rarely known today.

On a July afternoon, lying under the tractor, my hands smeared with the grease dropping on my shirt, runnels of perspiration stinging my eyes, my legs burning from the sun, my back aching, I struggled with a frozen bolt. The heavy wrench I used couldn't turn it.

I heard Mary calling me.

"Here . . . Under the tractor," I shouted, knocking my elbow sharply against a brace which held mowing equipment. The steel felt especially hard today. !%@#*!

"Where are you?"

"Where I said I was," I answered grumpily. "Under the cursed tractor. I wish the engineers who devised this contraption had to work on it with these conditions. It'd be a different story. All they do is sit in an air-conditioned office and figure out how to make my life miserable. I'll bet none of them have ever even driven one of these fool things."

I twisted my neck around to look up at Mary.

She had tears in her eyes. "It's three o'clock . . . You haven't been down for lunch. You ate breakfast at six . . . This is all wrong."

"I'm trying to get all these things done so I can get back to work on that magazine deadline this afternoon . . . We can't afford to have the mechanic up here every time something happens to one of the machines."

"But you're *not* a mechanic. That's *not* your job . . . I love this place. Just as much as you. But this isn't what you're meant to be doing. Like this today. If it happened only once in a while, it'd be all right . . . It might be fun. But it happens all the time. If it's not this, it's something else. It's endless . . . It goes on and on and on . . . We have to rethink our priorities." She paused and then added with emotional emphasis, "We have to sell the farm."

We looked at one another. It was out now. She'd voiced what we'd both dreaded saying. I nodded, sliding out from beneath the tractor.

She pointed to it. "Can you leave it here for a while."

"It's not going anywhere."

"Let's go down to the house. I'll make you a sandwich and some iced tea while you get cleaned up . . . We can talk on the terrace."

Jenny grazed near us, broom tail flicking away flies, her teeth nipping off the tops of the grass. "What about her?" I said of the little white burro.

"I guess it depends on where we move."

"It won't be a farm. There'd be no place for her."

"We could never sell her," Mary said, petting the small animal.

I sighed. "Maybe give her away?"

Life without Jenny. Inconceivable. My wits would grow dull without her challenges.

We sat on the terrace and talked. The decision was to sell

and to sell immediately if we could. We talked with our backs to the view.

The children were aghast. We were committing the most heinous of all crimes. How could we think of selling?

We explained.

They understood but still thought we were making a mistake. There'd never be another place like this. We'd miss it all our lives.

Yes, we did love it. We would miss it. But perhaps this is the way it should be. Every major religion teaches that we really own nothing; we're only caretakers of what's given to us, and so too we must share with others whatever it is we have. We must never be possessed by our possessions. What we have is temporary. What we are is eternal.

In the regional newspapers we advertised we had a burro to give away. We described the twenty-five-year-old Jenny as lovable and whimsical. Whimsical? Some of the word's definitions are: "characterized by capriciousness"; "oddly out of the ordinary"; "fanciful"; "freakish"; "subject to sudden change"; "unpredictable." All described Jenny. We hoped those who might be interested wouldn't bother to look up the word in the dictionary. If they knew what it meant they'd never call us. But caveat emptor. *Whimsical* sounds so nice. Beware of logodaedaly!

We stressed that she would be "on loan" as a pet to a loving family.

We had a myriad of telephone calls. I'd been right. No one ever bothered to check out the word. We settled on Angelina DiBianco and her four-year-old daughter, Karen. They fell in love with Jenny immediately. When they left, Mary said, "They're the ones. Angelina suits her name. And did you see how cute Jenny was with Karen. I'll miss Jenny, but if we have to give up our silly little burro, I won't worry about her with the DiBiancos." However, we asked them to wait until the farm was sold. We wanted her to be with us as long as we were on the farm. It would not be Good Ground without her.

Achilles ended up in a good home. Eleanor, with tearful teen-age wisdom, understood the necessity of passing her warrior along to someone else. You can only hope that your pets will receive loving care.

Several weeks later when I went to the barn I missed Hubert's honking his challenging welcome. I'd noticed that he'd been subdued for several days. I found him near one of the stalls lying on the cement, a watery discharge coming from his nose. He kept his eyes closed, breathing rapidly.

We took him to Alan Schuller immediately, who diagnosed a disease that came from pigeons. He said Hubert would die and he was right. I felt a little like Hubert when Babe had been sold. The barn was strangely empty for me. Supposedly he was Paul's pet and he'd been in love with Babe. Yet I had a special relationship with him.

For better or worse, our wedding anniversary coincides with Thanksgiving. We always have a cornucopia of people with us to celebrate our family fecundity. There are cousins by the dozens, aunts, uncles, grandchildren, grandparents. And always others who for one reason or another cannot be with their families and are enthusiastically adopted by us for the day.

This year our family grew with two daughters-in-law. Peter and John married—Peter to Diana and John to Taffy, each a daughter to us, each enriching our family in her own way.

We couldn't forget our sadness about this being the last Thanksgiving at Good Ground, but activity kept our minds on other things.

Thanksgiving on our farm evoked the spirit of a Currier & Ives print—an old farmhouse with wood neatly stacked under an overhang; smoke drifting from a chimney promising warm, cozy rooms; a cheerful family arriving in a sleigh welcomed by a barking dog; a clean tablecloth of snow covering the earth.

There were a few differences between our situation and the print. Snow was not always present and people arrived by wheels rather than sled runners. However, our house, built during Revolutionary times, was old. We cut and stacked our wood under an overhang. Six fireplaces kept the house warm when the ancient furnace took a holiday.

The background of bare, gray-dark woods, the slumberous russet-colored fields, and the smooth rhythmic curves of unadorned distant hills gave us winter's spare beauty.

This particular Thanksgiving Day came with lowering, blustery clouds and a damp, chill wind that sliced through outer clothing. Mary had us up early, separating us into different work groups.

"Mother is so well organized. I don't see how she does everything" is a frequent comment from our daughters. Occasionally they'll say to me, "Sometimes you are too." I think it's to encourage latent possibilities.

The girls were assigned tasks in the kitchen and to the details of amending the house for the imminent crush of people. We expected around thirty-five.

Mary has a way with plants, and unable to refuse the orphans people give her, she has an odd collection. Deciding to spread her indoor garden throughout the house, she directed her sons as to where they should go.

"John, I think Saint Francis should be in the playroom." She names plants and this happened to be a flourishing orange tree. "Peter, Montezuma (a Christmas cactus with brilliant red blossoms) goes on the hallway table."

"A hall is appropriate for Montezuma since Dad was in the Marine Corps," Peter smiled.

Gabriel, a large, thriving, pink-blossomed angel-wing begonia ended up in my house office. Mary Cabot Lodge, a stately Boston fern, temporarily graced a light corner of the living room. Other plants were clustered on the table and the broad windowsill of our back entrance hall near the circular stairway to the boys' former dormitory. Chrysanthemums were scattered throughout the house, their flowers visual reminders of sun-filled autumn days.

"She talks to them," Estelle explained once to a friend who had overheard Mary encouraging an ailing prayer plant.

The "men" under my supervision fed the barn animals, made fires, cleaned up the outside, set up tables, and pumped up the football. I had to intercept a few passes, break up spontaneous wrestling matches, and put the Ping-Pong balls in my pocket. I was glad to play the father again in this way.

My mother and father always arrived promptly, driven here by Uncle Bert, Aunt Gid's husband. She was my mother's sister. We were glad my father didn't drive. The way he handled a car resembled his maladroit efforts to shave. His mind would be on other things and frequently he'd nick his face, appearing at breakfast with bits of toilet paper plastered on his skin to stem the flow of blood.

Invariably they arrived in high good humor, generously bringing various items to eat and drink. Sometimes there'd be other gifts. This day my parents brought a set of twelve wine glasses. Mary was delighted, for we had a motley collection which we filled out with water tumblers.

My mother, after patting the dogs and complimenting them on their splendid qualities, looked around expectantly. "Where's Licorice? Why isn't she here? I just love that old black cat."

"*He's* around somewhere. Don't worry. *He'll* show up if he thinks someone's going to feed *him,*" I replied, emphasizing the *he.*

"But I want to say hello to her. I'm so diappointed."

To my mother, a cat is always a *she,* and a dog a *he,* whatever the actual gender.

Since neither the dogs nor the cats seemed to mind, why should I?

After stretching in his somewhat stiff way, my father sniffed. From the damp northeast wind he caught a whiff of the farmyard. He wrinkled his nose disparagingly.

"Give me the good clean smell of Forty-second Street in New York City." He glanced at the open country around us. "I don't know how we ended up with children living on farms. It must be from your mother's side."

It must be.

My father was the consummate urbanite. For him beauty and drama resided in cities—in crowds, in the noise of traffic, in the press of tall buildings, in the theater during those few moments just before a play begins, in the multitude of different restaurants.

"How I'd hate to be out here. It would depress me. You can't even see another house."

"But we have the trees, the fields, the sky, animals, ourselves, our dreams . . ."

"I like to be able to wave to my neighbors out of my window."

My mother could understand our love for the land. She always longed for a farm. My father refused. He maintained it would be a disaster, for she'd have ended up with a zoo for hundreds of displaced animals.

Curiously, however, in the unfathomable intricacies of the psyche, my father, a most graceful writer and a clever and accomplished poet, wrote romantically of the sea, of ships, of the flowers my mother loved and grew, of his children. Few of his poems ever referred to the city.

As a linguist, he became enamored with words and was one of the first to write popular books encouraging readers to build their vocabularies, enriching the minds of literally millions. It was he who developed and brought to *Reader's Digest* the monthly feature "It Pays to Enrich Your Word Power."

He was an intriguing, challenging, and often charming companion who excited affection. But like each of us, he too had the dark side of his moon.

"She's beautiful," friends say of my mother. And she is. A portrait painted in her thirties catches this essence of her. The artist put her in a delicate black dress, which contrasts strikingly with the yellow chair and her blond hair and pale skin. But the artist caught more than beauty. The picture reveals energy, determination, courage, and a touch of sadness. My mother sits straight and alert.

By your fruits you will be known. In her volunteer work with hospitals and numerous community projects, my mother produced an orchard of fruit. At one time she received an award as the outstanding citizen of her town.

Mary's mother and father arrived, the valorous producers of seven children, who spawned innumerable grandchildren.

Then cousins, Mary's brothers and sisters and their children, my sisters and their families from their farms, several young friends of our children, too far away from home to return for just a weekend. And Daisy Moore came also. She'd taught our youngest children piano lessons. Her husband had died several years ago. Being a widow and alone, the previous Thanksgiving she had her dog sit with her in a chair at the table while they both ate their Thanksgiving dinner. We did not invite her dog.

My cousin Fred Miller and I began to carve the turkeys when Paul hustled in from the kitchen. "Mom says she's in a predicament. She can't remember where she put the place cards for seating everyone."

"I remember she wrote them out last night upstairs . . . I'm not sure where she put them."

"By the way, Pop, what's the Latin root of *predicament?*"

Though I suspected Paul might be teasing, my immediate reflex was to reach for my pocket. I caught myself and laughed. Then I hesitated. "Actually it's an interesting root because I know it comes from *praedicare,* 'to preach' . . ."

Mary's head appeared through the door. "Darling, please . . . !"

My cousin laughed. "You never get your fill of words."

The kitchen was Mary's fragrant, busy command post. "You're right . . . I did them upstairs. I left them in the left side of my bureau . . . Could you get them for me?"

I saw my brother-in-law Karl standing in the doorway. "Do me a favor. You're an expert carver. Mary has something she wants me to do." I handed him the carving knife and fork and threaded my way through the crowd.

Tall, thin Uncle Bert called out to me, his face crinkling with enjoyment. "Your dad still doesn't believe you can think without words." He liked to bait my father into arguments, sometimes pretending to defend wildly implausible positions.

"Bert has such an abominably small vocabulary, he should know," my father's rejoinder reached me through the air, thick with conversation and smoke.

My uncle laughed at the acerbic remark, taking it as a jest.

On the way to get the place cards, I stopped off in my home

study and took Eric Partridge's book on word origins with me. I knew it came from *praedicare*, having something to do with predictions. But why does it indicate problems? I'd look it up later. Passing through the living room, I overheard Mary's mother talking to Celine. "I understand you're in Boston now . . . What're you doing there?"

"I'm studying at the Boston Museum of Art and Tufts University. It's a combined program."

"Will you graduate?"

Celine gave a low, warm laugh, amused at herself and her grandmother. "I hope so, Granny."

Her grandmother, friendly and gracious, joined her in the laughter. "No . . . No . . . I meant, is it a regular program leading to a degree?"

"Yes . . . I'll have an A.B."

Mark, looking like a golden-haired lion with his growing beard, shook his head mournfully. "Pop . . . I don't see how you could do it? How can you sell the farm? I can't ever think of living any other place. This is our last Thanksgiving here."

We'd always thought that Mark and Eleanor felt a deeper attachment to Good Ground than any of the other children.

Our meal began with a grace by Mary's father, a well-rounded talk to God.

Partway through dinner, Peter stood up, tapping a glass for attention.

"Well . . . As the oldest child, I'd like to make a toast to Mother and Dad," he said in his buoyant, pleasantly quiet voice. "As you know, this is their anniversary and so here's to many more wonderful years . . ." After our family toasted us, he nodded to Celine, who held a small box. "My brothers and sisters and I thought a particular kind of gift would be appropriate."

Celine gave the book-sized box to Mary, who unwrapped the present. She held out a darkly stained, exquisite wood carving of an open Bible. Each side contained a silver plaque, three quarters the size of the page. One contained the inscription: *To*

Mother and Dad on their Anniversary and included the signatures of all our children. On the other:

> *Bred of Love*
> *And brought to light,*
> *On a path set*
> *In knowledge and rejoicing.*
>
> *Unity in action*
> *And Words in abundance,*
> *Pages revealed for*
> *Constructive contemplation.*
>
> *We pause . . .*
> *Amidst our exertions,*
> *In gratitude and love,*
> *Today.*

Mary and I are as one, and so I knew what was in her heart. We were blessed beyond anything we could deserve. More than we could give thanks for.

The moment brought back another special Thanksgiving, nine months after my cancer operation. We'd gone to a ten o'clock Thanksgiving service in our small church. Only a few people attended. Perhaps a dozen. But each gave thanks for a special reason.

Mary's hand, warm and filled with love, held mine tightly. How different now than that day I struggled awake from the anesthetic, when her hand of life gently pulled me through the binding, smothering darkness.

I would not willingly endure that ordeal of sickness again. Yet in the curious paradoxes of life, how grateful I became for the experience, how blessed by all that happened. A garden of riches and beauty came out of what I'd believed to be the poisoned soil of illness.

For both of us—for Mary and me—God became indisputably the center of our lives. And the richness we experienced was the sustaining love that passes beyond understanding, that love that flows from God. Fears and anxieties dissolved gradually in this love. Into our lives came a joy we never knew existed; which we didn't have to work at or search for.

Whom have I in heaven but you, and having you desire nothing upon earth. You hold me by my right hand.

I felt well. I knew the nuts and bolts of my body were tight again and the machinery functioning smoothly.

I looked around the small church that Thanksgiving Day of several years ago, knowing that each of us had similar feelings, and we all gave thanks in our own way.

Fifteen-year-old Andrew sat behind us in the pew with his mother. Six months ago he'd been struck by a hit-and-run driver and hadn't been expected to live, let alone walk. He'd hobbled into the church on crutches. A young husband and his wife were in front of us. He'd survived an air crash. A friend kneeling close by discovered Alcoholics Anonymous and life was new and wonderful to her again. One person after the other had reason to give great and glorious thanks and we did.

We all sang the Thanksgiving hymns with gusto and feeling and our minds and emotions became one with the prayers we said together and heard from our minister.

My mind slipped back again into the present, into the midst of my family. As I listened to the blur of voices and laughter rising and falling as if shooting the rapids of time, I thought, with gratitude, of how every family is happy in its own way; of how ours is happy in our relationships, in our concerns for one another, and of how this center of love gradually expands to include the world.

"It's the way all of you feel about one another . . . You really like to be together and you're not jealous . . . How come? That makes us about as happy as anything else," I said to one of the older ones recently.

"You and Mother never had favorites. You loved and scolded everyone in just about the same way," came the reply.

I hoped they forgave our mistakes with them.

How much influence had Good Ground on our attitudes? Probably more than either Mary or I even realized.

"My turn for a toast," I said, rising. For a minute or so I talked about that paragon of love and joy in my life—Mary. And I welcomed our new daughters.

"Since we haven't been together for a while, I thought we might catch up your aunts and uncles and cousins and all as to your activities . . . After Peter left the Green Berets he matriculated at Bishops University in Canada, met his future wife, Diana, graduated taking the only English prize awarded, and is a first-year law student at Boston University.

"John graduated from Princeton University with honors, proposed to Taffy on an island in Narragansett Bay, straightened up the navy for a few years, and is a first-year law student at the same law school.

"A few minutes ago, Celine told her grandmother about her courses at the Boston Museum School of Art and Tufts. And along with only a few others, her sculpture was exhibited at the Municipal Building. She made it out of fifty pounds of rubberbands—a very unusual and intriguing design."

"You mean a *snappy* one," Paul called out.

Voices groaned.

"That's stretching it, Paul," Peter added.

"Estelle's nineteen and it's hard to believe. She's in college training to be a teacher and decided she'll go to England in her junior year as an exchange student. For several summers she's worked as a counselor with crippled children. And if she ever wanted to, she could also become a writer. We know she'll always have something to do with the church.

"Mark's the youngest person to have worked in the county hospital emergency room. He's getting ready to go to college next year as a pre-med. It's lucky we're moving, because Mark is the one who can repair anything. The farm will fall down without him.

"If Paul looks strange to you, it's because he's turned into a combination of a football, a hockey puck, a lacrosse stick, and a

goal. Whatever Paul does, he immerses himself in it. And someday he'll become a book as well. I can see indications. He's
asking about words now . . . And Paul, we never did finish
about *predicament.*" My dictionary of origins was under the
chair. I picked it up.

Mary cleared her throat. I put the dictionary back under
my chair.

"And by the way, sports has a rival in Paul's life. A new
interest has captivated him . . . a cute girl by the name of Jean
Beckwith . . . Incidentally, I don't have the time to go into all
the romances involving our daughters. We'd be here all day.

"Finally the caboose of the family. The way Eleanor mothers her animals, large and small, she has to grow up to be a real
one someday. But she mothers people too, and this year she's
been working under a special program with the elderly in a
hospital. And Eleanor, like Estelle, has writing ability. Will she
write the memoirs of the great Achilles?"

Though the day had been stitched together by threads of
laughter, we came now to the moment we couldn't avoid any
longer. We laugh sometimes in the midst of sorrow, for laughter
often plays the clown for tears.

Keeping my eyes on my plate, my fingers toyed with the
table silver.

"There's a word that's taken me a lifetime to comprehend
even slightly. It's one of the most important words of our lives. I
understand it intellectually. I *know* what it means. So do you.
It's such a simple word. Yet it's the stumbling block for so many
of us.

"How I accept and interpret and act on the consequences
of the word determines to a large extent the quality of my life.

"The word is *change.* And it's a very old word, going back
almost to the time when language as we know it was born. Its
Indo-European root is *kamb-,* which means 'to bend,' or 'to
make crooked.' And *change* does bend us . . . It bends us out
of routines we've become used to.

"And here we are now in a changing situation. Next year

this time, probably we will be celebrating Thanksgiving somewhere else.

"Change is like a river of moving water. It flows over river bottoms that differ mile by mile, through channels of varying widths, past diverse shorelines. The individual molecules of water are never in the same place.

"And time is a river flowing through us, carrying us along in the same way to new situations and challenges. Some people try to build a dam against the river of time. They are frightened of change. They resist it. They won't accept it. And for a while they may succeed. But *still waters* stagnate. Inevitably the dam bursts from the pressure, and their lives swirl out of control, lost in the boiling waters.

"When we first moved to Good Ground, we knew we were meant to be here. There were nine of us then, and we used the place fully in a life-style which we loved and learned from. But time has swept all of us along to new situations. In a few years Paul and Eleanor will have left. And your mother and I know . . . We know sadly. We know realistically. It is no longer the same. We're not meant to stay. There's been a change."

In early December, when we had several people genuinely interested in buying our farm—we were sure it would be sold by the month's end—I received a telephone call from a deacon in a Baptist church in a nearby town. He'd heard about Jenny and wondered if she might be used to play a part in a living crèche during the Christmas season.

I couldn't help laughing. Our whimsical Jenny in a crèche!

"It's going to be outside the church. We'll have real people playing the part of Mary and Joseph and the shepherds. We'll take very good care of her."

"I'm not worried about Jenny. What does worry me is that I'm not sure you can cope with *her.*"

"She won't be any trouble. I'm a farmer and have animals.

I'm bringing along some sheep too. We're going to have a fence around the crèche."

I wanted to suggest something like the Berlin Wall for Jenny. Anyway, the crèche idea appealed to us. Saint Francis dearly loved Christmas and it was he who thought up the idea of a crèche in the first place. The saint wanted to convey to people the sense of beauty and mystery and yet the reality of Christ's birth.

The DiBianco family agreed to take Jenny home with them after this event.

One evening, just before Christmas, we were on our way to Princeton where we'd bought a new home. A heavy snowstorm covered the area and the roads were empty of cars. We drove through Hopewell where Jenny took part in the crèche. As we drew alongside of the church, I turned off the engine and we stepped out of the car.

We found ourselves in the midst of a truly Silent Night. The snow falling muffled all sounds and we stood in hushed wonder.

Inside a small, barnlike shelter sat a live Mary holding the infant Jesus. Joseph, the father, stood alongside. Several shepherds stood watching, leaning on their staffs, occasionally shifting positions. Two sheep lay inside the shelter also.

Outside the lean-to, almost as white as the snow, we saw Jenny doing what she did so expertly and even at times gracefully—nibbling on a bale of hay—completely at peace, her skinny tail flicking at the falling snowflakes.

"She looks positively angelic," Mary whispered.

As if to dispel this unusual image of herself, she reached over and tore a tuft of hay from the manger itself. Jenny would be forever Jenny.

She played her role professionally, however. Before we returned to the car we couldn't help clapping. Thanks to Jenny and the "cast" of performers, we, and hundreds of others, were part of a scene that caught the true spirit of Christmas. It was a worthwhile recompense for all her escapades.

As we drove away, Jenny's whiteness faded into the whiteness of the snow . . . The fading of the dream.

Endings flow into beginnings.

In the beam of our headlights the swirling snowflakes wallpapered the ebony room of night in a mist of dancing gold. As we moved along the way, I had a growing sense that we were being drawn in a direction we were destined to go. Unlike Lot's wife, we would not look back to be frozen in a pillar of salt of the past.

About the Author

Peter Funk is a member of a distinguished publishing family. His grandfather, I. K. Funk, founded Funk and Wagnalls, the dictionary and encyclopedia company. His father, Wilfred Funk, not only followed in his father's footsteps in the publishing world but originated the famed *Reader's Digest* feature "It Pays to Enrich Your Word Power," which Peter has been creating for the past twenty years. So there is no mystery as to where Peter obtained his love for words. In addition to his work as a noted lexical semanticist, Peter has written five nonfiction books (four on vocabulary building) and two novels. He now lives in Princeton, New Jersey.

CHRISTIAN HERALD ASSOCIATION AND ITS MINISTRIES

CHRISTIAN HERALD ASSOCIATION, founded in 1878, publishes The Christian Herald Magazine, one of the leading interdenominational religious monthlies in America. Through its wide circulation, it brings inspiring articles and the latest news of religious developments to many families. From the magazine's pages came the initiative for CHRISTIAN HERALD CHILDREN'S HOME and THE BOWERY MISSION, two individually supported not-for-profit corporations.

CHRISTIAN HERALD CHILDREN'S HOME, established in 1894, is the name for a unique and dynamic ministry to disadvantaged children, offering hope and opportunities which would not otherwise be available for reasons of poverty and neglect. The goal is to develop each child's potential and to demonstrate Christian compassion and understanding to children in need.

Mont Lawn is a permanent camp located in Bushkill, Pennsylvania. It is the focal point of a ministry which provides a healthful "vacation with a purpose" to children who without it would be confined to the streets of the city. Up to 1000 children between the ages of 7 and 11 come to Mont Lawn each year.

Christian Herald Children's Home maintains year-round contact with children by means of an *In-City Youth Ministry*. Central to its philosophy is the belief that only through sustained relationships and demonstrated concern can individual lives be truly enriched. Special emphasis is on individual guidance, spiritual and family counseling and tutoring. This follow-up ministry to inner-city children culminates for many in financial assistance toward higher education and career counseling.

THE BOWERY MISSION, located at 227 Bowery, New York City, has since 1879 been reaching out to the lost men on the Bowery, offering them what could be their last chance to rebuild their lives. Every man is fed, clothed and ministered to. Countless numbers have entered the 90-day residential rehabilitation program at the Bowery Mission. A concentrated ministry of counseling, medical care, nutrition therapy, Bible study and Gospel services awakens a man to spiritual renewal within himself.

These ministries are supported solely by the voluntary contributions of individuals and by legacies and bequests. Contributions are tax deductible. Checks should be made out either to CHRISTIAN HERALD CHILDREN'S HOME or to THE BOWERY MISSION.

**Administrative Office: 40 Overlook Drive, Chappaqua, New York 10514
Telephone: (914) 769-9000**